Born Southern

Born Southern

*Childbirth, Motherhood, and Social Networks
in the Old South*

V. LYNN KENNEDY

The Johns Hopkins University Press

Baltimore

© 2010 The Johns Hopkins University Press
All rights reserved. Published 2010
Printed in the United States of America on acid-free paper
9 8 7 6 5 4 3 2 1

The Johns Hopkins University Press
2715 North Charles Street
Baltimore, Maryland 21218-4363
www.press.jhu.edu

Library of Congress Cataloging-in-Publication Data

Kennedy, V. Lynn, 1970–
  Born southern : childbirth, motherhood, and social networks in the
old South / V. Lynn Kennedy.
     p. cm.
  Includes bibliographical references and index.
  ISBN-13: 978-0-8018-9417-6 (hardcover : alk. paper)
  ISBN-10: 0-8018-9417-4 (hardcover : alk. paper)
  1. Childbirth—Social aspects—Southern States—History—19th century.
2. Pregnancy—Social aspects—Southern States—History—19th century.
3. Motherhood—Southern States—History—19th century.   4. Mothers—Southern
States—Social conditions—19th century.   5. Children—Southern States—Social
conditions—19th century.   6. Social networks—Southern States—History—19th
century.   7. Family—Southern States—History—19th century.   8. Community
life—Southern States—History—19th century.   9. Southern States—Social
conditions—19th century.   10. Southern States—Social life and
customs—1775–1865   I. Title.
  RG652.K46 2010
  362.198'200975—dc22   2009013966

A catalog record for this book is available from the British Library.

*Special discounts are available for bulk purchases of this book. For more information,
please contact Special Sales at 410-516-6936 or specialsales@press.jhu.edu.*

The Johns Hopkins University Press uses environmentally friendly book materials,
including recycled text paper that is composed of at least 30 percent post-consumer
waste, whenever possible. All of our book papers are acid-free, and our jackets and
covers are printed on paper with recycled content.

CONTENTS

ACKNOWLEDGMENTS

As I WROTE about the social networks formed by people in the Old South, I could not help but think about those who encouraged my own endeavors and tied me to a larger sense of community. At the University of Western Ontario and at the University of Lethbridge I have benefited from the generosity of many people. I am particularly grateful for the guidance of Margaret Kellow, who offered so much insight at all stages of this project and continues to be a source of support. Craig Simpson and Robert Hohner are also responsible for shepherding me from a naive undergraduate to the historian that I am today—I hope I have made them proud. Having Heidi MacDonald serve as my chair at the University of Lethbridge made my transition from student to teacher much easier than it might otherwise have been. She has set the standard for mentorship and collegiality that I hope to emulate in my own career as a professor.

A number of people have taken the time to read this entire project at various stages and to offer invaluable feedback. They included Michelle Hamilton, Heidi MacDonald, Janay Nugent, Jim Tagg, Catherine Clinton, Cindy Kierner, and Ben Marsh. At the Johns Hopkins University Press, Bob Brugger and Josh Tong have been models of efficiency and professionalism. I am also appreciative of the careful reading and improvements to the manuscript suggested by the anonymous reader at the JHU Press and by copyeditor Kathleen Capels. All have made important improvements and corrections; any errors that remain are my own. A grant from the Social Science and Humanities Research Council of Canada assisted in the research and writing of this study.

The women of the Old South with whom I have been engaged for the last ten years relied on a community of friends, family, and kin to get through their daily lives. I too have been blessed with a community of women who have offered many forms of assistance and encouragement, always when I needed it most. Michelle Hamilton helped talk me through many things and shared my interest, some would say obsession, with minute details. Marise Bachand shared my "Canadian Girl" enthusiasm for the history of the American South and has proven herself an excellent roommate. Claire Campbell reminded me that all can be done with style. Heidi MacDonald, Janay Nugent, Jan Newberry, and Anne Dymond have bridged the gap between colleagues and friends, offering advice, support, and tea in perfect balance. Gail Hepburn, Andrea Wojtak, and Christie Webster provided perspectives beyond the field of history and served as my cheerleaders when I needed that extra bit of encouragement. Finally, Amy Shaw has, over the course of a decade, moved from an office-mate to a sister-friend. I could not have completed this project without her unwavering support.

This book is dedicated to Barbara and Jerry Kennedy for all that they have done for me. It is they who taught me that family is the foundation for everything. My love and gratitude is beyond words.

Born Southern

Introduction

Mahala and Henrietta lived in the same household in ante-bellum Vicksburg, Mississippi. In July of 1856 Mahala, who kept a daily diary of her activities, recorded the birth of her fifth child: "Little John, born this morning at 5 am—before 5—he is a delicate poor baby, only weighs 3-1/2 pounds—Mother came down, but no one was here when he arrived but Margery and Henrietta." About nine months earlier, in September 1855, Mahala had written of a similar scene in which Henrietta had given birth to a daughter, also at five in the morning. Mahala noted that she had spent the afternoon taking care of the newly delivered mother. These women had much in common, sharing not only a household but the experiences of bearing and nurturing infants. They came to each other's assistance during the trials of labor and delivery. But Mahala Roach was an elite white woman and Henrietta was a black woman held in bondage.

The presence of free and enslaved women together in the same household created a uniquely southern narrative. Mahala's status and race gave her the power to shape many aspects of Henrietta's childbearing experience. As mistress, Mahala commanded the work Henrietta performed while pregnant, the length of her recovery period, and the time she could devote to nurturing her infant. But Mahala also depended on Henrietta to complete the necessary tasks of the household and to assist in her mistress's own mothering tasks. The relationship of these two women reveals the complexity of similarities and separations engendered by childbearing in the antebellum South.[1]

During the same period, the Jones family of Georgia exchanged letters that, among other things, detailed the reproduction of both white relatives and the enslaved women in their household. In 1859 their discussion turned to a more public incident involving infanticide. The Reverend Charles Jones wrote to his son, Charles Colcock Jones Jr., about a case that had caught the attention of the neighborhood. *"The infant has been found—the 12th day after its birth and secretion!"* he wrote with emphasis. "The guilty mother now confesses all, with the reservation that it was *stillborn!"*[2] While he prided himself on being a beneficent slaveholder, Jones demonstrated little sympathy for the enslaved girl's story that she had hidden the dead infant because she had denied her pregnancy and feared disclosing it when the infant was born dead. He concluded not only that the girl should be punished but that her mother and the midwife, who may have assisted her, should also be prosecuted. The elder Jones was a plantation owner as well as a minister, and his son was establishing himself in the legal profession in Savannah. Hence these men discussed this incident not just as a piece of passing gossip, but as a breach of the moral standards of their society, defying gender norms and patterns of racial control. As men, and as professionals, they believed it was their duty not only to discuss this birth, but to demand punishment for all those who had challenged the boundaries of proper behavior. In the public sphere, birth and motherhood narratives became an important means of both shaping and reflecting social mores.

In this book *birth* includes a broadly defined set of meanings and experiences, not merely a physiological event. It involves a sense of origin, with an emotional and symbolic resonance that ties an individual to a broader sense of social identity and community. In the antebellum South, birth and motherhood became a nexus of identities. Mothers, children, fathers, and family—in fact most community members—in some way shaped and were shaped by the meanings assigned to birth. Southerners based their understanding of childbearing not just on the physical experiences of women, or simply on the gender ideals that made childbearing central to the female identity. Rather, these ideas intertwined with social assumptions about race and class to shape an understanding of what birth and motherhood meant both to individual women and to society as a whole. *Born Southern* explores the pivotal roles of birth and motherhood in slaveholding families to assess how the power structures of race, gender, and class functioned to construct antebellum southern society, and how discussions of birth and motherhood became part of the development of a regional identity. Family formed a fundamental element of southern society, and childbearing by women, black *and* white, touched all members of this society.

The book next asks how antebellum southerners used birth and motherhood to create, justify, and replicate their community and their sense of identity. Women gave birth within a social network. The society in which a woman lived had a stake in her reproductive behavior, which indicated either a compliance with or a defiance of social norms and structures. Further, women's children became members of that community, assuming their social identity and status based on the family into which they were born. Popular perceptions generally acknowledge that birth creates ties to a family structure, which in turn links a person to a wider community. Yet how people negotiate these relationships on a daily basis and how the connections are shaped by the historical context in which they occurred have received only limited attention. Most contemporary and historical scholarship has concentrated on the biological and medical experiences of birth.[3] A narrow focus on labor and delivery, however, seldom illuminates the multiplicity of meanings women, and society as a whole, applied to birth at any one time or place. For most women, the birth experience represented a continuity—from conception through pregnancy, labor, and delivery to the nurturing of an infant. The specific historical context shaped not only the physical experience of these events, but the meanings that a woman and her social community applied to them.[4]

In the period between 1830 and 1861, southern social commentators showed a growing concern with defining what it meant to be a southerner. The South was a vast place, even in the mid-nineteenth century, stretching from long-settled communities to rough frontiers. Settlement patterns, agricultural interests, and living conditions all varied widely, both between localities and between class and ethnic groups within the region. Southerners remained a diverse group during this period. The author of an 1847 *DeBow's Review* article boldly claimed: "I am a southerner and my ancestors before me were southerners."[5] But what a southern identity, politically or socially, meant during this period remained debatable. Birth and motherhood became an important part of this discussion. Linking birth to a social identity allowed an organic sense of social hierarchy and defined one's place within it. Although elites dominated written narratives, available sources tend to indicate that the physical events and many of the social meanings of birth remained fairly consistent across boundaries.[6] The experiences of birth and motherhood tied individuals to their families, households, and communities; they also sometimes functioned to form a larger sense of regional identity.

The values and ideals southerners expressed around these experiences often bore a striking similarity to those expounded by other Americans in this period. Southern social commentators, however, emphasized their own superior ability to fulfill these values, if not a superiority of southern values themselves. Using sermons, stories and poems in magazines, and sentimental novels, southern authors created a didactic model for the meaning of birth and motherhood within their region. In 1856, an article entitled "The Duty of Southern Authors" in the *Southern Literary Messenger* called for a redoubled effort in producing a southern narrative, arguing that "the great armories and arsenals of literature" not only created a shared sense of identity, but offered a defense against external attacks on their character.[7] Small differences became building blocks for constructing a unique sense of regional identity. A continuing reliance on an agricultural economy stood in stark contrast to the shift to an industrial market economy in the North and allowed southerners to claim that only they maintained an orderly patriarchal society, in which the father protected the interests of women, children, and the entire family, black and white. Slavery made strong social structures and boundaries necessary. Southern apologists argued that this patriarchal authority ideally created a conservative social order in which everyone knew his or her place, being cast by virtue of birth into a predetermined, "natural" role within society.[8]

Narratives of birth and motherhood became an important means for southerners to link people together, establish southern social values, and differentiate themselves from their northern compatriots. Historians seeking to identify the emergence of a distinct southern identity have often focused on the Civil War and its aftermath. The memory of the Confederate experience seemed to provide a common basis of identity for many white southerners, while emancipation linked black southerners together. But while the formation of the Confederacy and its subsequent defeat undoubtedly represented a crucial moment in the history of southern identity, these events required a preexisting sense of common interests and values. Thus, while the southern identity may have emerged as most salient, or at least most active, around secession and war, the foundations of this identity developed in the antebellum period, in the individual southerner's inborn sense of self, family, and community.[9]

This book gives voice to the narratives created around birth and motherhood by individual women, their kin, and members of their social networks. In their letters and diaries, these southerners expressed their own ideas about what birth ought to be and how their own experiences aligned with these expectations. Within the southern household, and specifically in the birthing room, negotiations over the meaning of gender and race shaped each person's status and identity—their sense of who they were and where they fit into southern society. Southerners developed nuanced perspectives on the meanings of birth and motherhood in their own lives that complicated their understanding of the structures—particularly patriarchy and slavery—shaping their society.

Social ideals told white women in the antebellum South that they should remain chaste until marriage and embrace the role of motherhood thereafter. Few elite white women defied these norms, fearing the ostracism that came with a failure to live up to social expectations. Yet many white women privately expressed trepidation about giving birth and becoming mothers, hoping either to avoid birth altogether or simply to achieve some sort of control over the number and frequency of their pregnancies. The manner in which white women talked about these experiences in their letters and diaries shows how they often felt buffeted between the idealized identity of the southern mother and their own individual realities. Elite southern women sought to balance personal desires with a public identity that fit the social norms of the southern lady, constructed in opposition to the degradation of black enslaved womanhood. To challenge the honored position of white southern motherhood risked a precipitous fall from the pedestal, and leaving this pedestal meant losing the privileges of both sex and race.[10]

Black women also lived within the confines of an appositional social structure in the antebellum South. Although childbirth offered the same basic biological experience to all southern females, enslaved women faced a greater struggle to have their own perceptions recognized and their physical needs met during pregnancy and delivery. Slavery made their maternal experience even more precarious. Enslaved mothers passed on their condition of servitude to their children, and these mothers faced the real possibility that white owners would not recognize their maternal claims and would separate them from their children. Thus, while the slave system encouraged, even required, enslaved women to reproduce, it often denigrated and devalued their motherhood. Still, black mothers, and the larger enslaved community, cared for and formed emotional bonds with their enslaved children, negotiating their own experiences of birth and motherhood apart from the dominant southern narrative.[11]

Despite the systemic divisions between white and black women, complex interactions and relationships were formed among them within individual southern households. Women negotiated the boundaries and possibilities of these relationships on a daily basis. The commonalities of birth and motherhood, in particular, brought them together as much as it divided them. Recognition of their common struggles, mutual aid offered in the birthing room, and shared responsibilities for infant nurturing created bonds that seemed to defy the power relationships of slavery. Often the definitions of identity based on clear divisions and social boundaries did not mesh neatly with people's individual experiences. Women's narratives of birth reveal a complexity of experiences and meanings far beyond the assumptions expressed in the ideal.

While the experiences of birth and motherhood shaped the identity of women, black and white, within the household, the contested meanings of these events also stretched into the public sphere. Just as giving birth tied women to a larger network of family, kin, and community, these social structures looked to birth to form their own foundations. In order to ensure their patriarchal authority, white men sought to apply their own particular definitions to birth and motherhood. These men gained their first claims to social dominion through their role as fathers, in control of their own households. In contrast, the inability of enslaved men to assert ownership of their own children marked their lack of authority and ultimate degradation within the southern social hierarchy.

Some men, belonging to the growing number of professionals during this period, went further in demanding the power to define the meaning of birth and motherhood. For example, doctors, who wished to claim scientific authority regarding the human body and its ailments, saw a professed knowledge of pregnancy, labor, and delivery as a means of gaining a professional foothold. Although they faced continued opposition from older, women-controlled approaches to the birthing room, physicians continually made both public and private assertions of authority over childbirth in the antebellum period. Other professionalizing groups, including lawyers and planters, also used discussions about the control of birth and motherhood to claim jurisdiction in their particular spheres of influence.

A growing sense of regional identity became increasingly evident among southern elites and social commentators in the antebellum period. Just as the ideals of birth and motherhood told southern women how they ought to behave in their own society, contrasting the birthing behaviors of women in the North and South became a means of proclaiming regional distinctiveness. The war of words that developed between northern abolitionists and southern supporters of slavery frequently used birth and motherhood as a weapon. These attacks and counterattacks sought to claim the same set of values that idealized the roles of childbearing and infant nurture, each arguing that their region best supported these activities while the other region became a hotbed of deviance. In constructing their defense against external attacks, southerners also made birth and motherhood a fundamental piece of their self-identity. This identity, however, had not yet become *Southern*, in the sense of a political or nationalistic affiliation with a common, shared definition; *southern* remained a tenuous, complex, and contested adjective in the antebellum period. The ties to family and community that birth and motherhood created gradually extended to form links to a larger regional identity for women, their families, and the children that they bore.

This book, then, asks how discussions of birth and motherhood shaped the identities of all individuals within the antebellum South and how these experiences created family and community bonds that developed into the foundations of a broader southern identity. Within the household, women's birth and motherhood experiences formed part of their personal identities and required balancing their own desires with the ideals of their society. In the public sphere, southerners used the ostensibly natural experiences of birth and motherhood to negotiate personal and professional identities and claims to authority, both shaping and reflecting power relations based on hierarchies of race, gender, and class. The myriad and diverse discussions of birth by all members of antebellum society tied people together into family and social networks. These discussions began with the negotiation of the ideals of how people *ought* to behave within this society, to which the following chapter now turns.

CHAPTER ONE

Idealizing Birth and Motherhood in the Antebellum South

IN 1835, Thomas Dew wrote of a mother's love for her child. Having given the baby life, he suggested, she "feels the deepest sympathy with all its pains and wants, and carries in her heart, the most unbound and unremitting affection for it"; in her devotion "she notices with a tender anxiety all its little movements, and administers to all its wants." While still a schoolgirl in North Carolina, Mary Ezell echoed these sentiments in an essay entitled "A Mother's Love," in which she described a mother's feeling as "the tenderest, purest form in which the passion ever yet appeared. Love for her offspring was implanted in the heart of every mother by the giver of all good." Similarly, while Charles Jones Jr. of Georgia awaited the birth of his second child he wrote that "the tender love which a mother cherishes for her child—at once so pure, so disinterested, so self-sacrificing—is perhaps the holiest emotion of which this fallen human nature is capable."[1] Each of these authors used language that suggested the idealized vision of sentimental motherhood that shaped the identity of southern women, particularly elites, in the antebellum period. Narratives spoke in this vein of the values of the larger community, defining its boundaries by delineating how members of this society ought to feel and act. While these social ideals cannot tell us how people actually behaved, they often formed the beginning point of an individual's self-identity. Southerners defined their own behavior as either proper or deviant by measuring it against this paradigm.

While the figure of the flirtatious southern belle has gained a prominent place in the popular history of the Old South, this stage of development occupied only a brief season in the life of an elite woman. Instead, contemporaries celebrated domesticity and motherhood as the true identity of southern womanhood. An 1849 article in the *Southern Literary Messenger* conceded the excitement of being a belle but concluded that "the true sphere of woman is at home. There her loveliness is pure, bright, and unfading." A decade earlier the *Southern Literary Journal* contrasted the male aspiration for "thrones and large dominions" with a woman's desire to be "the queen of the household; her diadem is the social affections; her sceptre love; her robe chastity, pure as the driven snow, enveloping her form, so that the imagination can find naught to blush at, even in the impropriety of attitude."[2] Domesticity, and particularly motherhood, became the full flowering of the belle's potential. Social commentators tied the role of motherhood to additional ideals of womanhood, including virtue and piety. At the same time, they used social divisions to explain deviations from these glorified norms. While northerners, and residents of other Western nations, shared many of these domestic ideals, southern social commentators hinted at a distinctly southern meaning, tying a woman's fulfillment of or failure to achieve these standards of maternal perfection to her status and identity within this community. Taken together, the idealized narratives of birth and motherhood, and the policing of potential challenges, suggested the contested nature of southern identity during the antebellum period.

Virtue was both the first tenet of southern womanhood and intrinsic to the female identity. "The very term 'Woman,'" one author explained, "implies identity of moral existence."[3] This morality was closely tied to the motherhood role. Lydia Sigourney, a northern author widely read in the South, wrote: "My friend, if in becoming a mother, you have reached the climax of your happiness, you have also taken a higher place in the scale of being." In the same work she assured her readers that "to love children, is the dictate of our nature," and warned that the "total absence of this love, induces a suspicion that the heart is not right."[4] Not only did her virtue shape the identity of the mother, but it also molded the character of future generations. The mother was "a moral teacher" upon whom fell the task of giving "first lessons in virtue, temperance and patriotism; while the willing listener, in breathless suspense, feels that there is no eloquence like that which flows from maternal lips."[5] John Gunn, the author of a popular medical-advice manual, mixed physiological information about pregnancy and infant nurture with a moral message. "How all-powerful, for good or evil, is the influence of the mother," he counseled. "During those hours of infancy, passed in unavoidable seclusion, when the affections and mental powers can be molded into any form by the plastic hand of maternal love, then it is that the bent is taken for weal or woe, which all future life cannot alter."[6]

The feminine ideals of piety and domesticity also clearly shaped the way that southerners talked about birth and motherhood. An 1832 article in the southern youth magazine the *Rose Bud* lauded the love and care mothers gave to their children, and then asked, "But who is the parent of the mother?" The article offered the answer that "God is the parent of the mother. He is the parent of all, for He created all."[7] Individual southerners echoed this same language of devotion and religious purpose in their own writings on motherhood. After the birth of her first child in 1851, Penelope Alderman of North Carolina wrote: "May it please thee O Lord who has given her to us to bless her with life, health, prosperity, and happiness and above all to give her thy grace[.]"[8] Motherly love and religious devotion thus became intertwined, assuring women that in embracing the motherhood ideal they were fulfilling both the dictates of their nature and God's will. Nineteenth-century Americans understood biology, religion, and nature as intertwined in an orderly universe in which everyone had a place, based on physiological determinants such as sex and race. *Family* referred to more than private relationships; it was the primary unit of the southern social structure, forming the model for all other relationships of dominance and submission within society. Most social commentators believed that this ordering manifested God's divine will. Thus discussions of birth and maternity moved easily from religion to family and social order. This link to birth allowed commentators to make the social hierarchy seem natural and organic.[9]

Antebellum southern fiction became an arena for expressing these familial and community ideals. Female readers of domestic novels found messages about proper behavior, as well as warnings about the consequences of failing to live up to these standards. In 1840 the *Southern Ladies' Book* called for an indigenous southern literature reflecting their sectional values, "unless we are willing to occupy before the world the singularly inconsistent position of boldly asserting our natural and constitutional rights in politics and commerce, and yet tamely submitting to a most inglorious dependence for all the agencies by which taste is to be refined and sentiment cultivated." After the publication of Harriet Beecher Stowe's *Uncle Tom's Cabin* in the early 1850s, the calls for a literature in defense of the South intensified. Southern novelists adopted motherhood, a symbol used extensively by Stowe to chastise the slave system, to refute Stowe's accusations and assert the natural superiority of their own southern society.[10]

Novelist John Pendleton Kennedy equated reproduction with a white southern woman's contribution to her family. In *Swallow Barn* he introduces Lucretia, the matriarch of the Meriwether family, as "a fruitful vessel" who "seldom fails in her annual tribute to the honors of the family[.]"[11] Lucretia barely figures into the main plot of the novel, making her fecundity her entire story, yet her reproductive role is shown as essential to the continuation of this southern family. In her 1854 novel, *The Planter's Northern Bride*, Caroline Hentz portrays a broader, but still organic, social structure in which birth gives each person his or her social identity. In one notable scene a southern planter addresses his slaves on their different social positions:

> Listen! You are slaves, and I am free; but I neither made you slaves nor myself a free man. We are all in the condition in which we are born. You are black, and I am white; but I did not give you those sable skins, nor myself this fairer complexion. You and I are as God Almighty made us, and, as I expect to give an account of the manner in which I fulfil my duties as a master, so you will be judged according to your fidelity, honesty, and uprightness as servants.[12]

Through this scene Hentz proclaims the "naturalness" of the southern hierarchy, in which birth, and not avarice, malice, or even racism, determined status and social destiny.

Mary Eastman, like Hentz, used her novel *Aunt Phillis's Cabin* to show that each person in southern society held his or her position due to birth and blood. However, for emphasis, Eastman makes her assertions about hierarchy in the voice of an enslaved woman. Aunt Phillis, a faithful servant of the Weston family, confessed that she experienced discontent when she first became a mother: "When my children was born, I would think 'what comfort is it to give birth to a child when I know it's a slave.'" But Eastman then has Phillis opine that it was her own weakness, and not slavery, that caused her discontent. "I struggled hard though, with these feelings, sir," she admits to the novel's narrator, "and God gave me grace to get the better of them, for I could not read my Bible without seeing there was nothing agin slavery there; and that God had told the master his duty, and the slave his duty."[13] This passage, complete with suggestions of slave literacy and religiosity, clearly represented Eastman's wish to counter northern attacks rather than to portray the realities of the slave experience or the enslaved community's acceptance of their status within the social hierarchy.

Black women undoubtedly viewed their identity as mothers within the slave system quite differently, although they lacked the public voice of the white southerners who constructed the hegemonic ideal. Anti-slavery novelists occasionally gave voice to a counternarrative. These novelists claimed the same principles of virtuous motherhood for enslaved women that were more typically applied to white women. At the same time, they condemned the barriers and burdens that impeded the ability of black mothers to meet these standards. Anti-slavery novelist Kate Pickard's description of the first moments of motherhood for her black heroine Vina carried a marked similarity to idealized descriptions of white motherhood: "A new fount of love gushed up in her mother-heart, to bless the little trembler, and her frame thrilled with a delicious joy, as she proudly placed in her husband's arms his first-born boy." African American author William Wells Brown also celebrated the devotion of the enslaved mother, but he equally emphasized her hardships. The heroine of his novel, *Clotel*, drowns while attempting to rescue a child. Brown laments: "Such was the life and such the death of a woman whose virtues and goodness of heart would have done honour to one in a higher station of life, and who, if she had been born in any other land but that of slavery, would have been honoured and loved." While critiquing the slave system, these narratives claimed a positive maternal identity for black women that corresponded with southern paradigms of child-bearing and motherhood.[14]

Anti-slavery writers also suggested that in the slave community the ideal mother's love and nurturing was expansive, going beyond her own children to include other black children and even white children under her care. In her 1856 novel *The Kidnapped and the Ransomed*, Pickard celebrated the love that a black woman, Aunt Sally, had for both the white infant she tended and for her own children: "[T]he deep love of her nature was transferred to the sweet infant left wholly to her care; and though when her own children were born, a new fount of tenderness was opened in her heart, it was scarce deeper than that which had welled forth for the motherless babe she had cherished."[15] Such narratives suggested that black women's nurturing better met this principle of maternalism than the narrow devotion of white mothers, which was directed exclusively toward their own children. In this literature, motherhood created an identity for enslaved women shaped both by an adherence to southern ideals and opposition to the social structures that framed them.

As well as the moral identity embodied in the motherhood role, birth and infant nurture in the antebellum South rested on a gender identity shaped by biology. Thomas Dew's 1835 treatise on women presumed a biological mandate to bear children, for "to increase and multiply, seems to be the great law of animated creation[.]"[16] South Carolina planter J. H. Hammond, writing to his brother, expressed this sentiment more bluntly: "Women were meant to breed—Men to do the work of the world."[17] Although these men may have been writing specifically about the role of white women, this biological mandate had the effect of linking women, black and white, together in their motherhood role.

High birthrates became a sign to social commentators that southern women were fulfilling their proper gender role, doing what they ought. They wrote boastfully of the fecundity of both white and black women. The *Southern Quarterly Review* celebrated the growth of the white population of the South by 65 percent between 1820 and 1849. This growth, the author contended, outstripped northern growth when new immigrants were subtracted. Thus it followed that southern white women better fulfilled their reproductive function than did native-born northern women, a reflection of the beneficence of the distinctive social organization of the South. The author further claimed that the natural increase of the enslaved population, which he estimated at 61.5 percent between 1820 and 1840, provided incontrovertible proof of the slave system's benevolence, arguing that "we may confidently challenge the history of the world to produce a parallel instance of natural increase in any class or race of the human family." From these demographics he concluded that "we may as confidently rest on this single fact—no other being necessary—to demonstrate beyond all cavil, that everywhere, in whatever occupation and by whomsoever owned, our slaves are uniformly treated in the manner best calculated to promote their comfort."[18]

Southern apologists adopted slave fecundity as a common theme, openly discussing the reproduction of enslaved women and using the reproductive health of southern women, black and white, as a symbol of societal well-being.[19] In fact, in the South, as elsewhere in America, birth rates actually declined throughout the nineteenth century. Still, in 1850 American women bore, on average, over five living infants, and southern women of both races reproduced at rates higher than the national average.[20] Larger families in the South resulted from women, both black and white, bearing children earlier and more often than their northern sisters. These reproductive statistics became a mark of a unique regional identity in the minds of many southern social commentators.

Southerners in the antebellum period did not, of course, invent the idealization of childbearing and motherhood. In the years following the Revolution, some American writers advocated a "republican" motherhood responsible for raising worthy citizens, a recognition of the intersection of women's private actions and the public interest of the nation. By the early nineteenth century, a sentimental reverence for motherhood reigned throughout America, at least in the ideal. Eleanor Lewis of Virginia wrote in 1799 that "the idea of being a Mother, of watching over & forming the mind of Our little infant is a source of delight which none but those in similar situations can experience."[21] Such sentiments would continue to resonate generations later. Subtle shifts and intensifications did, however, occur in the antebellum glorification of childbearing and motherhood. While eighteenth-century parents believed that the survival of their offspring was in the hands of God, nineteenth-century commentators began to suggest that "good" mothering could keep children alive. At the same time, the view of children shifted from a natural depravity to a malleable innocence, demanding a mother's care to shape children's hearts and minds. Changing economic patterns also altered the mothering role, at least among the middling classes. As men increasingly went out to work, the home became the domain of the mother, who thus became the primary influence on the children.[22]

Both northern and southern social commentators made motherhood central to the female identity. The *Ladies' Repository*, a magazine published in Cincinnati, observed in 1861: "Of the many interesting aspects under which we may regard the female character there is none more striking and beautiful than that of the mother." The author added that "upon her devolves, under almost all circumstances, the early training of the young, and it is a mother's chief praise to see to her home and tend her children."[23] The overlapping rhetoric in the North and the South suggested a shared model, but context altered interpretations of the conventions across regional boundaries. The realities of slavery, plantation life, and higher fertility all shaped southerners' understanding of the essential principles of childbearing and motherhood in a way they believed distinguished them from northerners. Rather than seeing a shared American value system, those interested in constructing a distinct southern identity used ideals of childbearing and motherhood to assert that difference. They understood that from birth each person possessed an identity that tied them first to their families and then to a larger community of friends and neighbors. The next logical step was a link to a regional, and ultimately a nationalistic, identity. Thus in the antebellum years, a discussion about which society, northern or southern, best fulfilled the ideals of birth and motherhood became an important part of the public debate.

Commentators throughout antebellum America associated motherhood with the development of citizenship and urged female education as the means of preparing women for this role. By the 1850s some southern commentators advocated a southern education for the future mothers of the South. Female students, they argued, would become mothers, and in that role they would teach their own children not just values, but southern values.[24] As the sectional debate intensified, many southerners (and northerners too) would interpret the ideals of childbearing and motherhood through the prism of region.

Southern society promised women certain rewards for fulfilling their motherhood role. Such rewards were primarily emotional, especially the knowledge that their personal identity conformed to the social ideal. White women received accolades from their husbands, friends, and relations when they bore children. Robert Allston wrote from Columbia, where he was serving as president of the South Carolina Senate, to praise his wife Adèle after she gave birth: "Honor to your sex for its beautiful symmetry, its wonderful & admirable perfection in fulfilling the responsibilities imposed by nature."[25] Robert esteemed Adèle for bearing his child and, in the rhetoric of the ideal, indicated that she had fulfilled her "natural" role as a woman. Another South Carolinian, Elizabeth Perry, anticipated these same accolades as she awaited the birth of her first child in 1838: "How strange! in a few months I may be a *Mother*. God grant it! My husband will *love* me so. Even *more* than he does *now*; though I should think that *impossible*."[26] Southern sons were also said to reward maternal devotion with expressions of deep attachment to their mothers. Madaline Edwards of New Orleans observed that even adult sons, long removed from the maternal home, continued to be devoted to their mothers. She wrote that she had "often seen the husband forsake wife and children but would not cast off his mother, I have seen brutes who cursed and despised their father, but seldom one who spoke slight of his Mother."[27]

The ideal further rewarded white women by offering them the claim that through their instruction they contributed to the greater good of society. South Carolinian Laura Cole Smith wrote in her diary of a young woman who, at twenty-four, was raising four of her own children and two orphaned sisters. Smith concluded that "this is certainly a very early age to be so deeply involved in the cares and perplexities of life, but doubtless the pleasure of forming their young minds, and instructing them in the way they should go fully compensates for the trouble."[28] White southern mothers were thus assured that if they fulfilled this quintessential role they would ultimately be rewarded by both private devotion and a well-ordered society.

For enslaved women, as for free women, reproduction could provide the emotional rewards of creating a family and contributing to a network of love and support. Slaveowners, however, felt uncertain that such emotional inducements would suffice (particularly with the omnipresent threat of separation, which might make family ties a source of pain as well as of joy). Thus many masters offered more tangible rewards when an enslaved woman gave birth—a new dress or a sum of money might be given when each infant was born. Rachel O'Connor, a Louisiana plantation mistress, explained this system of rewards to her agent, along with her request for fabric, in April 1835: "I have always given a dress of such to every women after having a young child. I am now in debt to four that has young babes, *and fine ones too*. They do much better by being encouraged a little and I have ever thought they deserved it."[29] Former slave Dink Walton Young recalled that "every time a Negro baby was born on one of his plantations, Major Walton gave the mother a calico dress and a 'bright shiny' silver dollar."[30]

For multiple births, or for women who produced a set number of children, some slave masters offered additional bonuses. British actress Frances "Fannie" Kemble wrote that on her husband's Georgia plantation enslaved women "enjoy, by means of numerous children, certain positive advantages." She then delineated these "advantages":

> In the first place, every woman who is pregnant, as soon as she chooses to make the fact known to the overseer, is relieved of a certain portion of her work in the field, which lightening of labor continues, of course, as long as she is so burdened. . . . Moreover, they have all of them a most distinct and perfect knowledge of their value to their owners as property; and a woman thinks, and not much amiss, that the more frequently she adds to the number of her master's live-stock by bringing new slaves into the world, the more claims she will have upon his consideration and good-will.[31]

While failing to recognize the personal and emotional rewards enslaved women could find in bearing children, Kemble attested to the negotiated relationship between reproduction and tangible compensation.

P. C. Weston of South Carolina wrote into his overseer's contract rewards for reproduction and infant nurturing. It instructed that "[w]omen with six children alive at any *one* time, are allowed all Saturday to themselves." Several former slaves interviewed by the Works Progress Administration (WPA) in the 1930s (these and other narratives were collected by George Rawick into the multiple volumes of *The American Slave: A Composite Autobiography*) recalled that women who had given birth to a large number of children escaped field work. Former slave Phil Towns, born in Virginia in 1824, recalled: "Mothers of three or more children were not compelled to work, *as the masters felt that their children needed care*." Lucy Galloway's grandmother, Frances, bore twenty-two children and her master put her in charge of tending to all of the enslaved children on the plantation. Douglas Parish's master considered Parish's mother, Fannie, a "breeder," so "all she had to do was raise children." Everyone concerned in the reproduction of enslaved women might desire a similar outcome (the birth and nurturing of enslaved children), and they accepted rewards as part of this system, even as their rationales diverged. Whatever the intentions of white southerners in offering these compensations, it is unlikely that they changed the ideals, emotions, or social identity of black mothers within their families or communities. Like the differences between North and South, the differences between the paradigms of white and black mothers were more in interpretation than in actualities.[32]

While social commentators stressed the importance of the ideals of birth and motherhood, not everyone lived up to these standards. Elite white southerners turned to perceived class or racial differences to explain away behavioral deviancies. They hoped that even defiance of the pattern could be used to sustain the existing social structure if a woman's behavior was linked to her race and class identity. Some southern authors balanced the sentimental paeans to motherhood with cautionary tales of "bad" mothers. Faced with the existence of illegitimacy and infanticide, they evoked class and race behaviors, respectively, while maintaining the idealized identity of elite white women. At the same time, however, these "deviant" groups voiced a counternarrative that expressed principles better suited to the realities of their lives. Together these narratives demonstrated the fragility of the hegemonic ideal and the contested nature of a southern identity founded on birth and motherhood.

Illegitimacy was one of the greatest perceived threats to southern social identity. Specifically, it threatened the purity of bloodlines, which were intrinsic to conceptions of patriarchy, honor, and status. Elite white southerners used a rhetoric of bloodlines to explain the social hierarchy and their status within it. By linking status to biology, and thus birth, social elites hoped to naturalize not only their own social position, but also the place of every southerner, black and white, rich and poor. The planter class used their birth and bloodlines to justify their position through claims to "noble blood." They legitimized their privileged status not through the property they owned, or even the slaves they held, but through claims to aristocratic parentage and ancestry. In his 1860 work,

Social Relations in Our Southern States, D. R. Hundley explained that "family pride" was central to southern identity, particularly among the gentry. Robert Criswell, who identified himself in the preface to his 1852 novel as a man who lived in the North but who had traveled extensively in the South, wrote *"Uncle Tom's Cabin" Contrasted with Buckingham Hall, the Planter's Home; or, A Fair View of Both Sides of the Slavery Question* with the stated intention of easing sectional tensions. Colonel Buckingham, who represented the southern planting class, bragged of his kinship ties and "his ancestral blood, which, he often boasted, had *not* 'crept through scoundrels ever since the flood,' but was pure and aristocratic in its descent." Bloodlines provided social identity in these works; pure white women and virile but honorable white men formed the foundation of these bloodlines, and birth was the source of their continuity.[33]

Since illegitimacy threatened both the solidity of family structures and the "purity" of bloodlines, it became a source of some anxiety. A number of southern novelists reflected this concern by warning of the dire consequences of illegitimate birth for both mother and child. Ironically, illegitimate births were the only ones that had a direct physical presence in antebellum novels. Authors considered discussions of the bodies of unblemished women improper, whereas emphasizing the physical pain of illegitimate birth, followed by death or ostracism, served as a cautionary tale against straying from the ideal. For example, in George Tucker's 1824 novel, *The Valley of the Shenandoah*, the seduction of Louisa Grayson, formerly a paragon of virtue and southern womanhood, is suggested by her confession: "I saw him privately—I saw him too often—I—Oh! I'm the veriest wretch that lives." If the reference to illegitimacy is oblique, the consequences of Louisa's moral failure are not—her brother died defending her honor, and Louisa herself died two years after being "taken sick," having suffered diminished health and spirits. Her mother had to live with the shame, unable to "think of any plan by which the stain upon the hitherto unsullied honour of their house could be kept from the knowledge of the world, or that any thing like happiness or respectability could again attend her in life."[34] Illicit sex and the threat of an illegitimate birth virtually destroyed this erstwhile respectable southern family.

Other authors wrote even more explicitly of the consequences of illegitimacy. William Gilmore Simms's 1855 novel *Charlemont* portrays the seduction of the heroine, Margaret Cooper. Through her "fatal lapse of virtue" she becomes pregnant. In desperation, she contemplates suicide to "save her from that more notorious exposure which must follow the birth of that child of sin whom she deemed it no more than a charity to destroy." Her maternal feelings for the unborn child prevent this course of action, but the child dies a month after its birth, having drunk "the milk of bitterness" from its mother's breast. Margaret Cooper, while she survives, retires into a life of seclusion, vowing revenge upon the seducer who has ruined her life by taking not only her virginity but her claim to status and identity within southern society.[35]

Another Margaret, the heroine of "The Fatherless Daughter," a story published in the *Southern Literary Messenger* in 1841, also encounters a seducer. Upon discovering she had been abandoned without a proper marriage, Margaret "underwent the tortures of premature parturition, and gave birth to a dead child. In the agony of her spirit, she blessed God who had spared it the infamy and misery which must have been its portion in this world of woe." Although Margaret lives on as a decorous model of womanhood, "she was not happy. The idea that her once spotless reputation had been tarnished . . . that whenever she appeared in society, she was always the object of pity, sometimes of contempt; poisoned every fountain of enjoyment." On her deathbed a minister reveals that her marriage was in fact valid, finally redeeming her to unsullied womanhood and allowing her to die guiltless.[36] Yet the reader is clearly meant to receive a message about both the short- and long-term consequences that came with lapses of virtuous behavior; straying from the identity of idealized womanhood would result in misery.

In fictional accounts, consequences were equally dire for the offspring of illicit unions. As the above examples suggest, an early death was the usual fate for illegitimate infants in novels. But those who survived faced a challenging future. Commentators suggested that the taint of illegitimacy would permanently mark the identity of the child. Novelist Mary Eastman provides a clear example of this legacy. In *Aunt Phillis's Cabin* the young white heroine of her novel, Alice Weston, begins to develop tender feelings for a man named Walter. Her father, however, warns her away from this relationship by informing her that "Walter is not an equal by right of birth to those whose parents held a fair and honorable position in society." While Mr. Weston suggests the character flaws of Walter's father, it was the fact that Walter's mother "was not married, as far as is known," that condemned not only her but the child she bore. Based on these origins, no relationship with Alice, a true southern lady, would be possible. Her father reflected society's judgment by noting that "no woman of delicacy would ever think of marrying him with that stain on his birth." The message was clear: a person's birth laid the foundation for the social identity that shaped his or her position and possibilities within antebellum southern society.[37]

In the North, men's culpability in seduction was increasingly being recognized in the antebellum period, particularly among moral reformers. But the fictional tales recounted above suggest that southern authors still viewed illegitimacy as primarily a female crime. Illegitimacy seemed, to many social commentators, to be a willful leap off of the pedestal of idealized female identity. An author for the southern journal *DeBow's Review* wrote in 1852 that

> in all derelictions from the right, the just, the holy, and the true, woman is responsible for her own degradation; inasmuch as it entirely proceeds from her own act, in casting herself out from her true position. She is herself, we repeat, the sole cause of it; and we wish to lay a stress upon this, because we maintain her to be a responsible, reasoning being, and not man's puppet. It is no excuse for her that man tempts her into folly. Man is unfortunately ready enough to tempt woman to err, and does not always stop to calculate the possible evil resulting from his pleasures and amusements.[38]

Illegitimate birth offered incontrovertible testimony of actions contrary to the chaste ideal of unmarried southern womanhood; the proof of the transgression was written on her body. Childbirth within marriage could be attributed to wifely and maternal duties, but outside of marriage, only to licentiousness. And, of course, illegitimacy threatened not only gender paradigms, but the patriarchal, father-led household and the inheritance structures which rested on family bloodlines.

Interestingly, despite myriad warnings to the contrary, some women managed to retain their elite social identity despite the taint of illegitimacy. In practice, the ideals proved open to some manipulation. A timely marriage could remove much of the ignominy of the situation. Although the "hasty" marriage of his daughter Rebecca caused South Carolinian Francis Pickens, then ambassador in Russia, "pain and mortification," according to his wife, it created no long-term damage to the family's social position. Gertrude Thomas wrote of a former school friend: *"Five months and twenty days* after her marriage Ella became the mother of a little daughter who is still living—such an act required no announcement. What a shock it must have been to the family." While this birth may have ended the new father's ambition to become a Methodist minister, it did not end in the tragedy threatened by fictional sources. Rosalie Calvert even made a joke of such occurrences. Writing to her family in Europe of her brother's childless marriage, she quipped: "In America one expects better than that—two women of our acquaintance came to their confinements after only seven months of marriage!"[39] These situations undoubtedly caused gossip, but they did not automatically remove these women from their communities or from their social identity as elite southerners.

In fact, illegitimacy seemed to have been most problematic for elite southerners when it was combined with additional challenges to the social structure. Miscegenation committed by a white woman would have created the greatest defiance of social boundaries. "The white woman who marries a negro," novelist Caroline Hentz warned, "makes herself an outcast, a scorn and a byword." But most elite commentators assumed that this was a problem only among the lowest classes. Frederick Law Olmsted quoted a southerner who assured him that sex between white women and black men was only a problem among women "so poor that their favors can be purchased by the slaves."[40] Such occurrences were so beyond the pale, and relatively rare, that they received very little attention in the writings of southerners.

More typically, illegitimacy was tied to adultery. In 1842, Eliza Fisher implied that a Mrs. Willings's husband was not the father of her newborn son by writing to her mother that the comments upon it were "too scandalous to be repeated much less written."[41] While the child would not actually have been illegitimate, since the mother was married, such a contravention of the assurances of pure bloodlines represented a threat to familial structures. Eleanor Lewis did not share Fisher's reservations about repeating scandalous incidents. She recounted a sensational tale of a man who had intended to run off with his sister-in-law but had been thwarted when "Miss McC's unexpected confinement disclosed the nefarious business."[42] Lewis tied the illegitimate birth to infidelity and property fraud, all of which challenged southern social mores.

Illegitimacy hit closer to home for Moses Moore of Louisiana. He wrote of his nephew Newton's widow, who had "disgraced herself after which I did not think proper to countenance her—Indeed I never saw her after she brot [*sic*] forth an illegitimate child—I am told the Father afterwards married her." Yet his letter suggests that his outrage related as much to her leaving her older children with him as to her behavior in bearing an illegitimate child. The latter simply became an excuse for ostracizing her.[43] While social commentators and novelists predicted inevitably dire consequences, incidents of illegitimacy actually fostered complex responses. Family ties, social position, and community judgment combined in constructing an identity for the transgressing woman and for the child she bore.

Southern opinion-makers, faced with women who did not disappear in shame and death after conceiving illegitimately, as they did in novels, sought explanations in the existing social order. Specifically, lower-class women were blamed for the existence of illegitimacy in the South. The small number of wealthy planter households disproportionately influenced the ideals and norms of society. Elites also claimed a moral superiority, a better adherence to the standards that they themselves created. An article in the *Southern Literary Messenger* linked class position to claims of piety and virtue: "We cannot call a man *worthless* who is *worth nothing*, nor can we say a *poor* man is a *bad* man, though when we use the phrase poor *but* pious, we do hint in direct opposition to Scripture, that this is an exception, the general rule being rich *and* pious."[44] Southern elites thus had few compunctions about blaming most incidents of illegitimacy on the immorality of the lower classes. This blame focused particularly on poor white women, since all enslaved women's births, by legal definition, were illegitimate and did not threaten the social order.

While social and legal commentator T. R. R. Cobb of Georgia expressed the hope that the slave system made poor white women "not subject to as great temptations and importunities as they would be under other circumstances," Frederick Law Olmsted reported from his travels through the South that most elite southerners believed that "any white girl who could be hired to work for wages would certainly be a girl of easy virtue."[45] Such class distinctions allowed elite women to solidify their own claims to the virtuous ideal, strengthened in comparison to the purported immorality of the women beneath them. The argument became circular: any woman who gave birth to an illegitimate child was deemed lower class, and thus only lower-class women, and not ladies, were responsible for illegitimacy.

In March 1828 Sarah Gayle recorded an incident in her diary that reflected the links she made between illegitimacy and lower-class women, as well as the expectation that the immorality of the mother would be passed on to the offspring. Gayle wrote of being called to the bedside of a Mrs. Dann whose two-day-old infant was dying. She notes that "I could not but think it would be merciful in the Almighty to snatch to himself the innocent offspring of a guilty mother." She describes this mother, "the now Mrs. Dann," as having been "a young handsome & un-blushing prostitute" whose entire family was of bad character, and whose five-year-old daughter seemed destined to follow the fate of her mother. Gayle goes on to suggest the cycle of poverty, immorality, and illegitimacy she foresaw:

> How slight a cause, probably at first, led to this ruin of fame and virtue! Maybe an incautious word a light and unmeaning look—imprudence first placed the curse upon them—believing *all* lost, they became careless & callous—gave birth to unfortunate children whose fathers dared not lay their hand upon them, and say "it is mine," they in turn, after a course of preparation, more deeply damning than beginning them into the world, resign themselves, without remorse to a life of infamy, to the inheritance of which they possibly believed themselves entitled.[46]

As in the fictional accounts, Gayle saw the identity of both mother and child as irrevocably altered by these events, with their class, family history, and social identity intertwined.

Elite southerners also associated poorer women with an excessive fecundity. Although southern ideals lauded high birth rates, they contrarily condemned poor whites for producing *too many* children. Social commentators linked the latter's reproduction to licentiousness, loss of control, and an inability to provide properly for offspring.[47] In his novel *Swallow Barn*, John Pendleton Kennedy wrote of a blacksmith's many children, "barefooted, half covered with rags, and with smutty faces looking wildly out of mops of hair." Although Kennedy noted that this appearance proved "their legitimate descent," these offspring did not support the familial structure, as the ideal suggested the production of children should. Rather, "the heir-apparent and the rest of the progeny abdicated their birthright, and wandered off, it is supposed, in search of food." One southern doctor claimed that "if an accurate record could be had of the births of illegitimate children . . . it would be found to be as great, among the poor people in the part of the country in which he practiced, as of those born in wedlock." In fact, poor whites may often have put off marriage and childbearing until they gathered sufficient resources to form a household, thus reducing their average fertility rate; statistically, elite women generally gave birth to as many children as poor white women.[48] But a belief in increased fecundity, combined with a presumed immorality, made poor women the originators of illegitimacy in the dominant narrative.

Despite their marginalization in idealized accounts, poor white women made up a significant part of the southern population. A majority of white southerners owned no slaves, and the labor of women in these families was essential to the support of the household. Further, a significant number of women, particularly those living in urban areas, worked for wages at some point in their lives.[49] These women countered the portrayal of themselves as women of easy virtue with a narrative that reflected their own standards of behavior. They relied on their own values, as historian Laura Edwards asserts, "to negotiate their way through an often hostile world, to blunt assertions of male power in their own households and communities, and to maintain the economic and social status of their families."[50] For these women, fulfilling family responsibilities and ensuring material survival was more central to their identity than the values of virtue and modesty lauded in the hegemonic ideal. As a matter of self-preservation, some women purposefully chose to defy the dictums of "meekness, chastity, and self-sacrifice." Others embraced monogamy but did not seek the legal sanction of marriage, which made unions legitimate in the eyes of the elite. Members of this social stratum did not necessarily condemn women who bore children out of wedlock;

illegitimacy in such cases had legal but little social meaning.[51] Unfortunately, these poor whites produced few written testaments to their maternal ideals, so while their actions provided a counternarrative of sorts, the dominant accounts, which blamed these women for deviancy from society's standards of motherhood, remained largely unchallenged and shaped their identity both in the antebellum period and beyond.

Illegitimacy generally played a smaller role in structuring the identity of black women and children. While some elite narratives linked free black women with poor white women in this regard, the illegitimate births of enslaved women had a limited use in the ideal narrative of southern society, since it drew into question the slave system, which did not recognize the legality of any slave marriages and thus rendered all slave births illegitimate. Still, a number of southern social commentators ignored this legal reality and instead focused on "the natural lewdness of the negro" in an attempt to shift the blame for the perceived immorality of enslaved women from the slave system to their race.[52] Dr. William Holcombe wrote that the "want of chastity is by no means the result of slavery, but is a remnant of that barbaric character which estimates woman in the lowest and most sensual manner—indeed, as merely a beast of burden."[53] In an 1844 article in the *Southern Literary Messenger*, "An Essay on the Moral and Political Effect of the Relation between the Caucasian Master and the African Slave," its author emphasized the character improvements he believed could be attributed to slavery but concluded that "in the essential quality of female purity, the slave may come short of the class which fills the same place in society where slavery is not known; yet it is not with that class, but with the negro, in his primitive state of wild freedom, that the comparison is to be made."[54] These elite white southerners attributed lasciviousness to black women and then blamed "natural" propensities, rather than their social system, for sexual misbehaviors, including illegitimacy.

Writing of enslaved women in 1860, South Carolina plantation mistress Keziah Brevard claimed that "many of them set no higher value on themselves than the beasts of the field do—I know a family in five miles of me where there are six women who have & have had children for thirty years back & not one of them but have [been] bastards & only one ever had a husband."[55] Eliza Andrews of Georgia wrote in retrospect of the woman who tended her as a child: "I am sorry to say that my dear old mammy—Sophia by name—while so superior, and as genuine a 'lady' as I ever knew, in other respects, shared the weakness of her race in regard to chastity."[56] Elite white women may have perpetuated this image because it contrasted with the purity and virtue they claimed for their own race and class, justifying, in their view, their superior social position. But even James Redpath, an anti-slavery newspaper editor, observed that "chastity is a virtue which, in the South, is entirely monopolized by the ladies of the ruling race. Every slave negress is a courtesan."[57] Here, too, enslaved women may have been joined with poor white women in their alleged lasciviousness and propensity toward producing illegitimate children.

Generally, when plantation masters and mistresses discussed the illegitimate births of the enslaved women in their own households, they simply ignored the legal realities and their own control over the enslaved women's ability to marry. Caroline Pettigrew of North Carolina wrote a lengthy letter to her husband upon discovering that her maid, Ellen, was pregnant. The enslaved father of the expected child, Edmond, remained on the plantation they had left for the season. When Pettigrew asked Ellen why she had not asked to be married earlier, she replied, "you said Mam we was not to be married till Margaret was married." Ellen thus suggested Pettigrew's control of the situation, a responsibility Pettigrew immediately denied by claiming that she would not have objected under such circumstances. Pettigrew then reported a conversation with Ellen's mother in which she was told: "Why Miss Carey it is very bad & wrong to have deceived you, but you know when his Master gave consent Ellen was as good as his wife." Pettigrew used this incident to comment on the morality of all enslaved people: "And such are their ideas of morals, the very best among them seem not capable of understanding that a marriage ceremony is of any consequence." Then, since Ellen noted that Edmond had intended to make her his wife, Pettigrew simply declared them married and indicated that writing to her husband of the fact would make it so.[58] Thus, despite her assertions to the contrary, it was Pettigrew, and not Ellen, who put minimal emphasis on a marriage ceremony and who did not fully understand the limits that she herself placed on marriage between enslaved couples. Similarly, Mahala Roach of Mississippi recorded the marriage of Henrietta, who had borne at least three children, with the remark: "I think it is time!"[59] Both white women alluded to the immorality of the actions of the enslaved women while disavowing their own control, which allowed them to either force or disregard enslaved marriages. Neither woman acknowledged in her comments that these marriages were neither legally sanctioned nor had the power to make the offspring "legitimate."

In the antebellum period, southern social elites ascribed a shared identity of promiscuity and immorality to both poor white women and enslaved black women. But while the condemnation of poor white women tended to focus on the production of illegitimate offspring, some southerners blamed enslaved women for the more serious transgression of infanticide. These social commentators extended their belief in natural promiscuity to assumptions about a general lack of control, resulting in both careless and violent motherhood. White southerners almost always identified *overlaying*, or infant smothering, with black mothers. The social stigma attached to infant suffocation meant that southern elites, who kept such records, sought to protect the reputation of white mothers by underreporting its existence among whites. At the same time, they more readily labeled black women as bad mothers, even murderers. Louisianan Zenah Preston's plantation-diary entry for May 11, 1845, for example, recorded the death of a two-month-old slave and pronounced that "its mother overlaid it & smothered it to death." Yet rather than expressing moral outrage, Preston's concern seems to have been the fee he had paid to hire the enslaved parents.[60]

Elite southerners shared stories of more spectacular cases of infanticide and had a marked willingness to assign guilt to black women. Thomas Chaplin wrote of a suspected infanticide that occurred on his own South Carolina plantation in January 1854. "Helen's last child died today," Chaplin recorded in his journal, adding, "regularly murdered." As evidence, he stated: "The little thing was bruised & hurt in several places." Yet instead of legal prosecution, Chaplin concluded that "the mother deserves a good whipping, & I think she will get it yet."[61] Perhaps Chaplin did not seek legal punishment because his only proof was his own observation, although this did not prevent him from labeling Helen a murderer. More probably he did not seek legal interdiction because that would have meant the loss of Helen's labor, compounding the loss *he* had already suffered through the death of the infant slave.

Infant abandonment, sometimes resulting in death, was another accusation made against black mothers. In 1865 Eliza Andrews recorded rumors condemning black women for literally abandoning their motherly duties: "I have heard several well-authenticated instances of women throwing away their babies in their mad haste to run away from their homes and follow the Northern deliverers."[62] Her willingness to accept such stories as truth may have reflected her own sense of abandonment by the family's slaves. It also indicated a commonly held belief among former slaveholders that without their guidance, blacks would devolve into barbarity. Such descriptions of desertion should be contrasted with a story related in an 1833 issue of the *Rose Bud*, a magazine aimed at children. This tale told of an abandoned white infant who, ironically, was put under the care of "a colored woman, who has lost her own."[63] Unlike Andrews's general denigration of black motherhood, the author of this magazine story did not use the incident to comment on the mothering of all white mothers. But to many white observers, infanticide committed by a black woman was not an individualized act of desperation, but the fulfillment of the stereotype of black women as savage and incapable of the ideals of motherhood.

Just as members of the poor white community created their own set of principles to incorporate illegitimacy into their social identity, the enslaved community created a narrative that explained infanticide, even if it did not sanction it. A number of anti-slavery authors emphasized the conditions that made this solution seem acceptable. William Wells Brown offered one possible motive for infanticide in a lecture he delivered to the Female Anti-Slavery Society of Salem, Massachusetts, in 1847. "The mother has taken the life of her child," he explained, "to preserve that child from the hands of the Slave-trader." Enslaved mothers committing infanticide could believe that they were protecting their children from a fate worse than death. Most slave women nurtured their children in the best way they could, given their limited control over their own lives. But they did so in the context of a society that frequently degraded, when it did not deny, their motherhood. When enslaved women refused to bear children or let their infants live, they made a clear political statement about their unwillingness to support and perpetuate the system that would keep themselves and their children in a perpetual state of victimization.[64]

Yet memoirs and novels also emphasized the maternal devotion of enslaved women. Harriet Jacobs, for example, would not leave North Carolina until her children could be made safe, despite the grave danger of hiding nearby. She recorded the great pleasure she found just in being able to observe them through a peep-hole.[65] Abolitionist writings often portrayed women dying of a broken heart or committing suicide in despair over separation from their children. William Wells Brown, who was hired to a slave trader, saw a woman separated from her family "and having no desire to live without them, in the agony of her soul jumped overboard, and drowned herself."[66] Female readers of anti-slavery literature could relate to such tales as extreme examples of the care and concern they gave their own children and empathize with these enslaved women through their own identity as mothers.

Some white commentators, southern as well as northern, expanded the ideals of birth—and more particularly of infant nurture—to encompass some, if not all, black mothers. In these narratives, praise often rested not on an enslaved mother's emotional devotion, but on how she fit her children to behave "properly" as slaves. Mary Eastman lauded her title character in *Aunt Phillis's Cabin* as a good mother to her own children: "She had accustomed them to constant industry, and unqualified obedience to her directions, and for this reason, no one had found it necessary to interfere in their management."[67] Eastman's assessment of Phillis's status as a good mother, however, rested on her ability to inculcate her children with the identity of good slaves and teach them the values slaveowners sought. Similarly, John Pendleton Kennedy presented Lucy, a character in *Swallow Barn*, as a successful "negro mother" because each of her offspring had been raised to be "serviceable."[68] Lucy's only failure, as judged by her white owner, came in her devotion to her youngest child, Abe, who proved too disobedient and willful for his slave status. Rather than attributing this devotion to maternal loyalty, Kennedy wrote that her "affection for this worthless scion of her stock" demonstrated "how entirely the unreasoning instincts of the animal sway the human mind, in its uneducated condition." This contrasts markedly to an essay written in Mary Ezell's copybook that celebrated the devotion of the white mother who possesses a "fond heart bleeding over the error of her son who is treading slowly but surely the downward road to ruin."[69] "Good" mothering of enslaved children had a narrow meaning for white commentators, which involved preparing them to accept their "proper" identity in the social hierarchy.

Paradoxically, the idealized narratives of black mothers created by white authors often involved the care that these women provided for elite white children. *Mammies*, or black caregivers for white children, touched on some of the most basic ironies and contradictions in antebellum southern society. White women, who were idealized for their mothering, shared the care of their infants with women whom white social commentators frequently condemned as promiscuous, animalistic in their emotions, and—most importantly—unnatural mothers. Elites needed to reconfigure their paradigm of the mothering impulse for at least some black women in order to justify white mothers turning their infants over to the care of these women. Like a white mother, the quintessential black mammy was skilled at nurturing her white charges both physically and mentally. She taught them proper manners and behaviors suitable to their position within the elite. Most importantly, the ideal mammy, like the ideal white mother, was emotionally devoted to her charges. In poetry and in novels, white southerners combined praise for a mammy's loyalty with praise for her nurturing. Mary Eastman's *Aunt Phillis's Cabin* portrayed the epitome of the relationship between a slaveowning family and a black mammy. The wife of Mr. Weston had died shortly after the birth of their son, and Aunt Phillis, an enslaved mother of twelve, had stepped in and "nourished him as her own child, and loved him quite as well." Mr. Weston calls Phillis "a mother to my only child," and as proof of her superior nurturing he claims that "she always gave Arthur [his son] the preference, putting her own infant aside to attend to his wants."[70] The poem "A Southern Scene from Life" has a mammy stating: "My baby's face is white an' red / Her skin is soft an' fine / An' on her pretty little head / The yaller ringlets shine[.]"[71] She thus claims her charge as her own, disavowing any natural children she might have. Authors of such narratives intended to present a picture of racial harmony and loyalty. The mammy provided far greater symbolic currency than similar devotion shown by a field laborer or a cook. Southern society idealized the mammy role because she acted as a mother, and motherhood played a significant role in maintaining social and political structures.[72]

An 1838 article in the *Southern Literary Messenger* hinted at the broader meanings of bearing and nurturing children, counseling that "the ability or inability of woman to discharge what the Almighty has committed to her, touches the equilibrium of society, and the hidden springs of existence." An 1846 article in the same journal instructed its readers that just as the ideals shaped the woman, "she, by a reflective operation of moral causes, equally affects the state of the society in which she exists."[73] Motherhood created a central identity for a woman in the antebellum South, while also allowing her to form the identity of the next generation of southerners. An adamant insistence on the maternal ideal suggested not only the power of the dominant group to shape the social narrative, but also their fears that they could be defied and that social controls and structures could collapse. While these paradigms did not always describe actual patterns of behavior, they set the standards against which each member of society measured conformity or deviance.[74] The ideals of birth and infant nurturing were not solely responsible for creating a social identity for southerners in the antebellum period, but these guidelines did provide a foundation upon which individuals built their ties to family, community, and society. The following chapters trace the process through which these individuals negotiated their identities in this society, ultimately leading many to assert that they had been "born southern."

CHAPTER TWO

Conception and Pregnancy

Southern Women's Experiences of Reproduction

O N April 2, 1854, Mary Lydia Hauser wrote a letter of sympathy to her sister-in-law, Julia Conrad Jones, on hearing that she was pregnant again: "[W]ell do I recollect how I used to trouble myself about such things and how I suffered from the time that I was aware of my condition until I was delivered from it." And although she recalled that "many have been the tears that I have shed on that account," she counseled Julia that "I do believe it is not right to do so and I have thought perhaps that was the reason why I have been so unfortunate[,] nine times have I suffered this as I consider it almost intolerable sickness and now only have four children left."[1] Hauser's letter suggests the conflicted emotions about bearing children that many southern women experienced. They knew that the womanly ideal made this their primary role, but they also knew the physical and emotional demands of childbearing. In their discussions of conception and pregnancy, southern women negotiated between the ideals and the realities of their lives. In the process, they developed a self-identity that both created and challenged ties to family, to community, and to southern society.

Women in the antebellum South could not have escaped the message that motherhood was their destiny, the ultimate fulfillment of their role. Or, as Thomas Ewell, a Virginia doctor and father of nine children, wrote in 1817: "Nature has given you functions to perform, everybody knows you perform them."[2] Women who publically stated a desire to limit reproduction knew they risked social condemnation as "unnatural" and "unwomanly." Still, some women professed uncertainty as to whether they were suited to the ideal or, in some cases, whether the ideal suited them. Some feared the pain and potential dangers that accompanied birth in the nineteenth century; most knew someone who had died in childbed. Others disdained becoming a mother because it tied them to a role that, while much lauded in the ideal, could in reality mean both worry and drudgery.

While still a young woman, Sarah Morgan recorded her limited enthusiasm for motherhood in her diary. She conceded that older children could be lovable, "but before that, the days and nights of shrieking and squealing, the months of long misery during which all babies take a fancy to sit up all night and admire the moon—Merci, je n'en veux pas! I repeat, all mothers who survive their thankless task, should be canonized."[3] Similarly, Kate Edmondston was 37 and childless when she noted in her diary: "Children are blessings I suppose. I know that they are sore trials and a great trouble and anxiety. 'Sour grapes' perhaps, Mrs. E., but who wants grapes at all?"[4] Maria Bryan, who married twice but bore no children, expressed even less regret. Rather, after observing a pregnant friend she wrote that it was a shame "that the happiness of the conjugal relation was obliged to be bought at so dear a price."[5] When Caroline Carson found herself in just such a situation only four months after her marriage, her reaction more closely mirrored Bryan's attitude than the ideal of southern womanhood. According to her aunt, Louise Porcher, Carson was "not *pleased* with her prospects[.] You know she rather dislikes children & says the idea of a *baby* is odious."[6] These women recognized that regardless of the dictates of the social standard, motherhood was not *their* ideal identity.

Other women, in contrast, experienced childlessness as a profound failure and feared it would limit their claim to the identity of ideal womanhood. South Carolinian Mary Chesnut labeled herself a "childless wretch." She further demonstrated her belief that a failure to bear children would harm the reputation of a southern lady in recounting her intercession on behalf of another woman. She told a group of acquaintances that Mrs. Browne "was childless now, but that she had lost three children." She made her reasoning clear: "Women have such a contempt for a childless wife. Now they will be all sympathy and kindness. I took away 'her reproach among women.'"[7] Chesnut believed that childlessness caused condemnation both from a woman's own family and from society at large. Women only had to listen to discussions of childbearing, both public and private, to gain a sense of how closely society tied fertility to female identity, and how a failure to fulfill this mandate raised questions about one's role in society. David Meade wrote in 1799 of his newly married and pregnant daughter who "promises to support the credit of our race by duly answering *the most important purpose of her creation*—already she discovers strong indications of the disposition."[8] Eleanor Lewis passed the sort of judgment so feared by Chesnut when she wrote to the childless Elizabeth Bordley Gibson: "My friend, in never having been a *Mother, you cannot conceive* a Mothers [*sic*] trials." She added, rather disingenuously, "You have *cause* to rejoice your fate. Long may you have reason to rejoice in your *destiny*."[9] Lewis's remarks, in effect, excluded Gibson from a full claim to the gender identity linked to motherhood.

Fiction authors often made childless women comedic figures; denatured in their infertility, "old maids" became subjects of disdain and ridicule. George Tucker's novel, *The Valley of the Shenandoah*, included the elderly Buckley sisters, "the youngest of whom had seen her fifth lustre." Tucker described these sisters as "remarkably homely and fat, possessed of more good nature than protracted celibacy in females is apt to produce."[10] He thus suggested that single status, and by extension childlessness, was likely to produce bad temper and bitterness in women, not to mention ugliness. When Mary Eastman described the wife of a black carriage driver, she noted that she was "not a very amiable character, and she had never had any children."[11] It is unclear which condition had caused the other. Obviously, however, these authors presented singleness and childlessness as deviancies from normal gender identities.

It is thus not surprising that Mary Chesnut lamented her "uselessness" as a woman because she bore no children. Or that Keziah Brevard, living on a plantation near Columbia, South Carolina, compared her own childless state to the motherhood of her sister-in-law and found herself wanting: "I do not envy my sister—no—no—but she has been a useful woman while I have been a blank—my nature makes me shrink when I should not[.]" Elite white women who failed to produce children could feel excluded, emotionally if not physically, from the bonds of family and community that were supposed to provide their identity in southern society.[12]

Enslaved women who failed to reproduce could find themselves in even more dire straits. Like white women, enslaved women belonged to communities that valued their reproductive abilities.[13] Along with the emotional consequences of infertility that black women shared with their white counterparts, enslaved women faced the further threat of being separated from their families and communities. Former slave Barry Clay recalled that a master "always requested, or rather demanded, that they be fruitful. A barren woman was separated from her husband and usually sold." Similarly, Henry Banner, born a slave in Virginia in 1849, claimed: "If a woman didn't breed well, she was put in a gang and sold."[14] In his observations on southern life, Frederick Law Olmsted referenced a letter confirming that "[p]lanters command their girls and women (married or unmarried) to have children; and I have known a great many negro girls to be sold off, because they did not have children."[15] An enslaved woman who failed in her reproductive role could thus find herself both alienated from the enslaved community and penalized by those who held her in bondage.

It is difficult to determine exactly how many southern women remained childless in the antebellum South. Studies of age at first birth indicate that by the age of thirty-nine between 14 and 18 percent of enslaved women remained childless, as did 17 percent of white women in the South. Such findings roughly correspond to data collected in the 1910 census indicating that 17 percent of native-born white women had no children, 9 percent of whom were married. The figure was slightly lower for foreign-born women. Whether these numbers are representative of an earlier period remains speculative. The figure for married infertility may have been slightly lower in the antebellum period. According to one study, an estimated 7.7 percent of American women born between 1835 and 1839 who had ever been married remained childless. Whatever the figures, childlessness—the act of not becoming a mother either by not marrying or as a result of infertility—defied the ideals of southern womanhood.[16]

For most women in the antebellum South, however, controlling conception was a more pressing issue than infertility. Women's attempts to limit their reproductive rate affected their identity on the most personal level. While most publically accepted the social ideal that made motherhood a woman's central role, privately some women sought to exert some control and create their own parameters in the fulfillment of the maternal ideal. Just as the body politic encompassed diverse viewpoints and interpretations, so too did women who both bore children and ascribed to the social ideals of southern society hold diverse views of what was best for them.

Controlling reproduction was a deeply intimate matter, difficult for the historian to recapture from beneath the veil of privacy. Although southern newspapers and journals published advertisements for "Female Pills" which promised to promote "period regularity" while cautioning that "these Pills should not be taken by females that are pregnant, during the *first three months* as they are sure to bring on Miscarriage,"[17] few women mentioned the use of such methods to prevent conception. But a careful reading of women's diaries and journals does suggest that at least some of them sought viable methods of contraception, and by mid-century they had achieved some success, as marital fertility rates began to fall. Abstinence offered the most fail-safe method of birth control. Mahala Roach seems to have used this approach to lengthen her birth intervals. In February 1855 her youngest child was just over three years old, and she indicated that her husband shared a room with their eldest son Tommy. In October of that same year she wrote that "Mr. Roach moved into my room again." Approximately nine months later she gave birth to her fifth child.[18] The ideal—which emphasized the delicacy, virtue, and chastity of elite white women—also put them in a position to at least bargain for abstinence, but women with husbands who refused to cooperate, or women who were unwilling to forego sexual relations themselves, could not rely on this method. Elite women might use family visits to bring about long periods of separation intended to lengthen birth intervals, but this was a temporary solution at best. Thus abstinence may have been more commonly used as a method for increasing spacing between children than for preventing conception in the long term.[19]

Prolonged breastfeeding offered women another possibility for lengthening birth intervals. This method seems to have been used by enslaved as well as white women.[20] As a strategy, it required less cooperation from male partners, although it was also less effective than abstinence. While breastfeeding could reduce the risk of conceiving, more than one woman recorded the need to wean her child because she was pregnant again.[21] Still, despite the inefficacy of most methods of contraception, women continued to hope for the possibility of controlling fertility.

Gertrude Thomas, in many ways an ideal southern mother, intimated that she and her husband had broached the topic of birth control: "I do not wish an only child, yet I should not object to long intervals. I think Mr. Thomas views the subject with the same idea of myself and is gratified at the prospect."[22] After the birth of her fourth child in six years, Rosalie Calvert expressed the desire for "a longer interval of repose" between births. She agreed with her sister's advice that she "ought to close down the factory" and have no more children, and they shared information on potential methods of preventing conception. Although Calvert only achieved this goal with the onset of menopause, six years and four children later, her limited success should not obscure both her desire for and her attempts to control her fertility.[23] Accepting the idealization of maternity did not mean individual women were unwilling to seek limits.

Lizzie Neblett of Texas provides an avid example of one woman's struggle with a female identity that demanded that she bear and raise children. Before the birth of her first child she seemed to accept the role of motherhood, but as more children came she confessed her limited maternal feelings and increasingly dwelt on preventing conception. Her fourth pregnancy left Neblett on the brink of suicide, and her cousin recommended "the Sponge" as "a safe and sure preventive." Yet Neblett wrote of its failure: "My God why is it that every body who has tried preventives that I know of have succeeded but me—and they did not desire success half as ardently as I did, they did not hate children as I do, & yet they succeeded and I never delayed the matter but a few months, by the devilish things." Later, during the Civil War, she wrote of her relief that her husband was away serving in the Confederate army, since this separation would prevent more children: "God who knows my heart, knows that no wife ever loved a husband more fondly or was ever more willing to make any kind of a reasonable sacrifice for his sake, but Will, I had rather live in perpetual banishment, than have another child." She could only accept him coming home on leave with the knowledge that "I am armed with Ergot, and various other implements of or for safety."[24]

In her frenzy to prevent conception Lizzie Neblett clearly articulated the conflict between the identity laid out for her in the maternal ideal and her own personal sentiments. She wrote in her journal of her recognition that she could not reconcile expectations and emotions:

> I am not a true mother—in some things am wanting & God ought
> never to have given me a child. A year has wrought a great change in
> me. I am a much worse woman than I was one year ago—and another
> child would make a *demon* of me, provided I did not end my days
> before the nine months expired. . . . I declare I sometimes think I had
> rather bury my daughters now than to live to see them mothers, &
> know that they felt on certain subjects like I do, for their sakes I had
> rather bury them now.[25]

By projecting onto her daughters, Neblett turned her sentiments from a personal feeling into a statement about the limited choices of all women. While Neblett's position may have been extreme, the need to negotiate their own personal physical and emotional experiences with the dictates of the ideal shaped, to some degree or other, the lives of all women in the antebellum South.

The recollections of former slaves indicate that some of them also tried to control their fertility. Traditional African societies made efforts to lengthen birth intervals through breastfeeding, ritual abstinence, and abortion. At least some of these cultural traditions may have been transported to the New World by enslaved women.[26] A number of former slaves interviewed by the WPA made reference to attempts at controlling reproduction within their own families or communities. Lulu Wilson related the story of a woman who, forced to join with a man against her will, remained barren. But when her master allowed her to leave this first man and marry the man of her choice, she had children each year until emancipation. "De Marster never did learnt how come thar warnt any chils bo'n wid de furst man," Lulu coyly concluded.[27]

Other informants more clearly identified the methods they believed enslaved women used to prevent conception. Lu Lee explained that calomel and turpentine could "unfix" a pregnancy: "In them days the turpentine was strong and ten or twelve drops could miscarry you." When the manufacturers recognized this use of their product, Lee claimed, they changed the formula, after which women began to use indigo to cause miscarriages.[28] Several former slaves also identified cotton root as an effective abortifacient. "Then, our negro women they like to have de-populated this country of the negro race. They got to chewing cotton roots to keep from giving births to babies and they finally made a law against that but it did not help much," Anna Lee of Tennessee told her interviewer. "If slavery had lasted much longer they would not have been any slaves except the old ones they had here left, cause when slavery was ended they was not being any new slaves born, we had done quit breeding."[29] Lee's comments do not reflect a statistical truth, but they do indicate a belief that the use of contraception and abortifacients was widespread.

Mary Gaffney, born in Mississippi in 1846, related her personal experience, in which the use of cotton root was an act of defiance. After she was relocated to Texas, her master forced her to sleep with another of his slaves in anticipation of producing more slaves. She told her story to a WPA interviewer many years after the end of slavery:

> Maser was going to raise him a lot more slaves, but still I cheated
> Maser, I never did have any slaves to grow and Maser wondered
> what was the matter. I tell you son, I kept cotton roots and chewed
> them all the time but I was careful not to let Maser know or catch
> me, so I never did have any children while I was a slave. . . . Yes after
> freedom we had five children, four of them is still living.[30]

Despite the high birthrates and penalties for not reproducing, some enslaved women attempted to limit their childbearing, whether for physical reasons or as a matter of principle. These women may have viewed such attempts to prevent conception as only logical in a society that too often denied their identity as mothers. Most enslaved mothers could control neither the amount of care they provided for their infant nor the treatment of that child in later life. Not only did enslaved women face all of the pain that white women feared, but they also knew that the children they bore would be slaves. Elizabeth Keckley wrote of her struggle with the idea of bearing children while still a slave: "He [Mr. Keckley] sought my hand in marriage, and for a long time I refused to consider his proposal; for I could not bear the thought of bringing children into slavery—of adding one single recruit to the millions bound to hopeless servitude, fettered and shackled with chains stronger and heavier than manacles of iron."[31] Although she offers no details of the methods of birth control she used, Keckley did marry and managed to bear no children in the union. Making a choice about conception, whether becoming a mother or preventing the birth of children, could become a small political statement for enslaved women who lived in a society that often refused to respect their identity either as women or mothers.[32]

Whatever the desires of women, black or white, available methods of contraception proved only moderately successful at best. One southern woman, already the mother of thirteen children, lamented: "I have so many little children and no prospect of ever stopping."[33] Although birthrates were falling throughout the nineteenth century, most southern women could still anticipate having much of their lives dominated by pregnancy and infant nurturing. Both black and white women recorded patterns of childbearing beginning early in their married lives and continuing with regularity, approximately every two years, until menopause.[34] Rosalie Calvert of Maryland followed this model, marrying in 1799, having her first child in 1800, and giving birth every two years until 1816. South Carolinian Elizabeth Perry was seventeen when she married in 1837. During the next twenty years she gave birth to seven living children and suffered four miscarriages and two stillbirths. In Mississippi, Mahala Roach had her first child in 1845, at the age of twenty, and before the death of her husband in 1860 she had delivered five more children.[35] Privately, some women expressed mixed feelings about the toll that regular childbearing took on them physically, but in the eyes of society they were doing what they ought, and their reproductive success made them embodiments of the ideal.

For a southern woman, speaking of "family addition" became an enumeration of her contribution, not only to her immediate family, but to her community and ultimately to southern society. Women listed their children as a validation of their lives' work. Elizabeth Perry, mentioned above, recorded all the additions to her family in her diary. "I have been married 31 years," she began an 1868 entry. "I am about 48 or 49 years old. I have had 7 living children, two still born, & 4 miscarriages, so have been 13 times pregnant. My first child was a daughter still born; born 15 months after marriage. The 2nd a son born 11 months after, named

William Hayne, he is now, or will be in June 29 years old . . . ." Perry noted each of the children she had carried—a summary of her life through her reproductive activity.[36]

Praise for bearing a large family also came from others. Mary Chesnut's father-in-law praised his wife for giving birth to fourteen children by saying "you have not been useless in your day and generation." Upon hearing of her latest delivery, James Petigru wrote of his niece, Caroline North Pettigrew: "Well done for little Carey! Has she not done her duty by scuppernong—two sons and four daughters and only nine years a wife. Why, the Queen of England hardly beats her." Sophia Dabney's greatest achievement, according to her daughter's memorial, was being the mother of "16 living children—9 sons & 7 daughters" and leading "the life of the mother who during 30 years was never without an infant in her arms." The language of family increase suggested a positive addition to and the fulfillment of the idealized narrative.[37]

But as many women struggled to balance the idealistic social identity of motherhood with their own reproductive desires, the language of family increase could also suggest some negative connotations. Women knew the physical and emotional burdens that bearing a large number of children imposed upon a mother. "Adela is going to have another baby, this will be the 5th. It is really terrible," Meta Grimball penned in 1861. A half century earlier, Rosalie Calvert of Maryland wrote that "Mrs. Stuart hasn't had any more children, and it is high time she stopped since she has eleven living." Edward Conigland reported to his wife that "Mrs. Jack Tillery has added a daughter to her stock of 'responsibilities[.]'" He meant to be humorous, but there is an element of truth in his assessment of a new child's impact. Mahala Roach took the potentially negative effects of a "family addition" seriously. "The first news I heard this morning was that Sister Mary had *twin boys* last night—Dick and John! Twins! And her youngest before this is nineteen months! poor, poor, thing! sister, I mean!" Roach thus expressed sympathy for the responsibilities that this birth would cause.[38]

Alabamian Sarah Gayle similarly commiserated on the frequent reproduction of her acquaintances, noting in one diary entry in April 1828: "Mrs. Erwin has a third fine girl—her second is hardly 14 months old. Maria James too has a son, her second since her last marriage. Poor Lucinda has added to her already numerous family a daughter Helen Maria.

I pity her from my heart for she is ill able to attend them[.]" Just six years later Gayle had added herself to the list of women who ought to be pitied for over-fecundity, as she again suspected she was pregnant. "I am now just thirty years old, and have bred with *eight children*," she lamented, concluding, "I have a family large enough, Heaven knows, and they begin to make me feel great uneasiness." Mothers may have expressed pride in the children they bore, laying claim to the idealized maternal identity, but they did not always desire additions as they came.[39]

In a broader context, discussions that used a language of family increase emphasized a woman's contributions to the maintenance of the community. When Rachel O'Connor wrote that "Mrs. Cash and Mrs. Semple will both enlarge their families shortly," or when the Webb sisters received news that Mary Green "is going to have a young one," the emphasis extended beyond the event of pregnancy or delivery.[40] They instead focused on the long-term outcome. Women embraced similar sentiments when they recorded that they "expected to become a Mother" or were on "the eve of becoming a Mother."[41]

Pregnancy was the initial step in the transition to a maternal identity. A first pregnancy represented perhaps the most significant milestone, but each pregnancy was unique and shaped a woman's identity in different ways. By the mid-nineteenth century, elite Americans who embraced the ideals of true womanhood often used a language of sickness to describe pregnancy. Tryphena Fox, for example, wrote to her mother while pregnant with her first child, describing her health as "remarkably good," but then adding, "excepting that one sickness I wrote you about. Of course, I am all the time *complaining* but presume the little ailments of first one thing and then another are the every-day occurrences of any one in my condition." She mainly experienced nausea at the beginning of her pregnancy: "The first two months I *did suffer*, so I cannot bear to think of it now, but since have got along tolerably well & hope to do so." Anita Withers also had a mixed experience with sickness during her pregnancy: "Was a most lovely day. I felt perfectly miserable, as sick as I could be. My Husband took me out riding in the afternoon, Mrs. Govan went with us. Dr. Dean came to see me in the evening—he would not give me any medicine but told me to go out all the time . . . ."[42]

Other women experienced their pregnancies as a more debilitating condition, genuinely disrupting their lives. A pregnant Rosalie Calvert wrote early in the nineteenth century that "I was so sick *every morning* that I couldn't do anything." Approximately seven months before the arrival of her baby, Sarah Gayle described the physical symptoms of "constant lassitude, nervous weakness, and dreadful sickness under which I have suffered." Gertrude Thomas also made the connection between ill-health and pregnancy clear when she wrote in 1855: "I have a great deal of sick stomach and headache and find I am again destined to be a mother. . . . suffering almost constantly with sick stomach as I am I cannot *yet* view the idea with a great deal of interest or pleasure." Seven years later and pregnant again, Thomas noted: "I am suffering terribly from nausea and lack of energy—for the last six weeks I have been I cannot say blessed with the prospect of again becoming a mother—I am too sick and irritable to regard this circumstance as a blessing *yet awhile.*" Perhaps not surprisingly, Thomas also drew a link between depression and the early stages of pregnancy.[43] While the range of symptoms and suffering varied, the "natural" event of pregnancy could seriously disrupt the lives of women, suggesting why they might privately question the glorified versions of childbearing presented in southern society.

The language of sickness allowed women to distinguish between the southern ideals of a presumed "natural" ability to bear children and the physically arduous reality that labor and delivery entailed. In some cases, elite white women emphasized illness as a means of claiming the delicacy promoted in the romanticized model of southern womanhood. While perhaps not intentionally meant as a social commentary, the use of such language, and the behavior it described, resonated in the context of southern society. The delicacy or "sickness" of pregnant white women stood in stark contrast to the treatment of childbearing enslaved women. When an article in *DeBow's Review* counseled that pregnant enslaved women "are always to do *some* work up to the time of their confinement, if it is only walking into the field and staying there," differences between black and white women were both assumed and reaffirmed. The physical realities of pregnancy created a recognition of a shared gendered experience, while at the same time the differences in treatment sought to reinforce racial divisions.[44]

With no accurate tests, women had to use observable changes to their bodies to determine if they were pregnant. Besides the nausea implied by the language of sickness, the most common indicators of pregnancy were changes in the breasts, enlargement of the abdomen, missed menstrual periods, and perceived movements of the fetus. In his medical guidebook written for home use, Dr. John Gunn reassured his readers that if such symptoms appeared the woman was pregnant in "*ninety-nine* cases out of a hundred."[45] Women seem to have placed varying emphases on these physical symptoms when performing a self-diagnosis. Antebellum southern women, for example, only rarely mentioned an absence of menses in relation to pregnancy, and then only obliquely. Anita Withers was something of an exception, observing in her diary at the beginning of November 1862: "I missed my——this month of October." Still, she does not mention pregnancy at this point. Over the months, however, other activities, such as visits from a doctor or hiring a nurse, suggest her pregnancy.[46] Perhaps more frequently, women knew they were *not* pregnant by the appearance of their periods. Rosalie Calvert believed she was pregnant in the spring of 1805, but later wrote her sister, presumably after the resumption of her menses: "it was a false alarm which didn't last long."[47] Mention of this private bodily function may have been deemed inappropriate by some women, but its limited use as a sign of pregnancy also stemmed from the reality that the presence of a woman's period more reliably indicated the absence of pregnancy than the absence of menstruation proved conception.

Perhaps the most definitive sign of pregnancy for women in the antebellum period was quickening—the movement of the fetus that generally occurs in the sixteenth to twentieth week of pregnancy. On November 17, 1858, Mahala Roach noted in her diary: "I think I felt slight indications of a *new life* tonight." Just over a week later she confirmed that "[m]y signs of 'life' felt on the 17th were real, I have felt them ever since." Her child was born at the beginning of May. Traditionally, women had not declared themselves pregnant until they had felt these sensations.[48] Most antebellum women were fully able to make their own diagnoses of pregnancy, based on a knowledge of their own bodies and sexual activities and on information shared within the female social network.

While most of the written documentation of this self-diagnosis comes from white women, black women experienced similar biological symptoms and could clearly also determine for themselves if they were pregnant. For enslaved women, however, masters only partially accepted a woman's own observations of her condition. This represented part of the continual struggle between an enslaved woman's ability to define herself as a woman and the slave system's attempt to define her as a possession. Slaveholders and overseers, for their part, feared being duped out of the enslaved woman's labor. Within the plantation hierarchy, the ultimate determination of an enslaved woman's pregnancy came from her ability to persuade her master of her condition. This diagnosis privileged a white man's perception over that of the enslaved woman.

Yet enslaved women may also have used the knowledge of their own bodies to make decisions about timing the announcement of their pregnancies. Thomas Chaplin recorded the delivery of one enslaved woman on his plantation who "has stuck out boldly to the last that she was not in a family way, and may say so now, with some truth." It is unlikely that this woman, Elsie, did not know she was pregnant. Her denial, however, allowed her to defy some of her master's authority over her body. Enslaved women may have learned to recognize pregnancy early on, so as to gain release from work in the first two trimesters. Others did not mention their pregnancies until delivery was imminent. Controlling information about conception and pregnancy thus became a means of contravening undesired interventions from the owning class.[49] The inability to control the physical symptoms of pregnancy affected all women and offered a point of commonality, but the privileging of some women's bodily knowledge and suffering, and a disregard for the knowledge and experience of others, demonstrated the difference in their status within southern society.

Uncertainty over determining conception also affected calculating the exact duration of pregnancy. Women measured their pregnancies in weeks and months rather than days, but they still sometimes found themselves surprised by an early birth or frustrated by delays in an anticipated delivery. Eleanor Lewis's daughter Parke delivered a son in 1826, with Lewis estimating that he was two months early although he was fat and healthy. Rachel O'Connor announced in October 1840 that her niece Clarissa anticipated being confined in January. In mid-February Rachel wrote that she had "been on the lookout for better than five weeks, every hour expecting to hear" of Clarissa's delivery. The child, who only lived a week, was finally born on February 21. Mary Middleton wrote of her surprise that her daughter-in-law was still "downstairs" over "a month since she expected to be confined!" As Sarah Gayle awaited the birth of her child in January 1835, she experienced bouts of depression, seemingly compounded by what she termed the "perfect uncertainty as to the period of suffering—it may be the middle of this, may be the middle of next month." On February 6 she wrote that "my miscalculations were wide" and continued to express apprehension as to when her delivery would occur. Finally, on February 19, her daughter Ann Maria was born. Thus the idea of "early" or "late" represented a woman's knowledge of her sexual relations, and a sense of her body and when she should deliver, rather than a medically determined due date.[50]

While all women might share this uncertainty, a white woman's miscalculation generally only affected her own comfort level. In contrast, masters often accused enslaved women of being deliberately misleading on this matter. Thomas Chaplin recorded in his diary in early December that "Phyllis has been in the house for a month, expecting to be confined every day, but came out today, as she is rather doubtful as to the time." Less than two weeks later Phyllis delivered a baby girl.[51] While masters disallowed an enslaved woman's bodily knowledge in determining conception or in reducing her workload, they expected her to accurately predict her delivery date. What was merely uncertainty for white women became deliberate malingering in enslaved women. The tension between acknowledging biologically similar experiences and maintaining differences in social status determined treatments and activities throughout pregnancy, shaped by, and shaping, a woman's identity as free or enslaved.

The behavior of elite women reflected not only their own preferences, but their social status. Nineteenth-century medical-advice literature warned against excessive excitement or activity during pregnancy, and some elite women limited their social engagements and household activities. For example, a pregnant Gertrude Thomas wrote in February 1857: "This spring I will be compelled to remain at home a good deal for I will not only be unpresentable in the street but I will find being in town fatiguing."[52] Thomas's experience with chronic nausea and miscarriages may have influenced her decision to limit her activities. Her elite status and her ability to command the assistance of enslaved women to fulfill her household duties fostered her ability to make these choices for herself.

Other elite women elected not to restrict their activities significantly while pregnant. Mary Middleton of South Carolina scolded her daughter Eliza Fisher, living in Philadelphia in 1840, for engaging in a racket sport called battledore while pregnant. She also advised Eliza that she thought "four or five miles walking, rather too much for you just now."[53] But many white women living in the South did engage in physical and/ or social activities well into their pregnancies. Mahala Roach, for example, recorded in 1856 that the day before she gave birth she sewed all day and then considered going to visit her friend for ice cream but did not feel quite well enough, probably because she was in early labor. Similarly, before the birth of her next child in 1859, she continued to go on visits until a week before her delivery and received visitors, including Jefferson Davis, the day before the birth. Varina Davis rode daily with her husband during her first pregnancy, and only two days before her delivery in 1859 she received President Buchanan in her drawing room.[54] Like Gertrude Thomas, the social position of these women gave them the ability to choose or limit their activities.

Poor and yeomen white women, in contrast, had fewer choices. Their household duties required their productive labor regardless of their condition. Usually there was no one else to feed and clothe their families or care for other children. Poor families might also require a woman's labor in the fields well into her pregnancy. The Sloan family of South Carolina, for example, relied on the physical efforts of all of its members for its economic survival. The pregnancies of Mrs. Sloan, however, disrupted her contributions to the work of the household and may have led to the hiring of an enslaved girl to replace Mrs. Sloan's labor in the fields.[55] But since many women spent a large portion of their reproductive lives pregnant or nursing an infant, this became a normal state, one around which non-elite women learned to work.[56] Whether by choice or necessity, pregnancy did not radically change the behavior patterns of most white women in the antebellum South.

Most black women also had their productive activities altered only slightly by pregnancy, but their identity as slaves meant that this decision was not theirs to make. Enslaved women had a distinct disadvantage in pregnancy because they were unable to choose or exercise control over their physical activities. While white women, particularly those of the elite class, based their activities on their own assessments of physical well-being, enslaved women had no such choices. Both the work as-signed to them and their inability to demur marked their debased position within southern society. Slaveholders balanced their concerns for the well-being of the mother, and the future slave she carried, with assessments of their labor needs.

Many plantation owners ignored the condition of the pregnant woman if it interfered with their need for labor. Still, both enslaved women and the slaveholders who controlled their activities knew that changes to this heavy labor were necessary if pregnancy was to end successfully. The more often a pregnant woman was released from work, the better the chances of her infant's survival may have been. A release earlier in the pregnancy, rather than in the third trimester, would have had the greatest benefit in terms of preventing infant mortality, but a majority of people in the nineteenth-century South, as well as in our own time, believed that women were most in need of rest and relief late in pregnancy, when they were visibly pregnant. Thus any respite from heavy labor generally came only in the last trimester.[57] Seasonal patterns of childbearing, however, meant that labor demand peaked at the same time that many women were in their third trimester of pregnancy.[58] Thus sometimes the need for labor overrode any concerns for a pregnant woman's health, even in the late stages of pregnancy. David Harris of South Carolina, who struggled with crop failures and tight profit margins, recorded the activity of one of his enslaved women on June 15, 1863: "Ann is plowing sugar-cane." Just over a month later, on July 20, he wrote that Ann gave birth to a son, indicating she performed fairly heavy field work at least into her eighth month of pregnancy, if not later.[59] Similarly, Louisianian Rachel O'Connor recorded on June 22, 1829, that an enslaved woman, Bridget, continued to hoe despite a sore hand. She did not mention that Bridget was also late into her pregnancy, but on July 5 she gave birth to "a fine boy."[60] Both of these owners knew the enslaved women well and undoubtedly were aware of their condition, yet the need for field labor clearly took precedence.

In an essay written for the Southern Central Agricultural Society of Georgia in 1851, Nathan Bass warned his readers against expecting a continuation of heavy labor from enslaved women while pregnant. He counseled that "females, during a state of pregnancy should be exempt from all labor that would have a tendency to injure them, such as lifting heavy burdens, fencing, plowing and &c., and for several weeks previous to confinement they should be required to perform no out-door labor."[61] But even according to this prescription, pregnancy did not mean that slaveholders allowed enslaved women to work according to a woman's own assessment of her fitness, the deciding factor for elite white women. Instead, concerned slaveholders were instructed to assign "lighter" tasks to women in the advanced stages of pregnancy.

Former slave Adeline Jackson recalled that just before their babies were due, women might be taken out of the fields and set to work carding and spinning.[62] Other former slaves also recounted instances of lighter workloads for pregnant women. Morgan Ray of Georgia said of his mother: "Old Marse nevah made her do hard work when chillun wuz on de way. She nevah had to birth chillun in de fields, like some slave women I done hear tell of." Letha Taylor Meeks of Mississippi similarly acknowledged a lightened workload while also identifying the motivation behind the granting of this privilege: "An' dey's good an' careful bout womens when dey's gonna have a baby. She wuz jes given light work to do, cause dey wanted big healthy famblies." Yet stories of field births, a clear sign that women were forced to labor until the moment of delivery, persisted. Sam and Louisa Everett of Virginia told of a demanding overseer: "So exacting was 'Big Jim' that slaves were forced to work when sick. Expectant mothers toiled in the fields until they felt their labor pains. It was not uncommon for babies to be born in the fields."[63] Whether granted decreased workloads or forced to maintain their regular duties throughout their pregnancies, enslaved women lacked control over their own bodies and their labor, marking the difference between their pregnancy experiences and those of free women.

The physical punishment that some slaveholders inflicted during pregnancy was even more striking than overwork in signaling the powerlessness of enslaved women in this society. While southern rhetoric suggested that masters would avoid physically punishing pregnant women, if for no other reason than to protect their investment in the mother and child, this amnesty was not always observed in practice.[64] Lou Williams, born in Maryland in 1829, recalled: "De mamas what expectin' babies was whopped to make dem work faster[.]"[65] A number of former slaves, from all regions of the South, told their WPA interviewers of a specific method of punishing pregnant women. In each case, the master or overseer dug a hole in the ground to accommodate the woman's belly, then forced her to lie face down while she was beaten on the back and shoulders. In some cases, such treatment induced labor.[66]

Other slaveholders required no special preparations, but instead whipped pregnant women as they did anyone else, regardless of condition. This seems to have been the case with David Harris, who recorded in his diary on February 23, 1864: "Nerve is gone to the wood this morning on account of a little flogging I gave her on yesterday." He does not mention that she was over six months pregnant; she gave birth at the end of May.[67] Other whippings had more dire consequences. Mandy McCullough Cosby told the story of an incident which left a lasting impression: "One woman on a plantation not so far from us, was expectin', an' they tied her up under a hack-a-berry tree, an' whipped her until she died. Mos' any time at night ef you go 'roun' that tree, you could hear that baby cry. I 'spect you could hear it yet."[68] Other examples, while more prosaic, were no less tragic. Former slave Analiza Foster caught the awful irony of the abuse of pregnant women when she reported a conversation between a driver and a master over how to punish a pregnant woman who fainted while plowing. The master agreed that the driver might whip the woman, provided he did not harm the baby. Ultimately, the mother and her unborn child both died, so that in the attempt to grind a small amount of additional work from a woman unable to perform it, the master lost not just her labor, but the lives (and value) of two slaves.[69] Whether true or apocryphal, such stories suggested an identity for enslaved women shaped not by the maternal ideal but by the powerlessness of bondage.

For slaveowners, punishment of a pregnant woman offered short-term gratification for their anger, but a potential risk if the woman ran away, miscarried, or died. For the slaves who witnessed this punishment, the meanings were very different. Occasionally, former slaves recalled, enslaved men stood up against the aggression of the master or overseer. Marie E. Harvey told of the whipping of one pregnant woman, but added: "They tried to do my grandma that way, but my grandpa got an ax and told them that if they did he would kill them. They never could do anything with him."[70] For most enslaved men, however, such action would have been too dangerous for both themselves and the women they sought to protect. For the partners of these women (and the fathers of the unborn children), the whipping of a pregnant female emphasized their curtailed ability to protect those they loved, suggesting some of the limits placed on the masculine identity of enslaved men within this system. For pregnant enslaved women, punishment meant physical pain and the danger of miscarriage. It also emphasized that the society in which they lived would rob them of their ability to offer a mother's protection to her children. It is impossible to know how frequently such abuse of pregnant women occurred in the antebellum South, but even the potential for such behavior demonstrated the power differentials that shaped an individual's identity within southern society.

Besides changes in physical expectations and activities, pregnancy also signaled the need for women to make other forms of preparation. And like the changes in her work patterns, the advanced arrangements women made for their babies reflected their relative positions within southern society. Although it is now considered essential, antebellum women did not generally seek medical care throughout their pregnancies. They determined their condition by observing their own bodies, and while they may have discussed pregnancy in terms of "sickness," they did not generally view their condition as pathological or one requiring medical attention. Some elite women did seek out a physician for specific problems. Anita Withers, for example, consulted a doctor about her nausea. But such consultations were anomalies rather than a normal part of prenatal care for white women.[71] And although some owners relied on medical examinations to determine the pregnancy of enslaved women, regular medical care was not generally forthcoming for them either. Criticism of the lack of prenatal care for slaves tends to reflect an understanding of pregnancy shaped by the medical perspective of the twentieth century, in which such care is deemed essential for the health of mother and child. In the antebellum period, a lack of prenatal care did not significantly differentiate enslaved women from women of the white elite. And while enslaved women may have lacked ultimate control over their bodies, the existence of female-kin networks among enslaved women ensured the sharing of all sorts of knowledge, including information on conception, pregnancy, and birthing. The lack of interference by white doctors may, in fact, have offered enslaved women more control over their condition.[72]

One key element in preparing for a child was sewing garments and diapers. These activities seemed to allow women to prepare emotionally as well as materially. For example, on June 27, 1855, only a week before her son's arrival, Mahala Roach wrote that she had "finished a shirt I have been making for 'Johnny,'" the name she had given to her unborn child. But, she then admitted, "it is almost time for his arrival, and I am not quite prepared for him."[73] Varina Davis, pregnant for the first time, faced a similar state of unpreparedness. She wrote to her mother in 1852: "I have not more at the very farthest than three weeks to go on, and not a shirt, not a petticoat, or slip, and only twelve diapers altogether. Please don't think me importunate but the thoughts of it nearly sets me crazy." She ultimately took up the task because "I hate in case of my death to leave the poor little thing without common necessaries."[74] Davis's delays reflected not a lack of skill or time, but a degree of hesitancy about her approaching confinement and motherhood. These women were getting ready not just for a new baby, but for a new phase of their lives.

Enslaved mothers may also have wished to prepare materially for their babies' arrivals, but most lacked the time and resources to do so in any significant way. The records of the plantations owned by the Manigaults of South Carolina indicated that blankets and cloth were allocated for each infant, but only after his or her arrival. When Clarissa— an enslaved woman whom the Roach family in Vicksburg, Mississippi, hired out—delivered a child, Mahala Roach wrote that she "went down town to buy some things for Clarissa's baby—dresses &c." Clarissa was thus absolved of the responsibility for furnishing a wardrobe for her new infant, but she also missed the emotional bond experienced by Roach and other white women of preparing for her child during pregnancy. In her postbellum memoir, Susan Smedes congratulated white southerners on their generosity in this matter. Joking that enslaved families were so large that the fathers could not remember how many children they had, she added: "But not so on the days when blankets were to be given out. Then their memories were fresh. Then the babies that had not been in their cradles more than a few days, mayhaps hours, were remembered and mentioned in due turn, with no danger of being forgotten or overlooked because there were 'so many on 'em.'"[75] Of course, newborns required blankets and other necessities, and free people with any resources at all would have made these preparations *before* the child's birth, an option unavailable to the enslaved father and mother. Thus the provision of these "baby bundles" evoked mixed feelings. While they supplied infants with their material necessities, enslaved parents worried that such provisions legitimized a master's claims of ownership—and thus his right to interfere in the nurturing of the infant. The seemingly innocuous creation of a layette and infant clothes echoed with broader meanings, reaffirming the limits that southern society placed on an enslaved woman's identity as a mother.

Despite all of the differences of condition, control, and choice that existed for pregnant women in the antebellum South, pregnancy itself offered at least the potential for a recognition of commonalities between women. Through their similar physical experiences, women might see each other *as women*, removing, however briefly, the divisions of race. In 1865, for example, Gertrude Thomas recorded the pregnancy of two enslaved women in her diary: "[I]n that condition I think all women ought to [be] favoured. I know that had I the sole management of a plantation, pregnant women would be highly favoured. A woman myself, I can sympathise with my sex wether [*sic*] white or black."[76] Fannie Kemble expressed similar sympathy for the enslaved women owned by her husband, and she intervened on a number of occasions on behalf of pregnant women.[77] While neither Thomas nor Kemble ever fully escaped their racist conditioning, childbearing provided an outlet in which they could explore some alternative perspectives. Inside the birthing room, women relied on other women, and race could become secondary.

On the path to motherhood, women negotiated between the dictates of the maternal ideal and the physical and emotional realities of this condition, and between the commonalities of gender and the divisions of race. In doing so, women constructed a personal sense of self. At the same time, a woman's social and racial identity shaped how she would be treated and how her experiences would be interpreted. While southern social commentators sanctified motherhood as the proper identity for females, in practice this role involved complex feelings and experiences. It may be sufficient to study birth because of the centrality that it had in the lives of individual southern women. But in a society in which birth and motherhood formed an important part of the definition of one's social identity, these personal experiences provide insight into larger societal issues. In their reproductive experiences, women both supported and defied southern social structures. These experiences shaped the identity of childbearing women, which in turn created the principal identity of the children they bore. Birth further gave shape to the kinship and community networks that formed around these women, and ultimately it would provide the foundation upon which a nationalist identity could be built. But before any of this could occur, the child that had been conceived had to be born.

CHAPTER THREE

Childbirth

Commonalities and Divisions

THE EVENTS OF LABOR and delivery were both pivotal points in the lives of women and parts of a broader continuum in their reproductive histories. This time of physical and emotional peril generated the potential for mutual dependence and the creation of a community of women across race and class lines. The birthing room became a space where normal social rules did not always apply. Birth assistants were chosen for their expertise and their availability rather than for their social identity. But then, in the recovery period that followed birth, social divisions were often firmly reasserted. Stark differences in treatment in the days and weeks following birth marked the contrasts in the social conditions of free and enslaved women. Thus the few weeks around the events of childbirth became a microcosm of the complex negotiations over identity and community in southern society—between shared and diametrically opposed experiences, commonalities and divisions. These events moved the maternal identity of women into a broader understanding of their role, one shaped by household, kinship, and community networks.

If the experiences of conception and pregnancy allowed women to measure and define themselves according to how they lived up to the ideals of womanhood as individuals, the events of childbirth tied women to a broader group identity, creating a reason for women to come together and offer mutual support. The birthing room, in fact, formed a unique social space in southern society. Men, when not totally excluded, had limited authority during these events, where the usual patriarchal order was at least temporarily subverted. Jane North of South Carolina passed on a message to her sister Adèle Allston from another sister who had successfully delivered a son earlier in the morning. She wrote that Harriette "says to you that she had an hour of desperate pain and as no physician was by to make her ashamed she screamed at the top of her lungs, and that it did her good."[1] An all-female birthing room seemingly freed the female voice, even if only for screams of pain. This exchange of information also suggests the networks formed between female kin, in which even those who could not be physically present desired to be included in the events of childbirth.

Equally important, while birthing rooms created a degree of gender exclusion, they also occasionally allowed for some incidents of racial integration. In their daily lives a clear power differential existed between southern women in the slave system: black women labored at the behest, and to meet the needs, of white women and their families; white slaveholding women directed this labor and controlled the physical destiny of black women, thereby holding the power to provide and punish. In the birthing room the issues of control and power were less clearly defined. Many women valued skill over racial identity in selecting birth attendants, and they followed the instructions and advice of those who seemed most knowledgeable. Although southern women never completely overcame the issues of authority and choice embedded in racial identity, mutual dependence could, at least temporarily, be acknowledged. While southern women did not necessarily recognize their support network in the birthing room as having political meaning, they certainly recognized the personal and social import of this assistance.[2]

Throughout the nineteenth century, birthing women relied on their mothers whenever they could for both information and physical assistance. This mother-daughter bond was particularly strong because southern women married and had children so young that their reproductive lives could overlap. In 1802 Virginian Eleanor Parke Lewis announced both the birth of a son to her sister and their mother's delivery of her twentieth child. While this represents an extraordinary fecundity, the situation of mother and daughter bearing children at the same time was not so unusual. Varina Davis's mother, for example, was still having children when Varina gave birth to her first child in 1852. Rachel O'Connor reported that the wife of a neighbor, already the mother of thirteen, gave birth to twins even as her daughter was pregnant with her grandchild.[3] Women relied on the maternal presence as a source of wisdom and comfort during childbirth and recovery. Mary Jones attended the delivery of her daughter in April 1858, and in the fall of 1859 she also volunteered to attend of her daughter-in-law's labor and delivery. She wrote to her son: "I will certainly be with you in November, and trust I may be enabled to render to one whom I tenderly love the sympathy and kindness which should flow from a mother's heart and hand in such an hour of trial."[4]

White women, if they had the resources, might travel great distances to join each other for these events. The experience of Eliza Fisher and her mother Mary Middleton exemplified the efforts of mothers and daughters to be together at the time of delivery. Fisher, who lived in Philadelphia, wrote to her mother regularly during her first pregnancy to seek advice about birthing and mothering. She also pleaded with her mother to travel from the family home in South Carolina to attend her. Fisher's father, however, objected, and Mary Middleton wrote to her daughter that "I now believe he never meant that I should be with you at the time we both so much wished to be together." But much begging, and a baby who was born several weeks later than anticipated, actually allowed Middleton to arrive two days before her daughter gave birth. A similar conflict emerged in this family in 1844. On this occasion Fisher's father was backed by her brother, who told his mother that she "was not a proper person to attend to one in [Fisher's] situation." This time Mary Middleton made it to Fisher's bedside only after Fisher had delivered a daughter. The men and women in this family clearly placed a very different value on the desire for mothers and daughters to be together during childbirth.[5]

But even when dealing with the logistics of long distances, poor travel conditions, or recalcitrant family members, mothers and daughters attempted to share this experience. In 1826 Eleanor Lewis wrote that if her pregnant daughter Parke could not travel from Cincinnati to Virginia, Lewis would make the journey to Ohio herself in December. Mrs. Joseph Jenkins wrote to her pregnant daughter, Martha Cornish of South Carolina, in 1847, begging her to come home since Mrs. Jenkins was unable to leave her ill husband. She assured Martha that she wanted to "do my very best for you," adding, "I hope I need not now say how willingly I would, I would cheerfully go to you if there was nothing to consider but myself but I do not feel satisfied to leave your Father in his dependent and often painful situation." Mrs. Jenkins clearly felt torn between meeting the needs of her pregnant daughter and her sick husband. White birthing women who knew with certainty that their mothers could not attend them still attempted to communicate their experiences and emotions through letters. Tryphena Fox, living in Louisiana and expecting her first child in 1857, wrote to her mother in Massachusetts about everything from her physical well-being to preparing a layette for the new baby.[6] Such communications, and the desire to be together at this time, suggests the importance birth played in linking women together into a community of shared experiences.

The social networks of southern women extended beyond their nuclear families to included female kin, friends, and other neighborhood women.[7] This network reached into the birthing room, with the aid that was offered marking the birthing woman's place in a larger community of women. The Petigru family, for example, relied on sisters, aunts, and cousins to provided mutual support throughout their pregnancies, deliveries, and recoveries. In 1832 Jane North, herself a mother of three children under age five, went to offer assistance to her pregnant sister Adèle Allston, who in turn traveled to Charleston to be with her sister-in-law, Jane Amelia Petigru, during her confinement. Twenty years later, another sister, Harriette Lesesne, sought comfort during her pregnancy with female kin gathered at Jane North's house, and then Jane traveled to Charleston to be with Harriette during her delivery. In fact, over a thirty-year period there was rarely a year that one of the sisters was not pregnant, and the first generation's childbearing overlapped with that of their daughters, making reproduction a fundamental part of this family's interactions.[8]

In Vicksburg, Mississippi, in the 1850s, Mahala Roach recorded a long list of visitors, including both family and friends, after each of her births. She also wrote of reciprocal visits in which she went to visit and offer support to recently delivered mothers and babies.[9] If women could not be in attendance during the actual delivery, they often hastened to assist in the days immediately after birth. Such was the case with Roach's fifth birth in 1856. She delivered at 5 a.m. with only her two house-slaves present, but her mother came soon after and stayed for a week, and many other visitors also attended the new mother. In North Carolina, Penelope Alderman gave birth to her second son at 2 a.m., attended by "aunt Mary," but soon thereafter her husband brought her mother and sent the midwife home. In Alabama, Sarah Gayle noted that she had not visited a new mother, Mrs. Williams, writing in September 1833 that "I recollect to have heard her express her surprise at the southern custom of visiting a lady so soon after her confinement." Yet these support networks provided comfort and assistance for the southern birthing woman and bound her to a broader sense of community.[10]

Neither poor white women nor enslaved women had the ability to travel far from home to assist their friends or kin at the time of delivery. Yet their immediate community provided the same support and solace found in elite social networks. Enslaved women, particularly on large plantations, formed gendered communities in which black women shared information and offered mutual support. An enslaved woman gave birth at what one historian has called a "crowded bedside," which might include her mother, female kin, and friends.[11] Less is known about the birth rituals of poor white women in the antebellum period, but evidence of strong kinship and community networks in other areas of life suggest that such women would have drawn on these networks whenever they were available during childbirth. In fact, such kin support would have been particularly important to poor women, black and white, who could not rely on servants to tend to their family responsibilities. Yet historians still struggle to locate birth rituals among groups of black and poor white women.[12]

For those southern women who left records of their experiences, birth offered a point of commonality among women. They proffered each other gifts, advice, assistance, and moral support. Anita Withers, a Texan who relocated to Virginia during the Civil War, wrote of the support she received following her confinement in 1863: "My friends were *exceedingly kind* to me, sending me *nice* things, and coming to see me."[13] Offers of support and exchanges of gifts also occurred across racial lines. White women provided clothes, blankets, and other necessities for new black mothers and their infants. Mary Chesnut observed that a major activity of her mother-in-law, Mary Cox Chesnut, was cutting out clothing for enslaved infants. She then distributed this material to her daughters and daughter-in-law to be sewn up and given to the enslaved mothers on the plantation. Slaves reciprocated in some situations, giving gifts to their mistresses after they gave birth. For example, after the arrival of her first child, Varina Davis received eggs, chickens, yams, fruits, and flowers from those held in bondage on the Brierfield plantation.[14] While such exchanges might be seen as rituals of duty, power, and authority, they could also express genuine sentiment and a recognition of a shared female experience.

Beyond their circle of female friends and kin, many women also desired the assistance of someone with experience and expertise in delivering babies. Most southern women, black and white, continued the "old-fashioned" practice of relying on the services of a female midwife, maintaining the birthing room as a female space long after doctor-assisted births became quite common in the North. A number of elite southern women did, however, increasingly choose to have their births attended by physicians in the antebellum period, as a mark of status and delicacy.[15] Robert Mallard's letter to his father-in-law in 1860 suggested this Georgia family's reliance on professional medical opinion. Writing that "so far everything seems to be taking its natural course," he credited "a kind Providence" that had "provided what I feared might be unavailable at the emergency: the desired medical attendance." On another occasion, Mallard's parents-in-law, Charles and Mary Jones, invited their son's wife to spend her "hour of trial" at their home, "if we had only a good physician within reach at Maybank."[16] One of the Joneses' own sons practiced medicine, perhaps increasing their acceptance and expectations of a doctor's presence in the birthing room.

But even southern women who engaged the services of a doctor could find that rural distances and other unforeseen circumstances interfered with their intentions. Anita Withers lacked a doctor's presence at the moment of her delivery in 1863, although she had been attended by one leading up to the event. Gertrude Thomas faced a similar situation in 1858, recording later: "Thursday morning September the 23rd the baby was born. I was not in pain more than an hour but it is a fearful agony.... I sent for Dr. Eve, but he did not arrive in three quarters of an hour after the baby was born."[17] For both Withers and Thomas, the nurse-midwife they had also hired to be in attendance performed the role of the missing physician. The reliability of midwives (or monthly nurses) encouraged many white women to continue to seek out their assistance, even as they began to hire physicians as well. Female birth attendants generally took only one client at a time and would stay with the birthing woman, offering help beyond their physical assistance during parturition. They often arrived before the onset of labor and remained for some time after delivery. A week after giving birth, Tryphena Fox of Louisiana wrote that her female attendant had "washed all my bed & night clothes & the baby things, so I have not been worried about them."[18] Fox's husband was a doctor, but clearly this attendant fulfilled needs not met by a medical man.

Birthing women might also feel that some midwives had more competence than poorly trained doctors. Awaiting her confinement in 1853, Lizzie Neblett recorded the arrival of "the old midwife Mrs. Ford . . . who came here last Sunday the 27th, she was with Mother when she had Walter and Babe and Mother praises her very much, I had rather trust myself in her hands, and Mothers, than any doctor I know of."[19] Neblett's comments emphasized both the long experience and the individualized attention that this midwife offered. Present more than a week before the birth, the midwife would be there when Neblett required her services.

The arrival of Mary Holland, a seasoned monthly nurse, relieved Adèle Allston, who had feared the ministrations of an inexperienced country doctor at her delivery in 1840. Some years later, Elizabeth Allston Pringle, who had not even been born at the time, recounted her mother's desire to have this experienced attendant at the aforementioned birth. Pringle also recalled that Holland was "an old woman, but still tall and stately in figure, and with great dignity and poise. She was about the color of an Indian."[20] The latter observation suggests a consciousness of racial difference, but also that perceptions of skill could override, at least temporarily, the racial barriers in southern society. Both white and black midwives attended births across racial lines, becoming part of, and generally directing, the female-centered birthing room.

Often the choice of a midwife had as much to do with practicality as preference, shaped more by geography and settlement patterns than social boundaries. On the southern frontier, women might have to accept help from whomever was available.[21] On large, remote plantations, white women lived in isolation from other white women. They often controlled most of the medical provisions on the plantation, but during their own births they too found it necessary to rely on enslaved women for assistance. Black women on these plantations could also count on the services of an enslaved midwife. In contrast, however, enslaved women who lived as one of only a few slaves on a small farm or in an urban setting often had to depend on their white mistresses for aid, whereas a white woman in this situation could call on the help of her white neighbors. These variants suggest not only the influence of geographic location in receiving medical care, but also the complexity of relationships that could occur around the events of childbirth. Necessity often demanded adaptations of the social boundaries created by race and class within southern society.

Elite white women on large plantations might serve as the plantation midwife, or at least attend births in a supervisory capacity. White women would have seen this as one aspect of their job in managing plantation healthcare, as well as part of the nurturing intrinsic to the ideals of womanhood. Isolated on large plots of land, with trained doctors rare in rural areas, plantation mistresses relied on medical handbooks, homemade remedies, and personal experience.[22] Women who were outside of the elite but took up midwifery used their skills to supplement their household incomes. David Harris, for example, recorded hiring a Mrs. Bearden, the wife of the local blacksmith, to assist both his wife and his enslaved women during childbirth. In 1861 he paid her $3. Four years earlier he had paid another midwife $2 ($1 less than the doctor who also attended).[23] The families of white midwives undoubtedly welcomed this income in a cash-poor society. Their profession also allowed these yeomen women to make the same claim to the identity of nurturing as their elite counterparts.

Among former slaves, opinions about a white midwife's assistance (or interference) varied, particularly when that midwife was also their mistress. Winger Vanhook, born in Tennessee in 1849, described his mistress's role in plantation healthcare: "She wuz de bes doctor I eber knowed. When folks got sick she'd take charge an den effen her medicine didn't do de work, den she'd call a doctor. She took keer ob de sarvants as like de fambly." Similarly, John Brown from Alabama noted the helpful attendance of his former mistress, Miss Abby, at his own birth: "She was with all the slave women every time a baby was born, or when a plague of misery hit the folks she knew what to do and what kind of medicine to chase off the aches and pains."[24] Eva Martin, in contrast, disdained this method of care: "Ol' missus she do herself for a slave mudder when a li'l baby bo'n. Dey didn' care. Dat's slavery."[25] For some, the assistance of a white woman emphasized the bond of care that could develop between women across racial lines; for others, it represented inferior care and a lack of choice.

Some enslaved women did experience an increasing medical presence in their lives during the antebellum period, as doctors solicited business from plantation owners. But while a doctor's attendance during childbirth marked the elite status of a white woman, for an enslaved woman it represented yet another bodily interference, since she lacked the power to call for or refuse this physician's ministrations. Henry F. Pyles described a typical plantation arrangement: "We had a white doctor lived at de next plantation, and old Master had a contract with old Dr. Brown to look after us. . . . He came for all kinds of misery except bornings. Then we had a midwife who was a white woman lived down below us."[26] As this case suggests, many masters viewed a physician's attendance at an enslaved woman's delivery as an unnecessary expense, except in the case of emergencies. Frederick Law Olmsted recorded a conversation with a slave manager who said he never called a physician for the births of enslaved women because "the women, from their labor in the field, were not subject to the difficulty, danger, and pain which attended women of the better classes in giving birth to their offspring."[27] Thus the work of enslaved women became a justification for what might seem to be inadequate attention to their medical needs.

Enslaved women, however, did not necessarily resent limited medical attention from white doctors. A number of these women noted a preference for black midwives, or *grannies*, to assist at their deliveries. Surrounded by women of her own community, the birthing woman could express her own views on how things should proceed. Black midwives served not only as birth attendants, but as the guardians of rituals, traditions, and folk beliefs important to their community. Rebecca Hooks of Georgia told her WPA interviewer: "On the plantation, the doctor was not nearly as popular as the 'granny' or midwife, who brewed medicines for every ailment." Walter Leggett recalled: "A good granny woman helped with the babies and they had good healthy ones. Now days the doctors make them puny."[28] Whether or not grannies could ensure healthier infants, the presence of a black midwife generally offered enslaved women a more benevolent "interference" at birthing time.

The role of midwife shaped not only the experience of the birthing women, but also the identity of the birth attendant herself. As mentioned above, for white women this role was tied to the ideal of female nurturing; for enslaved midwives, this nurturing could be combined with a sense of power generally unavailable to black women in a slave society. A black midwife's attendance on other black women made her a powerful person within her community and a valuable contributor to the maintenance of her culture. Their practices included folk rituals as well as physical assistance and emotional support. They might offer pain relief, which ranged from cloves and whiskey to the use of herbs, salves, and home ointments, or to the more idiosyncratic practice of placing a rusty tin or ax beneath the mattress to "cut" the pains.[29] The significance of these methods in the deliveries of other black women was not necessarily their medical efficacy, but the ability they offered to black women to ritualize their births in a manner that made sense to them, maintaining cultural traditions and creating their own narratives of the experience. White doctors spoke of success in childbirth as the production of a living infant by a living mother. Enslaved women sought more from their birth experiences under a black midwife, valuing the process and how they were treated as well as the outcome.[30]

A black midwife's power and authority could also extend beyond the enslaved community. Narratives by and about black midwives often explicitly noted the interracial nature of their service. Rebecca Hooks recalled that "each plantation had its own 'granny' who also served the mistress during confinement." Midwife Clara Walker claimed that she "brought as many white as culled children."[31] In some ways this service represented an extension of the social system whereby house-slaves assisted white women in any number of intimate situations, from dressing to washing menstrual rags, but the singular circumstances of the birthing room altered this power dynamic. Birthing white women required not only physical assistance, but the emotional support and expertise of the black midwife; obeying the instructions of this black woman could prove essential to the well-being of both themselves and their infants. Gertrude Thomas admitted her reliance on black midwives, writing in 1858: "Aunt Tinsey's presence inspired me with a great deal of confidence." Later, in 1865, when the formerly enslaved Susan asserted her independence by leaving the family, Thomas wrote: "I am under too many obligations to Susan to have harsh feelings toward her. During six confinements Susan has been with me, the best of servants, rendering the most efficient help."[32] The citizens of Isle of Wight County, Virginia, highly valued the services furnished by the black midwife Lizzie Perdue. Freed upon the death of her master, the law required Perdue to leave the state, but the citizens petitioned the state legislature for her to stay, arguing: "She is useful in serving sick persons, and especially among ladies."[33] This extraordinary abrogation of the rules meant to ensure racial boundaries suggests that the relationship forged in the birthing room created a recognition of mutuality and interdependence that few other services could engender.

The presence of a black midwife on the plantation benefited not only birthing women but slaveowners; the latter could depend on the midwife to provide reliable and affordable (i.e., free) treatment. Besides the advantages she had for her own plantation, a skilled midwife could be a profitable venture for her owner, who could hire out her services to neighbors who did not possess such an asset. Clara Walker asserted: "I made a lot of money for ol' miss. But she was good to me."[34] Although some owners had misgivings about the midwives' knowledge, fearing that they might prevent conception or induce abortion as well as deliver babies, the advantages usually outweighed any doubts.[35]

The art of midwifery offered a small number of black women a privileged position and the potential to exercise a modicum of control. Some masters excused midwives from laboring in the fields. Cornelia Winfield noted that her mother, the plantation midwife, received a medical bag and a horse and buggy to take her to deliveries, which marked her elevated status. More important than material benefits, however, was the black midwife's ability to claim a voice for herself and her community. In Kate Pickard's semi-fictionalized account of the enslaved couple Peter and Vina Still, the slavemaster must ask Vina to resume her midwifery, a service she had withdrawn in protest to his treatment of another enslaved woman. He petitions Vina: "But your mistress says she would like to have you back. Several of the women will be sick soon, and she wants you there." Vina initially refused this request but ultimately made a decision to return, based on duty to her community rather than to her master. Vina Still is shown to have experienced numerous abuses as an enslaved woman, but this incident demonstrates the belief that her skills as a midwife created a moment in which power temporarily shifted, and the master had to request rather than demand her compliance.[36]

For white members of southern society, recognition of a midwife's vital position often conflicted with racist assumptions about the limited capacity of all blacks. Even the remarks of British actress Fannie Kemble, who was generally sympathetic to the plight of the enslaved, show this ambivalence. Describing the time she spent on her husband's Georgia plantation, she commented on the "ludicrous visit" she received from a black midwife, labeling her "a dirty, fat, good-humored looking old negress." Nonetheless, in the same passage Kemble conceded that this midwife represented "an important personage both to master and slave, as to her unassisted skill and science the ushering of all the young negroes into their existence of bondage is intrusted."[37] Subjected to ridicule, and with little power to affect change on her own, Rose, the maligned midwife, still took the initiative to put herself forward on behalf of her community. The power she had was small, but not insignificant. She used Kemble's shared experience in giving birth to gain her advocacy for pregnant and birthing women on the plantation, blurring, if only temporarily, the rigid hierarchy that separated these women.

Much of the basis for a recognition of a common gender identity among birthing women sprang from a shared sense of danger. Southern women, black and white, were linked by the real and perceived pains and physical dangers of childbirth. A woman's "hour of trial" put her in a liminal position between life and death, and in the process other boundaries became blurred. Women's narratives touched on both a belief in the inevitability of pain and a desire to ease this suffering.[38] The *Ladies' Repository* assured its readers that "the highest joy to the Christian almost always comes through suffering."[39] And some women may indeed have seen their birth pains as the cost of fulfilling the ideal of true womanhood, thus facing them with equanimity. Madge Preston, for example, was said to have dealt with "her protracted labor, difficulty, pain and anxiety, which endured forty eight hours, with calmness, courage, and fortitude."[40] Other women, however, shared the sentiments of Lizzie Neblett of Texas, who feared and resented the pain involved in birth.

Thomas wrote more specifically of her fears, recording in her journal in 1865: "I have thought of my dying when the hour of trial comes. Mr. Thomas says I always say I expect to die, but I don't think so. I know I have thought of it this time more than usual and if I do die, I hope that my baby will die with me."[48] In case of her death during childbirth, Madaline Edwards of New Orleans left a list of instructions for her lover, Charles Bradbury, in the back of her journal, explaining: "[M]y most beloved and adored Charley the time is close at hand that brings to me a period of suffering and it may be death also."[49] Women were aware that if complications developed, neither doctors nor midwives had much assistance to offer.

Many southerners knew at least one woman who had died as a result of childbirth, and both men and women recorded occurrences of such deaths. Some hit very close to home. Maria Inskeep of New Orleans wrote to her sister Fanny Hampton in 1825 about the death of her daughter Sarah. Inskeep noted that Sarah's labor was "not very severe," but afterwards she had never regained her appetite, and after several days "she was attacked with a violent colic, which through [sic] her into spasms, and she became very ill . . . everything that human aid could suggest, was done, but of no avail!" After bidding her infant son goodbye, Sarah died. Rebecca Singleton of South Carolina told a similarly heart-wrenching story about the lingering death of her daughter, Mary, after the birth of her first child. On July 8, 1830, she wrote: "I have the happiness to inform you, my dear Girls, that your sister is the Mother of a sweet little Girl." But by the twenty-sixth of the month Singleton began to write of the precarious health of this daughter, and in September she had to write of the "misfortune that I feared was inevitable, and Alas! My fears were too soon realized, for the next day, your beloved sister's gentle spirit winged its flight to regions of bliss!"[50] These women shared the pain and sorrow that could result from the loss of a family member during birth.

But even the death of an unrelated woman could stir empathy. S. Cassell of Gladsboro, Virginia, wrote to her sister of one such maternal death: "I suppose you have heard that Nannie Weddle died the 20th of last month. She died on the day she was married ten months. She had a little boy and she only lived about twelve hours after it was born. Poor Nannie, her pleasure for this life was but short, but it is to be hoped that she is gone where pleasure never dies. Her babe still lives and is doing well." Mahala Roach recorded similar sentiments in her diary in 1856: "Poor Mrs. Putnam dies today, she leaves an infant daughter, three days old—well, she was as good and pure a woman as ever lived."[51] Women recorded these events with tones of both sadness and resignation, expressing empathy for what they feared could be their fate.

South Carolina planter Thomas Chaplin also wrote of the death of a friend's wife while delivering their first child in April 1852. He added that "this is the second wife Perry has lost in the same manner & his brother Tom's wife died in the same way."[52] John Cornish's brother, the Reverend Andrew Cornish, wrote in 1850: "Mrs. Dr. John C. Calhoun whom you recollect I married last year is no more—She died in child-bed last Sunday under distressing circumstances. . . . Her child lies in the coffin by her side. The funeral, as you may suppose, was a most solemn one."[53] Both Charles Jones Jr. of Georgia and Bennet Barrow of Louisiana recorded in some detail the painful, lingering deaths of their own wives after childbirth.[54] Like women, these men, while not rejecting the childbearing imperative, created a narrative that included the perils as well as the rewards.

As was the case with the birth experience itself, white women who recorded the deaths of enslaved women or of their infants suggested conflicted feelings between a sense of commonality and a need to define themselves in opposition to these "other" women. Mahala Roach, for example, recorded the deaths of both black and white infants in her diary. She wrote of one white neighbor: "Mary Jack's baby died this morning! poor young Mother—I am sorry for her!" On another occasion she wrote: "Mrs. James Moore's sweet little baby died this morning! I am so sorry for her, this is the second child she has lost, and now has *none*." In contrast, Roach expressed limited emotion for Clarissa, who lived as a slave within her own household, when this black woman's child was stillborn, writing only: "Clarissa had a dead baby this morning. Mother went to see her and attend to her comfort." And of another enslaved woman, Roach recorded: "Henrietta had a boy baby today—it was premature and only lived six hours—she is doing well." Given no time to grieve, Henrietta returned to her tasks less than two weeks later, which Roach recorded without any apparent irony: "Henrietta came out to work this morning, and I felt so *free*."[55] Roach expressed concern for the enslaved woman's physical well-being, but her comments lacked the emotional empathy she expressed for white women in similar circumstances.

In February 1860, Tryphena Fox recorded her sorrow at the death of her own newborn son. She wrote that "although only two weeks old, the loss of my babe is to me as though I had loved & cherished him for years." Yet less than two months later, when an enslaved woman in her household endured a similar tragedy, Fox placed the blame on the woman's poor mothering and neglect. She showed no empathy for the woman's pain, but rather indicated that she believed the woman was using her situation to get out of work: "Susan is well enough to do anything, but it is customary to give *four* weeks & I am determined she shall have her month & *then* go to work in downright good earnest."[56] Constructions of both physical and emotional pain allowed for a retreat into differentiation and hierarchy, separating, no matter how invidiously, the experiences of birthing women. This conflict between a shared physiological experience on the one hand, and a need to clearly differentiate social identities on the other, suggests the complex negotiations of these identities that occurred in antebellum southern society. Birth was one of the most intimate of situations that, like other social and economic relationships, tied black and white women together even as white southerners strove to assure the differences in these women's status and power.

While an interaction between birth, gender, and racial identity shaped the experience of women in the antebellum period, during the Civil War a few southern women adopted a rhetoric that linked the pains of childbirth, the military struggle that surrounded them, and their nascent Confederate identity. For millennia, women had been attributing the pain and danger of childbirth either to nature or to God's will, but now some women placed the blame on the war, and more specifically on the northern invaders. Gertrude Thomas had suffered a number of miscarriages and premature births in the antebellum period, but in October 1865 she attributed the premature birth and death of an infant son directly to the "constant strain upon my nervous system" stemming from the war in Georgia.[57] When the pregnant daughter of Mary Jones fell from a wagon as she retreated from Sherman's army, Jones noted that they suffered "intense anxiety and distress" lest this incident had harmed the baby by the encounter with the enemy. Later, when she recorded the difficulties of her daughter's delivery, Jones felt compelled to add: "During these hours of agony the yard was filled with Yankees, it is supposed one hundred visited the place during the day."[58] The stresses of birth and of war were closely linked in the mind of Mary Jones. Emma LeConte also directly blamed the Northern Army for a difficult birth experience: "Poor Aunt Sallie suffered dreadfully, and her babe was born dead—the result of the fright she experienced when the enemy passed through Milledgeville."[59] These narratives suggest the dramatic flair that war often inspires. But they also indicated how southerners' comprehension of pain went beyond physical sensations, reflecting broader understandings of the contextual meaning of birth.

If labor and delivery offered a moment when some of the social boundaries could be tested, the recovery period generally represented a time when the social hierarchy was reasserted. Societal dictates regarding the treatment of postpartum women clearly reflected differences in status, based both on race and on class. The month following birth erased many of the commonalities of the birthing room and reestablished clear social differences between the delicate elite white women of the southern ideal and the poor and black women of whom hard physical labor was required soon after their children were born.

Childbirth could leave women physically and emotionally drained. Dr. Gunn's popular medical guidebook advised that if a woman's delivery had not been too difficult, she should be able to sit briefly in an easy chair by the third or fourth day after delivery, but she should not "stand or walk much for a week or ten days after her confinement[.]" After the tenth day, Gunn recommended a careful return to a woman's "usual mode of domestic affairs." Gunn preceded this advice with the proviso that "the length of time, as to her confinement, depends much on habit, as some women can do that which, in similar circumstances, others would suffer much from."[60] This may be read as respecting the feelings and experiences of individual women, but implicit in this statement was the understanding that only well-off white women had the "habit" of controlling their actions and domestic affairs. Enslaved women, in particular, were at the mercy of the decisions of others in determining the circumstances of their recovery period.

To some extent, however, even elite southern women had their recovery period shaped by social expectations. Like their counterparts in the

North, elite southern women recorded a gradual return to controlling the reins of their households and reemerging into society.[61] Ideals of womanhood meant that these women generally adopted a persona that emphasized delicacy and a gradual recovery, regardless of how quickly they actually regained their health. When Sarah Wadley recorded the birth of her youngest brother on April 6, 1860, she indicated that both her mother and the infant were "doing very well," yet two weeks passed before she recorded that "Mother begins to sit up a little." Kate Edmondston recorded that her sister-in-law was "still confined to her Chamber" with an infant a "fortnight old"; and Susan Webb received a letter reporting that a female relative was just "beginning to creep around the room" nearly a month after giving birth. In 1857 Tryphena Fox wrote of her recovery after birth: "as this is my seventh day I hope soon to get up & attend to my household duties & the claims of the little one."[62] While these women may have appreciated the opportunity to recover their physical strength in relative quiet, it must be remembered how closely this period of recovery was tied to the idealized dictates of feminine identity that elite white women alone could satisfy.

The main reason that these women could fulfill the expectations of a postpartum retreat was that they had access to a community of women to offer them assistance. While almost all southern women could rely on a network of female relatives and friends to temporarily care for their household responsibilities, women who had sufficient resources could also hire monthly nurses to assist with the birth and recovery period. In addition, women of the planter class could lean heavily on the support of their slaves. Mahala Roach, complaining of her own weakness twelve days after giving birth, expressed her dependence on the women she held in bondage: "[T]he servants have done well, *very* well, while I was sick, and feel grateful to them for it."[63] In general, however, such assistance received little comment, as most elite women took it for granted that enslaved women were there to help.

White women who lived in households without slaves, or in households that required all available enslaved labor for other purposes, enjoyed considerably shorter recovery periods. David Harris recorded the birth of his son on July 12, 1858. By July 21 he noted: "Our boy is growing finely, and Emily is well enough to attend to her business about the house."[64] Emily Harris could not afford to remain in bed two weeks after giving birth—her children and household needed care, and her husband needed the labor of the enslaved women who might have assisted her. Meta Grimball of South Carolina recalled in retrospect how financial concerns had shaped her recovery each time she gave birth:

> For the 12 confinements I had:—Motives of economy induced me to only 4 times have a regular nurse, and only twice for a whole Month, the others I had what I could get at home, & the regular nurse here was with me 2 weeks. I believe now this was a mistake, it was thought that I really did not wish a nurse, and *not* that I made a sacrifice to what I considered necessary economy.—I recollect now the feeling of nervous misery, when ill, with a baby's head paining, & the noise of children running up & down stairs, doors slamming &c., & that restraint which the presence of a stranger in the nurse would have occasioned in my sick room, not there; & the dreary details of expenditure discussed at my bed side. Well, I have had, & now have many blessings, but were I to begin life again, at such times I would have a nurse & I would nurse myself.[65]

Grimball's view of the recovery period had clearly altered from a luxury to a necessity. Yet for reasons of real economic shortfalls, many women could afford neither to hire assistance nor take time away from their household duties. Clearly, the ability to dictate one's recovery period marked class status in the antebellum South.

The differences between free and enslaved women's recovery periods made even greater distinctions of identity, both in terms of physical treatment and the exercise of control. The amount of time allotted to recuperation after birth clearly shows how the experience of southern women was defined in terms of the "other." If white southerners saw a slow recovery for an elite woman as a necessary result of her delicacy and a privilege accorded to her status, they insisted that enslaved women gave birth with greater ease and viewed any considerations that were granted to these women as acts of benevolence on their part. "The mothers themselves looked on these seasons as gala times," Susan Dabney Smedes wrote of the postpartum women on her father's plantation. "They were provided with flour, sugar, dried fruits, and often meals from the table, and a woman to do all their cooking, washing, and house-work for a month. During the rest of the year they did little more than take care of the babies."[66] These remarks may represent Smedes's postbellum fantasy of the beneficence of the slave system; they do not acknowledge that women of her own class would have considered such "privileges" unexceptional.

The narratives of other white southerners bemoaned the inconvenience that the recovery period for enslaved women created in their own lives. Sarah Wadley, for example, noted the birth of her enslaved servant's child and then followed it up with a comment about the extra work that this would require *her* to do: "To add to my cares Emmeline was taken sick Friday evening, and that night gave birth to a fine boy; deprived of her services about the house, Miss Mary and I have a great deal to do. I never before realized half the care of housekeeping, nor half the trial it is to the patience."[67] Similarly, David Harris closely monitored the recovery of his slave Minerva, fretting that she remained confined to the house in what he deemed a too slow recovery, meaning that the field work he required might go undone.[68]

Enslaved women could not help but note the disparity between their recovery periods and those of elite women, something that must have been particularly vexing to those who had observed the common experiences within the birthing room. Former slaves recalled a range of behaviors applying to black women recovering from childbirth. Gus Fester of South Carolina claimed that his master excused new mothers from field work until the babies could use a bottle, sometime after their first birthday. He concluded that "de wimmins in family way was better cared for den dose young niggers now-a-days."[69] In the opposite extreme, greed overrode even minimal concern for a woman's postpartum health, as Rosaline Rogers of South Carolina told her interviewer: "Slave mothers were allowed to stay in bed only two or three days after childbirth; then were forced to go into the fields to work, as if nothing had happened."[70] Such treatment could have severe repercussions. Hannah Jones claimed that her grandmother became blind after being forced to get up three days after giving birth to sew twelve shirts for her mistress's son to take to school.[71] The treatment of most enslaved women fell between these extremes of indulgence and abuse. Many former slaves recalled that new mothers remained out of the fields for approximately a month, but in that period they performed household tasks such as spinning.[72]

In general, behaviors varied at the discretion of the master. Eustace Hodges's mother, who bore eleven children in slavery, had different experiences under different masters: "She had a baby one day an' went ter wurk de nex' while she 'longed ter McGee, but at Marse Rufus' she stayed in de bed seberal days an' had a doctor."[73] Enslaved women, regardless of whether they experienced long or short recovery periods, received the time allowed for recovery at the behest of another. Fannie Kemble recorded that some of the women on her husband's Georgia plantation confronted her with concerns about the amount of time allotted for their recovery from childbirth: "The women who visited me yesterday evening were all in the family-way, and came to entreat me to have the sentence (what else can I call it?) modified which condemns them to resume their labor of hoeing in the fields three weeks after their confinement." Besides a lengthening of the recovery period, they also "implored me to have a kind of labor given to them less exhausting during the month after their confinement."[74] The appeals that these enslaved women made demonstrated an awareness of their unjust treatment (a four-week recovery period was more typical). Seeking out Kemble also suggested that they hoped gender solidarity, based on common experience, might garner sympathy. Indeed, Kemble recorded that one supplicant "spoke of my babies, and my carefully tended, delicately nursed, and tenderly watched confinement and convalescence[.]"[75] While she expressed concern, Kemble could not overturn the established plantation routine, and ultimately she made little difference in the material condition of these women. The enslaved women's appeal to a shared gender identity echoed the one made during labor and delivery, but in the recovery period racial differences seemed to trump similarities in physical experience, reaffirming rather than challenging social boundaries.

White southerners based stereotypes about the ease with which a black woman gave birth on her rapid return to her labor, but they also forced her resumption of these efforts with little regard for her physical health. Slaveowners thus created a self-justifying model for the work performed by their enslaved women that had little to do with the actual recovery needs of these women. Further, at the end of the recovery period enslaved women might be immediately thrust back into heavy labor, leaving them little time to nurture their infants.[76] The recovery period of women was not a neutral medical event; it reflected southern society's racial assumptions and was used to justify the social hierarchy and power relations.

While the support offered during the physical experiences of labor, delivery, and recovery formulated an immediate community of mutual assistance around birth, the news of these events created a larger sense of kinship and community. Inclusion (or exclusion) from this network could shape a woman's sense of who she was and where she belonged in antebellum southern society. Both the words that they used, and who received the information, became imbued with larger meanings in this context. In February 1855, for example, Carey North Pettigrew wrote to a number of female relatives, asking about a rumor that her Aunt Harriette was "contemplating an addition to her family." When she still had not heard by March 1, she wrote again: "You did not answer my question about Aunt Harriette, I really do very much wish to know, do tell me?"[77] Pettigrew's questions stemmed not just from idle curiosity, but from a desire to feel connected to her extended family. Discussions of birth formed an important facet of a female network of communication in the antebellum South. The language these women chose, the narratives they constructed, and the relationships they formed offer important insights into both their birth experiences and their assessment of their socially assigned role or identity.

Nineteenth-century Americans used a wide range of words and expressions to describe the birth experience. Pregnant women might be labeled as "in an 'interesting' and promising 'situation'" or with the rather lyrical "in the way that ladies love to be who love their lords." Their experience could culminate in an "hour of trial," a "severe trial," or in a "borning"; and the anticipated result was an "addition to her family."[78] Their choices reflected understandings about class, physicality, womanhood, and both the speaker's and subject's place in their society. Antebellum southerners themselves understood the potentially constructive power of words. An article reprinted in an 1861 edition of the *Southern Planter* observed that language "can paint with vivid truthfulness the objects of the external world, it re-acts at the same time upon thought, and animates it, as it were, with the breath of life. It is this mutual re-action which makes words more than signs and forms of thought[.]"[79] Thus the language choices of southerners, both in what was spoken and in how it was said, offer some important insights into how birth affected a woman's identity and position within the southern community.

Perhaps the most common word used in describing delivery in the antebellum period was *confinement*. In countless diaries and letters, the writer, or a female friend, "expected to be confined." Some women saw pregnancy itself as a form of confinement. In September 1855, a pregnant Gertrude Thomas wrote that she did not need many new winter clothes, "having to be confined to the house until after February."[80] In the fourth or fifth month of her first pregnancy, Elizabeth Perry began to plan where "to be confined."[81] New mothers also marked time in terms of their confinements. Penelope Alderman recorded on November 16, 1851, one month after the birth of her baby: "Paid my first visit after confinement to Mother's."[82] Here her confinement lasted not just during the time of labor and delivery, but stretched through her recovery period.

For reluctant mothers, such as Lizzie Neblett of Texas, confinement represented not just the events of pregnancy or delivery, but an ongoing confinement within a social role. Neblett wrote that she would rather be confined in a penitentiary than face another confinement in childbirth.[83] The language of confinement reflected, perhaps subconsciously, an aspect of the physicality of birth for nineteenth-century women; since labor, delivery, and recovery could keep some women in their beds or houses for long periods of time, the idea of confinement had resonance. But it also reflected the social and emotional reality of many women who felt confined by their motherhood role.[84] For enslaved women, the term confinement also offered a bitter irony, embodied in the recollection of a former slave whose mother "was confined in de field and dy got her to the de house." While they lived their entire lives in the confinement of bondage, enslaved women lacked the ability to plan their own "confinements" or to confine themselves to their own homes while they recovered.[85]

According to Virginia Clay of Alabama, Mrs. Keitt, the wife of a congressman from South Carolina, introduced "the fashion of sending out birth-cards to announce the arrival of infants" to Washington society.[86] If these were indeed the first formal announcements, informal communications abounded in the letters of southerners throughout the antebellum period. The diaries of southern women recorded births to female acquaintances and relatives so frequently that the language became almost formulaic. Women noted the timing of delivery, the sex of the infant, and, most importantly, the survival of mother and child: "Mrs. Balfour had a daughter today! they think of calling it 'Emma'"; "My cousin Eloisa has a little daughter, and is quite well"; "Aunt Jane has a little daughter born on the 16th of the month"; "Mrs. Young has a baby boy, born today."[87]

Some announcements involved little information, such as a letter received by Mary Eliza Tillery that announced simply "Lucy Ann Ellis has a fine son."[88] Others offered more detail, as must have been the case in a letter by the Reverend Charles Jones describing the confinement of his daughter, for he received the reply: "Mother thanks you for your *graphic description* of the little lady's arrival."[89] Birth announcements passed from person to person. Eliza Fisher reported hearing "the news of the birth of Paolina's little girl from Mrs. Smith, who recd it from Mrs. Blamyer." Similarly, Sally Taylor wrote to Marion Deveaux of South Carolina to congratulate her on the birth of a son, having "accidently heard through Mrs. Gen. Hampton yesterday, who called here with Mrs. Preston, that you were confined." Such patterns of communication marked a community of women sharing their experiences and information.[90] The prevalence of these announcements demonstrates the centrality of the birth experience in the antebellum South, both to women in their individual lives and to broader social patterns.

The importance of the communication network surrounding birth may best be seen in the behavior of white women who felt left out. Their reactions demonstrate the importance of the bonds formed in sharing birth experiences, either by a physical presence or through the exchange of information. Circumstances of war excluded Mary Bethell from her daughter's bedside. Her inability to attend her daughter, compounded by a lack of information, caused Bethell much distress. She recorded on March 3, 1862: "I long to be with my daughter as she expects to be confined this month, it is a great trial to me that I cannot go." By the end of the next month, Bethell's emotions alternated between resignation and despair. On April 17 she wrote: "I have not heard from my daughter in six weeks, this suspense and anxiety of mind is very unpleasant, but I look to the Lord in this great trial, I put my trust in him, he is my only help." But by the end of April, even this source of hope seemed depleted. "The Lord's face is hid from me, darkness and gloom surrounds me, I cannot get any tidings from my daughter in Arkansa [*sic*], have not heard from her in near two months." Fortunately, Mary Bethell received word that her daughter had delivered a son on April 14 and "was doing tolerable well."[91] The failure of Mary Jones's son and daughter-in-law to tell her that they expected a child in the immediate postbellum years left Jones feeling hurt and resentment. She wrote to her daughter about this omission: "A friend tells me *Eva* is to be *confined* in July, and said she supposed I knew all about it. But not a *hint* even has been given to me." Her son did not inform her until over a month later, shortly before the baby was born, allowing Jones little involvement in the experience.[92] The reaction of these women at being excluded from the information grapevine indicated the emotional importance of sharing birth information within the female network of elite southern women.

Illiteracy kept most enslaved women from participating in this form of communication network, and although the births of most black women went unmentioned except in the plantation record books, some white women did note such births in their letters and diaries. These white women generally focused on birth as a physical or emotional experience rather than as the production of assets, suggesting a possible recognition of commonalities. Many of the language choices made in describing the births of both black and white women could be ascribed to fashion or serendipity. But these language choices also illustrated both presumptions and ambiguities about the status and the racial identity of the birthing woman. Rachel O'Connor, for example, used "in the family way" to describe Bridget and Harriet, two enslaved women on her plantation. She also used this phrase in reference to her nieces Charlotte and Clarissa. O'Connor held a strong regard for family ties, both within her white family and among the families of those she held in bondage; she carefully recorded all birth dates and lineages. In general, the language with which she discussed the pregnancies and births of enslaved women cannot be differentiated from that which she used to describe her white relatives.[93] Yet she could also lapse into the terminology describing enslaved children as assets, as when she wrote to her brother, the *de jure* owner of her slaves: "Harriet has been delivered of a little daughter . . . which adds one more to the stock of Negroes and much to my comfort to see them doing well for the sake of you and yours."[94] For those enslaved women with even less-considerate owners, being described as "in the family way" could only have rung with cruel irony, since those held in bondage had no family ties that those who held them were legally required to respect.

Historians might also ask if it was mere coincidence that Gertrude Thomas wrote that her enslaved women "have had babies," while a few months later she recorded that she, herself, had "become a Mother"? Did Thomas's language indicate her assessment that while her status in society had clearly changed to the role of Mother, the enslaved women remained her servants first and mothers only incidentally? Undoubtedly Venus and Charity, the enslaved women held by Thomas, would have made different language choices, asserting their own claims to motherhood.[95] Historian Bertram Wyatt-Brown argues that "the importance of language in the enunciation of basic beliefs cannot be exaggerated. The words used are not empty gestures."[96] Within these language choices are clues about the personal and social experiences of birth, the meanings individuals ascribed to them, and the role that birth played in the formation of identity in the antebellum South.

The ideals of southern society dictated that all women should bear children, but the treatment and choices of birthing women depended largely on their status and identity within southern society. Women constructed a community around giving birth, and during the singular circumstances of labor and delivery women made connections that sometimes contravened the normal social boundaries. In the less-harried recovery period after birth, white southerners reasserted these clear lines. In the process, the social identity of the birthing woman came into play, defining her experience in relation to that of other women. Thus childbirth had the power to both unite and divide women. The shared experiences in this context suggested that southern women possessed a degree of mutuality based on their gender. But at the same time, the differing treatments of these women marked them as virtual strangers, separated by vast gulfs of status, rights, and privilege. This complex identity formation would be passed on to the children these women bore, beginning with how they were nurtured as infants.

CHAPTER FOUR

Motherhood

Infant Nurturing and Identity

I n 1799, Eleanor Lewis observed: "The idea of being a Mother, of watching over & forming the mind of Our little infant is a source of delight which none but those in similar situations can experience." Alabamian Sarah Anne Gayle suggested a similar pleasure when she wrote about a friend in 1833: "what a thrilling and interesting occasion is the birth of a first child, especially in one who feels so tenderly and thinks as deeply as Julia!" In June 1862, Kate Edmondston, who never became a mother herself, noted in her journal that "children make a vast difference in people's character."[1] These comments all evince the strong connection southerners made between the bearing of children and the development of a woman's identity. But birth did not merely shape the identity of the mother, it also laid the foundations for the status and identity of the children she bore. This transferability made birth a pivotal element in defining both who belonged in the southern community and one's own status within that society. This was, in part, a legal question—sorting infants, from their birth, into the categories of free or enslaved was fundamental to the foundations of the southern social hierarchy. But the responsibilities of nurturing infants, black and white, belied many of the clear distinctions that these legal determinations might have imposed. Both mothers and infants had their social identities defined through the tasks of infant care. Faced with individual difficulties and socially imposed impediments, white and black mothers turned to a wider community for support and assistance. The complex interrelationships that developed around the tasks of nurturing, like those around birth, created behaviors within the household that both reflected and shaped patterns of belonging and exclusion in southern society.[2]

The ideals of antebellum southern society suggested that all "good mothers" would be directly involved in nurturing their infants, providing both physical and emotional well-being. In 1840, the *Southern Ladies' Book* offered this counsel to its readers:

> During the plastic period, when the first and most enduring impressions are made—when the foundation of all that can be valuable in future character is laid, the child is necessarily the companion of its mother. How interesting and momentous then is her duty to train its mind and heart in the 'good and the right way.'... Your early lessons will in a great measure control the destinies of your sons, and the formation of the character of your daughter is to you alike a matter of the highest interest and the highest duties.[3]

Instilling the proper values and providing the correct care required a mother to devote her time and energy to her children.

Despite these glorified ideals, the letters and diaries of white southern women dwelt on the difficulties of infant care, accenting the limited knowledge and abilities of new mothers. For example, after recording the birth of her niece's baby in 1827, Eleanor Lewis added: "she is a helpless Mother, she cannot suckle it, & knows very little about the care of children." Similarly, Elizabeth Pringle wrote that her mother "spent a very anxious time in the first year of her eldest child's life. He was very delicate and mamma knew nothing about babies."[4] These narratives questioned the naturalness of the role of motherhood and the skills it required. Even experienced mothers wrote of the difficulties of balancing care for their infants with their other duties. After the birth of her fifth child, Mahala Roach wrote: "I would always enjoy nursing him, but it so fully occupies my *hands* and not my mind, that I can work at nothing but the nursing, while my thoughts are often dwelling on duties neglected for the other children—or something omitted which might add to the happiness of my dear good husband."[5] While the idealized rhetoric emphasized the complete mental and physical devotion of a mother to her new infant, personal experiences challenged these ideals, with the demands of day-to-day life getting in the way. Yet despite these difficulties, most white women in the antebellum South still took primary responsibility for the children to whom they gave birth. Few had any other option, having neither money to hire outside help nor slaves who could be spared from other labor. But even women who could afford to turn their children over to others often did not do so, because their identity as women was so tied to this maternal role.

Enslaved women in the South faced even greater struggles in aligning their maternal identities, and their identities as enslaved laborers, with the feminine ideal. Black women shared many of the same cares and concerns as white mothers. They focused on nurturing their infants, physically and emotionally, and ensuring that they had the ability to survive within this society. Enslaved mothers worked to teach their children behaviors that would facilitate their ability to survive as an enslaved person without losing themselves in what one historian has called "the paternalistic drama of southern race relations."[6] An enslaved mother's lack of power exacerbated her worries, since she rarely controlled allotments of food, clothing, or punishment. Moreover, labor expectations meant that enslaved mothers were often separated from their infants for long periods of time.

Former slave Steve Robertson of Texas recalled that he only saw his mother on Sunday; the rest of the time he lived in a "nursery" while she worked. Julius Jones lived in the same house as his parents, but he too recalled seeing them only on Sundays because of their work schedule: "they left in the morning for the fields before I was awake, and when they got back I was asleep."[7] On large plantations, owners often instituted communal childcare to enable enslaved mothers to return to work as soon as possible. The meaning of these "baby houses" varied, depending on the observer. Some slaveowners presented their child-supervision arrangements as models of efficiency, magnanimity, and good management. Mrs. Henry Rowe Schoolcraft praised communal care as particularly beneficial to the child:

> On all well-regulated plantations there is a large house expressly to
> receive all the infants, and their young nurses, when their mothers
> go out to work. An old, black, medical crone is at the head of this
> establishment, and she is required to keep up large fires, to feed,
> watch over, and report any sickness or accident to her young charges,
> while their mothers are absent in the fields. The little girls on the

plantation, between the ages of nine and fifteen, runabout with and amuse their mother's infants, or those of other relatives. Every baby has thus its own nurse.[8]

Former planter Duncan Clinch Heyward also emphasized the good care received by enslaved infants, contending that "the most intelligent and trustworthy Negro woman on the plantation was always in charge of the nursery[.]" He added that this arrangement allowed for supervision by the planter's wife, thus revealing his assumptions that white women naturally provided better care than the black mothers of these children.[9] No white southerners, it should be noted, advocated this form of communal care for *white* children.

The narratives of some visitors to the South disputed the contention that infant houses provided the best possible care for enslaved infants. In his travelogue, Edmund Kirke remarked on the plantation nurseries, noting that this system separated children from their mothers and "herded" them together under the supervision of "feeble, sickly women, or recent mothers."[10] Emily Burke, in her 1850 *Reminiscences of Georgia*, wrote: "I doubt not from the cries I have heard from those nurseries, that those helpless little ones often suffer from want of nourishment nature has provided for infancy."[11] Fredrika Bremer condemned this system of care in a letter she penned in 1851 to Carolina Amelia, Queen Dowager of Denmark:

> It is a universal custom on the plantations of the South that while the slaves, men and women, are out at labor the children should all be collected at one place, under the care of one or two old women. I have sometimes seen as many as 60 or 70, or even more together, and their guardians were a couple of old negro witches, who with a rod of reeds kept rule over these poor little lambs, who with an unmistakable expression of fear and horror shrunk back in crowds whenever the threatening witches came forth, flourishing their rods. . . . And yet these were *human beings*, capable of the noblest human development as regards sentiment and virtue—human beings with immortal souls![12]

While the physical conditions described by Bremer do not differ radically from Schoolcraft's description, these women clearly drew different conclusions about these nurseries. To the outside world, the childcare provided for enslaved infants was not the shining example of the slave system's beneficence for which slavery's defenders hoped.

In the 1930s, a number of former slaves recalled that they had, as children, been cared for in plantation nurseries. Henry Brown, a small child when slavery ended, provided a relatively neutral account of this system: "The babies were taken to the negro house and the old women and young colored girls who were big enough to lift them took care of them. At one o'clock the babies were taken to the field to be nursed, then they were brought back to the negro house until the mothers finished their work, then they would come for them."[13] Other former slaves spoke of the inadequacy of the care they experienced. On smaller plantations or farms, slaveowners often left childcare to whomever was available, sometimes children not much older than their charges. Silvia Witherspoon recalled that her mother "would tie de smalles' baby on my back so's I could play widout no inconvenience."[14] Even when caregivers were of an appropriate age, other obstacles stood in the way. Owners often expected the nurses to look after too many young ones or to complete other tasks while tending the children. Also, some caregivers took out their frustrations with their situation by abusing their charges.[15] Yet even those children given the most conscientious supervision lacked the individual attention and emotional devotion lauded in the ideal of the southern mother. This experience shaped an enslaved child's understanding that he or she was viewed as less valuable than white children within southern society.

For enslaved mothers, the available alternatives for the care of infants often proved just as problematic as communal nurseries. Some women had to carry their infants to the fields, leaving them on quilts or suspending them from a tree in a makeshift cradle. Such solutions allowed the individual mother to attend to her infant in short breaks from her toil, but it exposed the infants to the sun and rain, as well as to insects, snakes, and other potential predators. Sara Colquitt, a former slave from Virginia, told her interviewer: "I worked in de fields every day from 'fore daylight to almost plumb dark. I usta take my littlest baby wid me. I had two chilluns, and I'd tie hit up to a tree limb to keep off de ants and bugs whilst I hoed and worked de furrow."[16] Alternatively, enslaved mothers might leave their children alone in their cabins. Kate Pickard, in her semi-fictionalized account of slavery, wrote of a situation in which "every mother, when she went to the field in the morning, locked her little ones in her cabin, leaving some bread where they could get it when they became hungry." According to Pickard, this practice ceased when an infant died in a cabin fire while his mother was away working. The owner then ordered the enslaved mothers to leave their infants in the kitchen with the cook.[17] Clearly, none of these situations met the standards of individualized attention embedded in the southern ideals of motherhood and infant care.

Yet when enslaved children could be worth hundreds of dollars, and their lifetime earning potential was usually far greater, keeping black infants alive made good fiscal sense, a fact acknowledged both by white women and those they held in bondage. This led to some caregiving arrangements that suggested a direct exchange—white mistresses tended black infants so that black mothers could perform other labor. Former slave John Beckwith recalled: "De missus, she raised de nigger babies so's de mammies could wuck."[18] Such patterns were particularly useful on small plantations and within yeoman households, where the number of black infants was small and the need for black women's labor great. White women took a more supervisory interest in black infants on larger plantations. During the time when Ann Coleman's husband served as an overseer on a Louisiana plantation, she noted her own value to the slaveowner:

> There were but few little children on the place when I first went to Mr. W.'s. Perhaps they might have numbered 15 or 20. In one year after I went there, there were 50. This pleased Mr. W. much, as they had never raised as many before in the same time. They had never had the attention they needed until now. They were all as fat as little pigs, clean and well clothed.[19]

Former slave Mariah Calloway observed a similar situation from the opposite perspective, recalling that "the mistress would keep a sharp eye on the children alot to see that they were well cared for. A slave's life was very valuable to their owners."[20]

Even mistresses who stressed their paternalistic interest in the lives of enslaved children could not avoid the economic motivations in tending for them. "It takes a great deal to feed so many children," Rachel

O'Connor wrote from her Louisiana plantation in 1843. "[S]till it is my greatest pleasure to take care of them and to see them look well." While her sentiments may have stemmed from a sense of care and concern, they were also based on fiscal interests. The latter were revealed in a letter to her brother, who held the deed to the plantation and its slaves. She wrote to him of the birth of an enslaved infant, concluding that the birth added "one more to the stock of Negroes[.]"[21] O'Connor's care for the enslaved infants on her plantation was a tangle of compassion and economics. Similarly, Gertrude Thomas expressed sympathy at the death of an enslaved child whom she had personally nursed. Yet she added to these comments the observation that "[a]side from being interested in him I disliked to write Mr. Thomas of his death for he has been so unfortunate since he left. We have lost three horses that I have had to tell him of . . . ."[22] Regardless of their empathy, southern white women could not escape the idea that black infants were property, and as former slave Cato Carter observed: "They was money tied up in li'l nigger young 'uns."[23]

Economic explanations were sometimes also assigned to the motherhood of poor white southerners. In the short term, childbirth might cause some hardship in poor families, limiting a woman's ability to complete the other labor required of her. But over time a woman's reproduction increased her family's productive capacity; a large number of children contributed to the family's economic status. This was particularly true in frontier regions, as the *Democratic Review* averred in 1844: "The poor man in the new country has one aid not dreamed of in the older settlements—his children."[24] Childbearing thus had a dual potential: immediate emotional rewards and additional workers who would enhance the household economy in later years.

Economically, benefits accrued directly to the parents of poor white children, unlike the situation for enslaved children. But these parents still found that they had to defend the status of their offspring within southern society. Edmund Kirke, a northerner traveling in the southern backcountry, observed a poor mother standing up for her children. His slaveowning host had labeled her children "young scare-crows" and ordered them to "clear-out" of his way. Her response was direct. "'They arn't no more scare-crows than yourn, Cunnel J—,' said the mother, in a decidedly belligerent tone. 'You may 'buse my old man—he kin stand

it—but ye shan't blackguard my young'uns!'"[25] Kirke had previously remarked on a corner of a poor family's dwelling "whose finer furnishings
told plainly it was the peculiar property of the 'wee ones' of the family—a
mother's tenderness for her youngest thus cropping out even in the midst
of filth and degradation . . . ."[26] Kirke's descriptions of these incidents
revealed the tensions between maternal sentiments within the household
and the status assigned to offspring in a broader southern society. His
observations demonstrate that social and economic status could miti-
gate the privilege offered by a white skin.

The care offered to infants in their first year of life frequently negotiated the boundaries between racial divisions and cooperation. Practical
concerns, parental resources, and personal sentiment all combined to affect the treatment received by infants and to establish the foundation of
each infant's status within southern society. Equally important, this care
and treatment shaped both the self- and the communal identities of the
female caregiver. The ability to protect and tend her infant was the first
mandate of motherhood. The idealized white mother cared for her own
children and possessed a maternal spirit that extended to her "family,
black and white." In reality, white women struggled with infant care and
often depended on the assistance of others in the rearing of their children.
Enslaved women fought against an idealized rhetoric that characterized
them as bad mothers and threatened to separate them from their children. They, like their white counterparts, often relied on a community of
women to attend to their children. Social status shaped a woman's ability
to nurture, governing the time and material resources she could devote to
her child, further shaping the identity of both mother and infant.

Fredrika Bremer lamented this disparity in the patterns of infant
care. She contrasted her elite southern hostess's role as mother with the
care provided for the enslaved children on the estate. The house in which
she stayed was "full of gay, youthful countenances, six boys and two
girls, the youngest of which is the image and delight of her father; and
Mrs. C. is a youthful pretty, and happy mother of this handsome flock of
children." In direct contrast, Bremer noted that "not far from the house
is a troop of little black children, 70 or 80 in number, whom I visited
this evening, *and who wanted mothers*."[27] This situation, as presented
by Bremer, deprived both black children and their mothers of the all-
important family bond. For white southerners, who believed most enslaved

women could neither meet the ideal nor even attend to their own children adequately, these limitations did not seem contradictory. Many black mothers, however, must have resented the limited opportunity to oversee the care of their own children.

Despite the common identification of mothering as an intrinsic task of all women, women in the most privileged classes have historically delegated the actual physical labor required by this role, while lower-class women have been required to balance their mothering with other activities necessary for their economic survival.[28] Thus while southern social ideals suggested that mothering was the primary activity of all women, black women were expected to combine their mothering with other labor demands. Further, elite women might command the aid of others in tending to their children, an option often unavailable to less-privileged women. Antebellum southern society clearly valued some women's motherhood over others. Yet southern mothers, black and white, sometimes also shared the tasks of infant care, creating tenuous bonds across socially constructed boundaries. The relationships between mothers, and between caregivers and infants, created a complex network of women and children that did not always fit neatly into the idealized patterns of southern society.

The motherhood role helped to define a southern woman's individual identity in relation to the feminine ideal of nurturing and domesticity. Motherhood also contributed to a communal identity in which peers offered mutual assistance, creating a sense of inclusion within a gendered community. Similar patterns and meanings of motherhood could be found throughout the United States in the nineteenth century. Southern motherhood, however, became unique in the context of a slave society. An interaction across racial lines meant some recognition of commonality existed, even as attempts were made to define a woman's mothering in contrast to the racial "other." The tensions between these two views were most apparent when a woman, either through choice or compulsion, cared for an infant of a different race.

White women often depended on a wide network of other women in performing their maternal role. Anita Withers, for example, relied on her mother for assistance if her child became ill or if she needed a babysitter. When she moved with her husband from Texas to Virginia, the loss of this support seemed more daunting to Withers than the actual relocation.[29] Mahala Roach, the mother of several children by 1857, offered her knowledge to less-experienced women in her community. When a new mother could not stop her baby's crying, she sent for Roach, who went immediately. Finding the baby screaming, Roach "gave it some *oil* to soothe it, got it to sleep and remained there three hours," the latter gesture intended probably to comfort the new mother as much as the infant.[30] Virginia Clay's memoirs suggested how even a woman with no living children could become part of a maternal network. While living in Washington, D.C., she became close friends with a young mother. She recalled that "Benny Fitzpatrick was at once the idol of his parents and the terror of the hotel." She then described her own role: "[A]s Mrs. Fitzpatrick and I were cordially united in other interests of life, so we shared the maternal duties as became two devoted sisters, 'Our boy Benny' receiving the motherly oversight of whichsoever of us happened to be near him when occasion arose for aid or admonition." Clay had been taken in by maternal relatives after the death of her own mother, and she participated in the maternal network without becoming a mother herself.[31]

Yet white women often demonstrated a reluctance to admit their reliance on others of different races or classes, afraid that they would be eclipsed as the ideal mother figure. They sought to differentiate their maternal identity from that of black women, or even poor white women. Elite white mothers feared that their motherhood, and thus their idealized identity, would be usurped. Mahala Roach noted several times in her diary that her son John appeared to prefer the ministrations of his enslaved nurse Ailsie to her own care. She finally decided that "John needs my nursing, and attention, for he is growing to be so wilful [*sic*] that he ought to be 'taken in hand.'"[32] The tenderness which endeared the child to his nurse thus became a failure to build character, which only his "real" mother could correct. Eliza Fisher faced a similar threat from a white wet-nurse whom her daughter appeared to prefer. "The little monkey is beginning to love her Nurse so much better than me that I am quite mortified," she wrote to her sister in 1844, but Fisher then concluded that her mortification was unnecessary, "as the preference is as yet purely *physical*, and when her *morale* is more developed, I need not fear the continuance of it—therefore as long as she continues to thrive as well with the Alderney I must not let my *jealousy* get the better of me."[33] By labeling the nurse, undoubtedly of a different class, merely a breed of cow and not a moral influence, Fisher soothed the fear that she had lost her mothering role. These elite women willingly enlisted the aid of others in caring for their infants, but they were far less willing to cede claims to the devotion that the idealized role of motherhood promised them.

This reluctance may have been because they feared the assessments both of other women and of society if they appeared to have given up their idealized role. Such was the case in an 1850 journal entry written by Miriam Hilliard. In it Hilliard passed judgment on a Mrs. Polk, who, she noted, "has a faithful nurse (negro) to whose care she abandons her babes entirely. Only when she has a fancy to caress them does she see them. Eight children and cannot lay to their charge the loss of a single night's rest."[34] There was no way for Hilliard to know what generally occurred within Mrs. Polk's household, but her critique suggests her belief that a white mother ought to be the primary caregiver for her own children.

The ubiquitous presence of enslaved women in elite households often rendered this assistance nearly invisible to those who leaned on it most heavily. Eliza Fisher noted that the illness of her black nursemaid Anne "has interfered a good deal with my leisure lately," and Mahala Roach frequently noted that the occupation of her child's nurse at other tasks left her tending her own baby.[35] Yet neither of these white women would have considered that they were co-mothering with these enslaved women. Caroline Hentz's 1854 novel, *The Planter's Northern Bride*, provided a fictionalized model for the denial of black women's assistance in relation to the celebration of white motherhood. Hentz lauds a white woman, Eulalia, as a devoted mother, yet her fretful infant drives her to exhaustion when the black nurse, Aunt Kizzie, goes out for an evening. Eulalia's husband also insists that she travel with a nurse for their son, because "I do not intend that you shall endure the fatigue of a mother's cares unassisted." Still, Hentz's readers would have recognized Eulalia as the ideal mother, bearing "the crowning grace of maternity," while the enslaved caregivers remained in the background.[36]

The letters of the Jones family of Georgia demonstrated attitudes similar to those suggested in Hentz's novel. Charles and Mary Jones brought home their granddaughter after their daughter-in-law died in childbirth. When this infant was just over a month old, Charles Jones wrote to another granddaughter: "Do you want to know who takes care of Mary Ruth? Grandmother takes care of her. She sleeps in the little crib every night by Grandmother, and sleeps so good she does not wake at night more than two or three time, and then don't cry, or cries very little, and goes to sleep again."[37] While Mary Jones had a great interest in the care given to her infant granddaughter, several enslaved women had the responsibility for meeting all of the infant's needs, including feeding her. Yet white southern society would have recognized only Mary Jones as the mother to this motherless child.

Some white women had the option of hiring assistance to supplement that offered by enslaved women. Elite southern families may have preferred white nurses who, at least physically, more closely resembled the biological mother.[38] Carey and Charles Pettigrew employed Mary Armstrong for fifteen years to care for their children because her skills and educational background made her an excellent teacher and governess. Other members of the Petigru clan sought white nursemaids as companions on their isolated plantations; the comfort of "having a white face in the house with her," as one family member put it.[39] Frederick Law Olmsted encountered one southerner who told him that hiring white nurses was a matter of fashion with "the swell-heads" who had "got to think that their old maumy niggers were not good enough for their young ones."[40] Some families, however, believed that white nurses were more competent than black caregivers, thus requiring less supervision from white family members, as Mary Jones implied: "Yesterday the *black* nurse was dismissed, and a very clever white one has taken her place. She is very competent, and I am now relieved of all care of mother and infant, who are doing as well as possible."[41] Hiring a white nanny avoided the racial incongruities of having a black woman tend to a white infant. Further, in hiring a white woman, the employers could also fire her if she did not suit their needs. These white nurses were employees, not substitute mothers or "members of the family," designations which complicated the relationships between white mothers, infants, and their black caregivers. Yet many white southerners had difficulty dealing with the independence of white employees, particularly when enslaved substitutes were readily available.[42]

Thus in many slaveholding households, infant nurture became a cross-racial prospect. While differences in the treatment of black and white infants reinforced their disparate status, turning one's infant over to another woman, particularly one of another race, also held the potential to shake social hierarchies and loyalties at their foundations. This was a point made by social critic G. W. Henry, who described a situation in which a black woman raised a white boy. He then demanded of his readers "[w]hether the hen which laid the eggs or the one which hatched and scratched for them, or brooded them under her fostering wing, was the true mother of the chickens[.]"[43] Rather than conceding the assistance received from black women, many narratives written by or about white southern women emphasized the expansive nature of *their* motherhood. An elite white woman's claims to a maternal identity extended beyond her immediate family into the broader household and across racial lines. "Her motherliness encompassed the whole plantation," Susan Smedes wrote of her own mother. "She had a special eye and care for any neglected or unfortunate or ill-treated negro child, and would contrive to have such cases near her."[44] Such care had symbolic value in pro-southern rhetoric, reinforcing the claim to the paternalism (or rather the maternalism) of the plantation system and the reciprocal relationship between master and slave. In providing for the physical needs of infants, southerners—black and white—affirmed the identity of both the caregivers and the children receiving their care.

Southern society, as has already been suggested, placed many restrictions on the attentions enslaved women were able to offer their own infants, and it often also limited the interactions allowed between enslaved women, particularly beyond their owner's property lines. Yet whenever possible, enslaved mothers relied on a circle of other women to help fulfill their mothering role. This assistance became an important facet in the creation of a communal identity.[45] Like the network enjoyed by white women, this mutual aid centered on emotional and practical support from kin and other female members of the community. Although white owners often controlled the plantation nurseries, enslaved women relied on the black caregivers employed therein to provide the best care possible, given their limited resources, and to instruct their children on how to survive within the southern social system. Mutual support also existed in incidents of forced separation. Laura Clark, who was sold away from her mother, told her WPA interviewer: "I recollect Mammy said to old Julie 'Take keer my baby chile (dat was me) and iffen I never sees her no mo' raise her for God.' Den she fell off de waggen where us was all settin' and roll over on de groun' jes' acryin'."[46] Enslaved mothers often had to rely on other black women to be there when they could not.

In the best of situations, maternal empathy, and a recognition of the shared position of "mother," could also motivate white women to assist enslaved mothers. Elizabeth Perry used her diary to record the births of her children; in some entries she also registered that of the enslaved women in her household. On June 6, 1848, she wrote: "Mary's child I took as soon as it was born, & nursed it & attended it until Mary was able to take it, when it was five weeks old it was suddenly taken sick and died, & the poor little thing has gone from a world where it would have known sorrow & trouble, to a better one." Although the child did not survive, Perry's intention had been to assist both mother and child, motivated by maternal sympathy.[47] Yet a white woman's choice to act in a maternal manner toward black children had a number of motivations, and each affected whether black children, and their mothers, experienced these acts as aid or interference.

A number of former slaves reported that they had been "raised" by their white mistresses, often after the death of their own mothers. Mittie Blakeley told her WPA interviewer that her mother had died when she was a baby, "and she was taken into the 'big house' and brought up with the white children. She was always treated very kindly."[48] Morris Hillyer's story suggested the mutuality which often inspired this mothering: "My mother died when I was only a few days old and the only mother I ever knew was Judge Hillyer's wife, Miss Jane. Her nine children were all older than I was and when mother died Miss Jane said mother had raised her children and she would raise hers."[49] While some former slaves expressed regret at not being raised by their own parents, and others recognized their care as economically motivated, at least some enslaved children experienced the maternal care of a white woman as an extraordinary act of personal kindness.

Some slaveowners worried among themselves that the "assistance" they provided black women negatively affected their ability to mother. "I am satisfied that I have endeavored to take too much care of the negro children," southern planter J. H. Hammond claimed. "It has made parents careless. They rely entirely on my management and will not learn to manage themselves." Yet his reaction to slaves trying to defy his dictums and manage their own health and lives suggests how closed he was to enslaved parents actually tending to their own children.[50] Thomas R. R. Cobb addressed the same concerns in his examination of the laws of slavery. He conceded that "the inability of the slave parents to control and govern their own children from the intervention of another power, the master's, has been considered an evil of this social system." He argued, however, that "the master never interferes with but rather encourages such government," and that this was necessary because "the negro has no disposition to control his waywardness or his vices."[51] For white southerners, interference in the mothering of enslaved women accented, but also compensated for, what they anticipated would be a natural failure in a black woman's maternal abilities. Mothering thus provided a forum in which to argue the positive good of slavery.

In a unique variation of this caregiving, some elite southern women, particularly those who had lost or never had children, adopted an enslaved child as a "pet." Keziah Brevard, a wealthy South Carolina widow with no children, took a particular interest in a sickly boy named Harrison. She lamented in her diary: "Oh if I could only take time & give him more attention." She remained devoted to his care for a month, ending only at his death.[52] Eliza Andrews's aunt chose her pet not because of his sickliness, but for his liveliness: "She had no children, but a little pet negro named Simon, the son of a favorite maid who had died, filled a large place in her affections and used to 'bull-doze' her as completely as if she had been the mother of a dozen unruly boys of her own."[53] Rachel O'Connor had her "little favourite *Isaac*," but she expressed a maternal affection that seemed to encompass the majority of the slaves on her plantation. She wrote to her plantation agent in 1836: "You will (no doubt) find yourself disgusted with the acknowledgment I make of the attachment I feel toward those Negroes on this place, but I do not see that I could be otherwise after the care that I have taken to raise them and the blessings the lord of Heaven and earth bestowed in causing them to prosper under my care." Eight years later she wrote to her nephew William Weeks: "I cannot part from my Negroes. I have raised all but a few and I love them. They have their faults, and I have mine. All living have faults."[54] O'Connor's statement of affection seems genuine, but the explanations she felt compelled to make indicate that she believed these bonds would not be viewed as entirely normal by southern society. Yet choosing a pet or mothering their slaves allowed these women an outlet that they would not otherwise have had for the maternal identity which society told them was part of their nature.

The few enslaved children who were singled out as a pet might have developed a unique identity within southern society. Those so chosen recalled the privileges that this status garnered them. Lizzie Polk explained: "I was raised by Miss Emily, who made a great pet of me and called me 'her Lizzie.' As long as she lived, she was always ready to protect me."[55] Other former pets recalled "privileges," such as having their own bed in the big house, being taught to behave "right," and being excused from field labor.[56] Yet just below the surface of these narratives lay the capriciousness of the relationship and the status of these children as "property" within the slave system. Georgia Flourney, adopted as a pet by a white woman after the death of her mother, recounted: "I was named a'ter her sister, Miss Georgia. I slep' in her room an' I was a house nigger all my days. I neber went to a nigger chu'ch 'till I was grown an' ma[rr]i[e]d, didn' sociate wid niggers 'cause I was a nu[rse]maid." Similarly, Laura Redmoun, who had been raised by her mistress's daughter, recalled: "Law, I didn't know I was no slave. I thought I was white and plumb different from the Niggers." Her confession that she was "right 'sprised when I found out I was Nigger just like the other black faces" revealed the deception in the treatment of these pets. For, regardless of the kind treatment and privileges, these children remained black and enslaved in a society that determined the value of a person based on race. They remained property, and their mistresses' whims determined the fate of these children.[57] Such relationships offered a form of nurturing, but they did so within a broader social context that valued a white woman's mothering over a black mother's and viewed black infants as property without a claim to an identity of their own.

For black mothers, making pets out of their children was just one of the interferences that they faced in their nurturing efforts. Former slave Caroline Hunter identified the dilemma of the enslaved mother when she lamented: "During slavery it seemed lak yo' chillun b'long to ev'ybody but you."[58] Whether for benign, selfish, or malicious purposes, white owners encroached on the motherhood of enslaved black women. This involvement could stray into all areas of childcare, from feeding schedules, to cleanliness, to punishing children for misbehavior. Some mistresses even took the privilege of naming the child.[59] Former slave Sally Murphy noted that this involvement of the white mistress often created more labor for enslaved mothers. She recalled "de wimen folks whut had families wus 'lowed to go home half-hour by sum to wash and ev'y Sunday morning all de little chillun had to be bathed and carried to de big house for Mistess to inspec dem."[60] Fannie Kemble expressed the view of many white women when she remarked on enslaved mothers' "helpless and inefficient" efforts, continuing, "they actually seemed incapable of drying or dressing their own babies." Yet Kemble does not acknowledge how slavery interfered with the provision of clothing or sanitary conditions.[61] Enslaved women who failed to meet the standards of their white mistresses faced scoldings or worse; mistresses, deeming "deficiencies" of mothering as personal failures on the part of black mothers, rarely considered or critiqued the material, physical, and even psychological conditions of slavery that made good mothering so difficult.

One of the first, and perhaps most important, tasks of mothers—both black and white—in the antebellum South was the nurturing of infants through breastfeeding. Most women nursed their own children. Medical-advice literature promoted mother's milk as the best source of nutrition for infants, and many antebellum southern mothers viewed this task as their "sacred duty."[62] Eliza Fisher moved her second child Sophy's cradle into her own room to more easily "satisfy her *cravings*," and she nursed the infant five or six times a day. Eliza's mother, however, objected to her nursing practices, suggesting that the elder daughter, Lily, should instead sleep near her mother: "Why not have Lily by your bed side, instead of being so often awoke by feeding little Sophy? Anne [the nurse] used to keep Lily quiet by giving her the Bottle, & why should she not manage the other child in the same way?"[63] Fisher may have felt instead that she breastfed her infant as much from devotion as from necessity. While some mothers faced opposition to their individual breastfeeding choices, southern society's interest in the moral motherhood of white women and the health of white children generally encouraged breastfeeding as both a physical and a symbolic act.

In fact, many southern women suggested that they weaned their infants only reluctantly. Some associated this event with the potential of increased health problems for the infant. Louisianian Maria Inskeep witnessed the weaning of several of her grandchildren in the spring of 1848: "poor little things I felt so sorry for them; Fanny and Isabelle bore it very well tho they exerted their *lungs* pretty well the two first nights." Her granddaughter Mary Palfrey, whose mother had died, did not adapt so easily. Inskeep reported that she was "very ill, she refused food, and her bowels and stomach became very much disordered—we had to recall the Nurse, she is now better, her stomach seems stronger, and she eats a little and only nurses twice a day—we shall have to wean her very gradually." Caroline North Pettigrew of North Carolina also viewed breastfeeding as a source of both nutrition and comfort. She wrote to her mother that she weaned her son Charley gradually, noting that nursing soothed him when teething pained his gums.[64]

Richmond resident Anita Withers weaned her child because of concerns for her own health. Although her doctor advised her to wean her son at seven months and get him a wet-nurse, she lamented the necessity in her diary. Reflecting their ongoing debate over infant feeding, Eliza Fisher wrote to her mother: "You will be glad to hear I daresay, what I am quite sorry to tell you—that I am about weaning dear Baby—I found that Nursing her 6 & 7 times a day weakened me so excessively, that I have had her fed oftener lately—& now my milk is diminishing so much that I cannot look forward to having enough to supply her during the summer[.]" Even women who nursed as long as they wished found weaning a noteworthy moment, an end to one of the first of their maternal duties. Penelope Alderman recorded that her first son "sucked for the last time" at fourteen months. Although she had ceased writing in her diary in February 1856, she added the fact of the weaning of her second son at eighteen months in August of that year.[65] Clearly, many women saw breastfeeding their infants as a significant part of their maternal identity, and weaning represented a significant change in the mother's relationship to her child.

Breastfeeding not only affected the mother's self-identity, it also shaped the experience of the infant who was thus nurtured. Limited knowledge about sterilization, and the availability of only cow's or goat's milk as a substitute, made bottle-feeding a dangerous prospect for any infant. Anne Webb perceived the difference the form of feeding made when she wrote of a family with three children. The two oldest were "very fine healthy children, the youngest a daughter 5 months old is not so healthy, she has had to nurse her with the sucking bottle."[66] A wet-nurse offered another possibility, particularly for those who could command such services with relative ease. Some women, such as the wife of James L. Petigru, welcomed this option. Jane Amelia Petigru made a conscious decision not to breastfeed, remarking that she did not nurse because she did not wish to be made "a slave to ones [sic] children." Petigru, throughout her life, proved herself to be a woman more interested in her own comforts than in fulfilling the self-sacrificing ideal of southern womanhood. Gertrude Thomas provides a more typical example of a southern mother's carefully made decision on the necessity of finding a wet-nurse. She expressed a self-disgust for her inability to nurse her own child, and although she found it relatively easy to find a suitable wet-nurse from her father's large slave population, she did not do so lightly.[67]

Often the death of the mother was the cause for seeking a wet-nurse for an infant. When Mary Singleton McDuffie sickened and then died shortly after giving birth in 1830, her family found a wet-nurse for the three-week-old infant, also named Mary. In a subsequent letter, the infant's grandmother, Rebecca Singleton, remarked on the things she herself was doing for the infant, noting, "this has served to attach her to me, more than to any one else, even Amy who is her wet nurse." This remark, perhaps inadvertently, revealed the bonds that could form between a white infant and her wet-nurse and the potential jealousy it could evoke in white family members.[68]

Interestingly, on some occasions elite white women nursed not only their own infants, but a black infant from the plantation. Although relatively rare, this activity suggested some of the complexities of identity and interrelationships in the antebellum South. According to her mother, Mary Sharpe Jones Mallard had "such an abundance of nourishment that she has had to nurse one of the little Negroes." In this case, Mallard was motivated by physical discomfort. Other white women may have had economic interests, or they may have been impelled by a concern for preserving the life of an infant. They always exercised choice when they nursed a black child, and the infant might eat or not, at the whim of the mistress. Yet in the intimate act of personally feeding and tending to the needs of an infant, there existed a recognition of the humanity of the child and at least the possibility of seeing the common interests of all mothers.[69]

The symbolism may have seemed even greater for the black infant thus nurtured. Susan Smedes, a white woman, wrote that a family slave named Isaac always boasted that in the arms of his mistress, Smedes's grandmother, he had drunk the same milk as Smedes's father.[70] Former slave Mack Brantley's mother died when he was only six months old. He told his WPA interviewer that while his sister "nursed" him, "Miss Mary Ann Roscoe suckled me wid Miss Minnie."[71] Former slave Lizzie Bennet identified herself as "Miss Fanny's child" because that white woman had breastfed her while her own mother worked in the field. A white woman also nursed Bessie Lawson so that her mother could labor elsewhere.[72] These later reminiscences suggest that former slaves recognized the economic value white women received in nurturing them, even as it created a bond between them. Like so many relationships in slavery, complicated and individualized motives affected racial interaction, creating a pattern with mixed social messages—the black infants these white women nursed were precious human beings and equally precious economic investments.

A somewhat more typical pattern on most plantations was a black woman nursing a white woman's infant, although it has been estimated that only one-fifth of white mistresses used a wet-nurse, even part time.[73] The limited use of such assistance did not stop many visitors to the South from commenting on black women nursing white infants, perhaps as a result of the novelty of such an occurrence in the outsiders' experiences. Fannie Kemble, the British actress who lived briefly on her husband's Georgia plantation, wrote that the racial hierarchy southerners used to justify slavery "does not prevent Southern women from hanging their infants at the breasts of negresses."[74] Despite the growing contention in the nineteenth century, based on scientific racism, that race was a biological determinant that justified slavery, and despite the even older folk belief that character traits might be passed on to infants through breastmilk, few objections emerged within the South about mothers nursing infants of another race.[75] For critics of southern society, however, the image became symbolic of the moral decay of southern motherhood, and thus of the region as a whole. G. W. Henry, a vociferous critic of the slave system, decried the moral harm hiring a wet-nurse caused women: "the fountains that the God of providence caused to flow, must be dried up; and the unnatural mother must sink into a degradation far below the beasts of the field, for nothing but death will prevent the streams of natural affection, even in brutes, from flowing for their offspring, the pure milk of a mother's love."[76] Other comments condemned what outsiders perceived as overly close racial interactions in the South. The intimacy required in nursing an infant, when it crossed racial lines, belied the strict dichotomous boundaries of southern society and revealed some of the interdependencies that linked people in this region together.

The black child-nurse, or *mammy*, charged with seeing to all of the other needs of the white infant was a more common figure than the wet-nurse in southern society. This role, in particular, demonstrated a negotiation of identities across racial lines, as well as one of the great ironies in antebellum southern society. For while elite southerners frequently denigrated a black women's ability to care for her own children, many willingly let an enslaved woman tend white infants. The idealization of the mammy—kind, nurturing, and utterly loyal to the white family— provided a rationale for white mothers turning their responsibility over to these surrogates. The ideal suggested a racially harmonious world in which mutual trust and caring existed for the benefit of all involved. In reality, of course, this interaction between white mothers, black nurses, and their white charges engendered complicated patterns of care, devotion, resentment, and abuse. Infant care reflected an understanding of social position in the antebellum South, and, as such, this care could also shape the identity of everyone involved in this relationship.

As discussed in chapter 1, the ideals of southern society celebrated the loyalty and caring that mammies offered the white family they served. Some elite writers clung to this image, particularly in their postwar memoirs. Both Caroline Gilman and Susan Smedes recalled that black nurses referred to their white charges with an affectionate possessiveness that "seems to claim us still as her babies." Smedes added:

> The devotion of the nurses to these foster-children was greater than
> their love for their own. One of them, with a baby at home very sick,

left it to stay with the white child. This one she insisted on walking the night through, because he was roaring with the colic, though the mistress entirely disapproved, and urged her to go home to her own child, whose illness was more serious, if less noisy, than the white nursling with its colic.[77]

Despite the apparent celebration of the care that this nurse gave her white charges, Smedes's comments suggest that the mistress really knows best for both the white and black children; the black nurse's maternal judgment remains suspect.

The affection between black nurse and white child purportedly flowed in both directions. Duncan Heyward wrote that "some children used to love their nurses, those faithful old black maumas, as much as they loved their parents."[78] In these recollections white southerners ignored the compulsion under which enslaved women acted. Black nurses had to exhibit the requisite affection and loyalty or face possible punishments. Mammies might express a possessiveness for their charges, but in reality their charges owned them. Yet these white southerners clung to the idealized illusion of their mutual relationship with the loyal and affectionate mammy both to justify elite mothers' reliance on this assistance and to bolster the social structures that purportedly rested on these demonstrations of racial cooperation and mutual benefits rather than on duress.

The experiences of antebellum southerners, however, frequently belied such ideals. Finding the right mammy often proved troublesome. Anita Withers praised her nursemaid Pattie as "a most excellent servant," but less than a month later Withers had to send her home for fear Pattie would miscarry. Withers then hired Louisa for a month, and although she characterized her as a "good servant," she also lamented that "we have had a great deal of trouble with servants, I have been worried to death." Next came Susan, who proved capable but had to be sent away five months later because she was about to deliver her own child. Thus in his first year, Johnny Withers had not one but four nurses or mammies.[79]

In Texas, Lizzie Neblett's brother lent her an enslaved girl to assist with childcare, but this girl was of limited help, since she was only eight years old: "Polly is too small to do anything for the baby but hold her &

consequently my attention to the baby takes up so much time."[80] For other women, the demands of the field competed with their need for assistance, particularly when the family owned a limited number of slaves. Ann Coleman, also from Texas, was pleased that her husband bought her a six-year-old girl to help with her infant son. She wrote that "I was very glad of this as I found her very handy about the house." Her pleasure was short-lived, however, because "cotton picking time arrived and my nurse was put into the fields to pick cotton."[81] Her husband clearly set the priorities, and in his assessment his requirements in the field outweighed her need for help with childcare. The ability to command the assistance of a black mammy became a mark of the superior resources, and thus the elite status, of a white mother.

But while elite southern women welcomed the extra assistance, they also denounced black women for not providing the best care. For white women, a number of different ideas had to be addressed: they had to balance their identity as ladies with the fulfillment of the maternal ideal, and each of these roles was also defined in contrast to the roles and behaviors of black women. White southerners often reported incidents of poor care given to their infants. While one might read these occurrences as an abdication of the white parents' responsibility, white southerners seemed to use them as indictments of the capacity of black women to provide proper care. Gertrude Thomas, for example, fretted that her daughter Cora Lou "fell down several times and yet had her face scarred up from a fall," because other tasks, undoubtedly assigned by Thomas, occupied her caregiver Patsy. Other reports of neglect threatened the child with more permanent damage. Bennet Barrow wrote that "Lavenia our nurse gave the baby a large dose of paregoric near Killing him." Sarah Gayle blamed the enslaved nurse when a straight-pin was found stuck in her newborn's ear. The Reverend Charles Jones reported that his infant granddaughter had been found with tobacco in her mouth, "a piece she got hold of about Susan's person someway. . . . Mother has hung the piece of tobacco up by a string in the closet, that Susan may see it morning and evening and at other times when she is washing and dressing the baby. As might be supposed, Susan has not the most remote idea how the baby came by the tobacco." Jones clearly blamed Susan for the incident, but he did not consider it serious enough to remove her from her duties or to have himself or his wife take on her responsibilities themselves. Admitting that their mammies acted purposefully in these incidents would have required the slaveowners to admit the limited loyalty of these women; denial may have been easier than questioning their own judgment or reflecting on the roots of this behavior.[82]

Similarly, in a postbellum memoir Caroline Merrick recalled an incidence of violence directed toward her nine-month-old child at her sister's wedding. She saw "a heavy blow administered in anger to the little creature" by the nurse Julia. Perhaps unintentionally, Merrick's account provides insight into the complicated relationship between a white mother and a black caregiver. Merrick wrote that she immediately told Julia, "you shall never touch her again. You are *free* from this hour!" On the return trip, Merrick "held the child during the long drive to Clinton, though I was very tired, and installed another nurse as soon as I reached home, ignoring Julia's existence." Julia, according to Merrick, became despondent at being removed from her duties and came to her "in a deluge of tears begging to be forgiven and to be allowed to nurse her baby again." Restored to her position, "Julia always resented the slightest reproof or adverse criticism administered to that child by parent or teachers." Merrick thus turns a tale of violence (and possible neglect on her own part), into one of devotion and loyalty from a black nurse, redeeming the ideal mammy. Portraying this abuse as an isolated incident avoided deeper questions about Merrick turning her child over to the care of others. Rather than questioning the tenuous bonds and potential for violence in this arrangement, Merrick instead clung to her own identity as the ideal mother supervising the less-than-competent but ultimately loyal black caregiver.[83]

Criticisms of the mammy's performance served a purpose for white women. By idealizing the mammy, white mothers could assure themselves that they were turning their children over to women who loved them as much as they themselves did. Even so, white women only reluctantly admitted their reliance on black women. Thus complaints about how black women performed these duties allowed white women to cling to their own professions of superior motherhood, claiming the role of "mother-managers."[84] White women adopted the mantle of teacher and corrector of the mothering skills of black women. From the white perspective, the mammy role required a careful balancing of social and gender stereotypes with the realities of infant care.

The enslaved community, not surprisingly, had quite a different interpretation of the identity created through the caregiving offered by black women. Some acknowledged that the role of the mammy offered rewards for individual women, including authority over, and affection from, the white community and special care in their old age.[85] Just as often, however, they commented on the negative aspects of this task. Several black women who nursed white children recalled that they were given responsibilities far beyond their years, a far cry from the middle-aged, maternal figure of the white ideal. Former slave Lou Williams told her WPA interviewer that her career began when her mistress identified her as a potential nursemaid at the age of five, and at "eight years old she trusts me with dem white chillen."[86] Elizabeth Keckley was even younger when her mistress allowed her to tend her infant: "True, I was but a child myself—only four years old—but then I had been raised in a hardy school—had been taught to rely upon myself, and to prepare myself to render assistance to others." Told to rock the child in her cradle, Keckley did so with such enthusiasm that the infant fell to the floor, and Keckley received a whipping.[87] Mattie Brown recalled that her sister "was the regular little nurse girl for mother's mistress." Her tasks included sitting up all night to rock the "sickly and fretful" infant, and, Brown added, "Mother thought she was too young to have to do that way."[88] These recollections illuminate the hardships of children set at responsibilities beyond their capacities. Equally important, they suggest a negative assessment of the white mothers who turned the care of their infants over to children, chosen because they were too young to work in the fields and who needed a mother's care themselves.

Older caregivers faced a different set of difficulties. Often black women could not attend to their own children because of the demands of their white charges. Former slave Katie Sutton recalled: "My mammy was good to me but she had to spend so much of her time at humoring the white babies and taking care of them that she hardly ever got to even sing her own babies to sleep."[89] Other children of former mammies recalled a sort of co-mothering in which their mothers tended to them and the white children at the same time. Owners presumed, however, that the needs of the white children would come first. Although white writers insisted that black nurses favored their white charges out of emotional devotion, black women faced a compulsion to treat them preferentially, knowing that their care for the white children subjected the mammies to scrutiny and possible punishment.

Kate Pickard expressed the hypocrisy of the slave system, which demanded an enslaved woman demonstrate emotional devotion and tender care for white children while denying her the opportunity to attend to her own babies. Vina, the heroine in Pickard's semi-fictionalized anti-slavery biography, had once served as a nursemaid, but under a new master she worked in the fields. Faced with leaving her infant a month after giving birth, Vina contemplated the inequities of her situation: "How tenderly, when she was employed as nurse in Courtland, had she cared for the little ones entrusted to her care! How anxiously had she watched every indication of uneasiness, lest they should be sick! . . . Now that her own babe needed her constant care, she could not be spared. *The cotton must be picked*."[90] For black women, the social system, which tore them away from their own infants to care for white children so that white women could be free of the task, revealed the hypocrisy of southern society's idealization of motherhood.

Many enslaved caregivers were undoubtedly frustrated by the inequities both of their own treatment and of the differences in attention and supervision that marked the status of black and white infants. Some black caregivers, however, adopted the mammy identity as their own. By providing skillful care they defied a society that labeled them "unnatural" mothers and denied them their own children. Ex-slaves lauded former mammies for their care and affection for all children, black and white. Moses Slaughter, for example, recalled:

> My mother was the sweetest woman that God ever let live. She was gentle, loving, always smiling. She was the Mother of ten children of her own, which she nursed and tended and also was wet nurse of ten Fauntleroy children of Master Joseph and Mistress Fauntleroy. All of us children, black and white, called my mother 'Mamma' and she never turned a deaf ear to a child.[91]

In this narrative, Slaughter's mother, not the white mistress, was the ideal southern mother. For black women, their families, and their communities, the mammy role represented not loyalty and devoted caregiving, but their own superior maternal instincts and the hypocrisies of mothering within the slave system. While only a small number of black women fulfilled this role throughout the South, both their real and their symbolic experience resonated within the enslaved community—in ways quite different from the meanings applied by white society.

The example of the "runaway mammy" illustrates the fault lines in the various understandings of the mammy role. For elite white southerners, the caregiver's abandonment of her charges threatened any illusions of loyalty and domestic harmony. In the late antebellum period, novelist Mary Eastman tried to calm these fears by placing the blame on individuals rather than on the system as a whole. In her tale, a master took his slave Susan to Boston to nurse his sick child, as "its mother, a very feeble person, had placed her dependence upon her." Through the interference of abolitionists, Susan "was finally convinced that though born a slave, it was not the intention of Providence, but a mistake," and she ran away. As a result of her desertion, the child dies and Susan suffers from self-reproach and unhappiness. Who is to blame for this sad tale? Certainly not the white mother, nor the slavemaster who had trusted Susan. Susan is at fault for her folly, but she is punished by remorse and by her own abandonment by her former masters. Abolitionists are the real villains in Eastman's tale; they enticed and then deserted Susan, and upset the social order. Thus the ideal of the devoted mammy, while challenged, remained intact.[92]

Most black caregivers, in contrast, did not define themselves in terms of loyalty to their white charges. While they might do their job skillfully, they possessed identities as individuals and as members of the enslaved community that had little to do with their mammy role. These other identities, however, became clear to whites only when the onset of the Civil War allowed blacks an opportunity for self-assertion. The "abandonment" by all slaves became an issue for elite southerners, but the departure of a mammy figure struck many particularly hard. Susan, who had been with Gertrude Thomas during six confinements and acted as "Kate's nurse, Ma's most trusty servant, her advisor, right hand woman and best liked house servant," left the family in 1865. Although Thomas blamed the influence of Susan's husband Anthony for the departure, she added her father's telling comment that "in case of a revolt among Negroes he thought that Susan would prove a ringleader."[93] Doubt and suspicion, it seems, lay just below the presumption of aid and loyalty.

In 1865, Georgian Eliza Andrews's family lost their mammy figure with a sense of resignation and inevitability:

Caesar Ann, Cora's nurse, went off to Augusta this morning, professedly to see her husband, who she says is sick, but we all think, in reality, to try the sweets of freedom. Cora and Henry made no effort to keep her, but merely warned her that if she once went over to the Yankees, she could never come back to them any more. Mother will have to give up one of her maids to nurse Maud, but I suppose it is a mere question of time when we shall have to give them all up anyway, so it doesn't matter.[94]

Kate Edmondston expressed the bitterness of many white southerners at the departure of enslaved women in these positions: "And as to the idea of a *faithful servant, it is all a fiction.* I have seen the favourite & most petted negroes the first to leave in every instance."[95] White southerners, who in the antebellum period proclaimed the mutual beneficence of the slave system and the loyalty that it engendered, found themselves disillusioned as the war freed those they thought they controlled.

For southern whites, the mammy and the care she gave represented racial harmony and loyalty; for the enslaved community, the black woman's care for white children, like the way she tended to her own children despite all obstacles, defied stereotypes about her mothering abilities. Thus the mammy, or black nurse, became the symbolic nexus of infant nurturing in the antebellum South, in which competing understandings about race, mothering, loyalty, status, and power both challenged and supported social boundaries and structures. The care mammies provided was at once private and personal, and of much broader significance within the society of the antebellum South.

Despite the great differences in their circumstances, black and white women in the antebellum South shared many of the same concerns and strategies in nurturing their infants. The ability or inability to control their work patterns, material resources, and in some cases their physical proximity to their children, however, created significant disparities in these experiences. White southerners drew on race-based assumptions to justify their apparent abandonment of their societal ideals in their treatment of enslaved mothers and infants. Slaveholders viewed black maternity in ways that served their own interests, postulating that black mothers were inadequate, incapable, and emotionally uncommitted, thereby requiring the oversight of whites, particularly "naturally good" white mothers. This rationale justified both their interference in the lives of enslaved women and their claims to ownership and control of these women's children, bolstering the patriarchal social structure. But black mothers created a counternarrative by defying these stereotypes and the social obstacles to caring for their children; in striving for the ideals of southern motherhood, enslaved women challenged presumptions about their value in southern society.

The realities of southern motherhood frequently proved far more complex than the ideals allowed. The various patterns of infant care raised questions for all southerners about race, gender, hierarchy, and their social values. The experience of motherhood in the antebellum South represented a balancing of expectation and ideals with the needs of mothers and infants and the conditions in which they lived. The experiences of early infant care not only shaped a women's sense of self, and her position within her community; it also laid the foundation of her infant's status and social identity, reinforcing the patterns of the southern social system.

CHAPTER FIVE

Fatherhood and the
Southern Patriarchy

W HEN CAROLINE NORTH PETTIGREW of North Carolina gave
birth to her second child in 1855, many in her extended family
expressed disappointment that the baby was a girl. Her husband's
brother, Johnston Pettigrew, summed up these sentiments when he
wrote that he could not "refrain from regretting" the infant's sex since
boys were "the thing for the world."[1] The ideals of patriarchy, male dominance, and paternal authority formed an important backdrop for southern society, and birth both shaped and was shaped by this social organization. As the words of Johnston Pettigrew suggest, gender preferences
were expressed in reaction to an infant's arrival—women may have been
the focus of the maternal ideal but, in the view of many southerners, they
fulfilled that ideal by producing male citizens. Equally important, the
southern social system relied on a racial hierarchy that sought to give
white men a position of ultimate authority. White southerners expressed
these racial beliefs in metaphors about blood, suggesting that social as
well as physical traits were passed on through birth.

But birth did not just reflect social boundaries; it also shaped the
identity of individual men by making them fathers. For white men this
role became a basis for their power, while for black men fatherhood often
demonstrated their ultimate powerlessness. Not merely a tale of wom-
en's experiences, birth in southern society established the authority and
social position of men, shaping the way each person understood his or
her place within the family and within the household to which that family belonged. Ultimately, maintaining control of these structures formed

the foundation for a white man's claims to patriarchal and political authority in the antebellum South.

In societies in which the inheritance of property and of surnames pass through the male line, families generally invest the birth of a male heir with great importance. Sons represent a continuity of the family and, therefore, presumed security for parents in their old age. In many societies the birth of a male child evokes celebrations, while female children receive no such welcome.[2] The antebellum South followed many of the tenets of such a traditional patriarchal society, based around agriculture and land ownership. Southerners valued male heirs who could maintain property holdings both through legal inheritance and labor. Even poor whites viewed the potential labor of sons as a means to better their circumstances; the labor of daughters, while often fully utilized, could be lost through marriage. Further, women working in the fields marked the lower social status of poor white farmers, so this tended to be ignored in public discussions, particularly by the elites who hoped to gain the political support of the yeomen class.[3] Sons, in contrast, were openly acknowledged as assets to the family. Carey Pettigrew may have meant to be humorous when she wrote to her husband of their son as their "heir apparent," yet these sentiments fit well with elite southerners' concerns about inheritance and their related preference for male children.[4] For white southerners in the antebellum period, gender was not merely an incident of identity, but identity itself, determining intellect, emotions, and one's place within society.

A preference for male infants existed to some extent throughout antebellum America, motivated by both a belief in male superiority and inheritance concerns. James Smith of Philadelphia, for example, wrote his friend Levi Lewis the morning after his wife gave birth: "This morning at quarter of 5 my wife presented me with a what—a-a-a-little baby—one of the human species and unquestionably and unexpectedly a girl—No boy this time and I feel confoundedly disposed to let baby making alias boy making alone for the future—I succeed only in girl making[.]"[5] Sex preference was clearly not limited to the Deep South. Yet certain elements of southern society—the agricultural economy, the celebration of masterhood, and a system of honor that associated virility with the production of male heirs—made the desire for male offspring resonate in this region.

The shaping of this sex preference began with expressions of the ideal future progeny. Married under a year, Elizabeth Perry's husband promised her in 1838 that "when you present me with a little son, I will make you a present of a *handsome* Rocking chair." In 1839, Louis Wigfall of South Carolina wrote of his dreams of the future which included his "lady" and a boy child: "& when they ask him what his name is he shall answer 'John Manning Wigfall, Jr.' Ma foi! I'll be a happy fellow yet!" Such fantasies could cause disappointment, and even hostility, when the new child was a girl. Lizzie Neblett wrote that when a neighborhood acquaintance had another daughter, "all [were] mightily disappointed that it was not a boy." Virginia Meade Gordon wrote to her sister of their cousin Laura, "who had just given birth to another daughter much to cousin Bolling's annoyance I can assure you."[6]

In 1841, Susan and Oliver Middleton, already the parents of four daughters, awaited the birth of their fifth child. Oliver Middleton's sister, Eliza Fisher, wrote her mother: "really I trust she will present him with a boy instead of a 5th girl . . . ." Fisher thus revealed not only the hopes resting on the birth of a boy, but also that others held the birthing woman as somehow responsible for this outcome. Replying to his sister's "condolences" when the child was another girl, Oliver Middleton sent the message that "he is very well satisfied with the little babe being a girl, & is not disappointed at not having a son." Ironically, Fisher faced similar expressions of disappointment from her own mother-in-law when her first three children were girls, prompting a shift in her attitude. She wrote defensively in response to a note that she received from a male acquaintance, reporting that his wife had

> "added another female to the inhabitants of this planet" & "begging me to caution all those *I might have any influence with* against such a needless multiplication of the gentle sex in families that are boyless"—I am sorry for his disappointment, but really think people ought to be satisfied that Providence orders these things much better for us than we could for ourselves—& I mean to be content with *whatever* comes to me, & hope Fisher will be equally so—or at any rate *resigned* if he has another girl instead of a boy[.][7]

Eliza Fisher's ruminations reveal the mixed feelings about sex preference during the antebellum period. A shift in attitudes toward children meant that all infants were viewed as precious, but the desire for male heirs lingered. The production of boys remained central to narratives of birth, indicating the continuing power of the patriarchy to shape sentiments. Birth clearly laid the foundation for an infant's self-identity, and future expectations for the child were based on gender norms.

Yet while a preference for males remained as the dominant narrative throughout the antebellum period, statements refuting such a bias became more common. In many cases this denial of sex preference denoted the increasingly emotional attachment between parent and child, a re-envisioning of children as gifts rather than assets. Thomas Kennedy, already the father of four daughters, wrote to his wife from Mississippi after the birth of their first son. He assured her that his joy at the birth did not stem from the child's sex, "for I would not if I could change my daughters for all the sons in existence." A month later he again reassured his wife Nancy, writing: "You say I must not love him better than my daughters[,] that was needless for I am satisfied it is impossible for me to love him or to have my love increase for any person (except my Nancy) greater than it is for them[.]"[8] American fathers, the Swedish visitor Fredrika Bremer wrote from South Carolina, had "a charming weakness for daughters."[9]

Perhaps not surprisingly, it was women who most avidly sought to change how sex preference defined the identity of their children. White southern mothers welcomed daughters as companions for themselves. Even women who voiced a preference for male children twisted the patriarchal narrative slightly. Rather than lauding the intrinsic superiority of men, they suggested that the structures of their society made life easier for men, and thus male children could anticipate a brighter future than females. Rosalie Calvert wrote of her children in 1813: "Sometimes I am sorry that they are not all boys, who—with a good education—can always carve their way in this country."[10] Lizzie Neblett of Texas expressed regret that the child she bore in 1863 was not a boy. In a letter to her husband she declared: "God knows I wish I had been placed in my grave before I ever brought one of my sex in this world." Similarly, in a diary entry from ten years earlier, when her first daughter was still an infant, she had noted: "Oh my daughter I would that you had been a boy, for 'woman's lot is hard to bear,' and I would save you from what I have endured, and should life be prolonged must still endure."[11] The desire for male children stated by Calvert and Neblett did not represent an unconditional preference for boys; instead it was a recognition of the power of patriarchal structures in shaping opportunities based on gender.

Notably, although discussions of a sex preference for infants were sprinkled throughout the diaries and letters of white southerners, there is limited evidence of this tendency in the enslaved community. The only clear references to a sex preference appear in the works of anti-slavery writers, who often imposed a patriarchal order in their compositions, aligning the gender roles of enslaved people to the expectations of their white audience. Thus they might introduce the image of a "first born boy" to evoke the ideals of family formation and its trials under slavery. Others associated the birth of a girl child with the sexual abuses they believed to be inevitable under this system.[12] But there are few indications that most enslaved parents adopted this mode of thinking. Inheritance and opportunities for advancement held little import within the enslaved community. Enslaved men asserted authority where they could, but patriarchal structures generally offered more impediments than rewards. Gender roles determined certain job assignments, yet owners expected the majority of enslaved women to "work like men" in the fields. The narratives of former slaves lauded the skills and contributions of enslaved women as frequently as those of men, in everything from excellence at field work, to skills at doctoring, to self-defense.[13] The enslaved community did not ignore gender, but they reshaped the ideals to suit their lives, and in this context they welcomed both male and female children.

While sex preferences for infants seemed to have softened somewhat in the antebellum period, racial distinction, expressed through metaphors about blood, remained undiminished. The link between birth and blood clearly shaped the identity and the destiny of southern infants. Elite white southerners used a rhetoric of blood to assert a social hierarchy based on biological differences. In their view, being born white and free proved their superiority; and its basis in birth proved the "naturalness" of this social order. Conversely, they claimed that birth and biology, not white southerners' actions, were responsible for the subjugated position of blacks within southern society. The servitude of slaves thus became a preordained—and presumably immutable—function of their own birth and blood. An 1860 article in the *Southern Literary Messenger* entitled "The Negro Race" asserted this proposition: "Slavery seems to have been emphatically the *history* of this Race; and who, thrusting himself into the Divine councils, will undertake to say that slavery is not their *doom*?" In an 1861 speech, Alexander H. Stephens, soon to be vice president of the Confederacy, demonstrated a similar desire to render this status beyond questioning. He argued that "the negro by nature, or by the curse against Canaan, is fitted for that condition which he occupies in our system." He then counseled his listeners that "it is not for us to inquire into the wisdom of His ordinances or question them. For His own purposes He has made one race to differ from another, as He has made 'one star to differ from another in glory.'" White southerners used the metaphors of birth and blood in an effort to portray the South as an organic society, one in which every member had a suitable and just position.[14]

A potential challenge to this neat explanation of a social identity determined by blood was the existence of miscegenation, or *mixed blood*, within southern society. It became a particularly potent symbol of the artificiality of bloodlines in determining—and justifying—status. Antislavery novelist Richard Hildreth observed southern society firsthand while recuperating from tuberculosis on a Florida plantation in the 1830s. He has the hero of his novel, *The Slave*, question the claims of a society supposedly based on distinctions of blood. This character, Archy Moore, asserts that he has "running in my veins, the best blood of Virginia," but in the slave South, "though I might count all the *nobility* of Virginia among my ancestors, one drop of blood imported from Africa—though that too, might be the blood of kings and chieftains,—would be enough to taint the whole pedigree, and to condemn me to perpetual slavery, even in the house of my own father!"[15]

Elizabeth Keckley, who would become a seamstress for and confidante of Mary Todd Lincoln after buying her way out of slavery, recalled her anger about the injustice of "blood" in a slave society. In a memoir published in the postbellum period, she wrote of her mixed-race son, the result of an unwanted relationship with a white man:

Why should my son be held in slavery? I often asked myself. He came into the world through no will of mine, and yet, God only knows how I loved him. The Anglo-Saxon blood as well as the African flowed in his veins; the two currents commingled—one singing of freedom, the other silent and sullen with generations of despair. Why should not the Anglo-Saxon triumph—Why should it be weighed down with the rich blood typical of the tropics? Must the life-current of one race bind the other race in chains as strong and enduring as if there had been no Anglo-Saxon taint? By the laws of God and nature, as interpreted by man, one-half of my boy was free, and why should not this fair birthright of freedom remove the curse from the other half—raise it into the bright joyous sunshine of liberty?[16]

Keckley's reference to the "taint" of Anglo-Saxon blood gives the idea of white superiority an ironic twist. Bloodlines appeared to be a mark of hypocrisy, rather than a natural ordering, to those who bore witness to the "mixing" of this blood.

The birth of mixed-raced children represented both the great power of, and the greatest challenge to, the racial hierarchy of southern society. Southerners once again had to negotiate between ideals and realities in determining who they were as individuals and as a community. A few white southerners completely denied the existence of miscegenation, intent on maintaining blood as a marker of social distinctions. For example, an 1845 article in the *Southern Quarterly Review* insisted that "the nonsense of abolitionists about amalgamation is as stupid as it is nauseous. It violates the common instincts of our nature."[17] Most southerners, however, while they did not openly acknowledge miscegenation, also did not overtly challenge its existence. Zealous in their defense of this particular ideal against outside attack, among themselves white southerners rationalized miscegenation, based on the stereotypes that pervaded their society. Few were willing to address the behaviors of slave-masters and their right to use their "property" as they wished. While a flaunting of miscegenation might cause polite society to wince, it rarely meant exclusion for the white male transgressor. The existence of mixed-blood individuals might have become a powerful symbol of the South's inability to maintain its strict categorizations and controls. But rather than concede this failure, powerful southerners sought both to silence the discussion and to justify the existence of miscegenation.

Despite references to birth, blood, and what was "natural," southerners actually relied on the legal system to assign a racial and social-status identity to each southerner. The law dictated that any offspring of a white man and a black woman was black; further, if the mother was enslaved, so too was the child. Thus white men who engaged in sex with enslaved women need not fear that their activities threatened the South's racial dichotomy.[18] In a lengthy exposition in defense of slavery, Judge Chancellor Harper of South Carolina even suggested miscegenation might offer some good to society, arguing that the sexual availability of enslaved women ensured the idealized purity of white womanhood. "And can it be doubted," he queried his readers, "that this purity is caused by, and is a compensation for the evils resulting from the existence of an enslaved class of more relaxed morals?" Harper further argued that not only had the enslaved woman "not impaired her means of support, nor materially impaired her character, or lowered her station in society," but "her offspring is not a burden, but an acquisition to her owner; his support is provided for, and he is brought up to usefulness."[19] Southern legal scholar Thomas R. R. Cobb also sought to emphasize positive aspects of miscegenation, suggesting that a child of such unions possessed "greater intelligence, and being indeed a superior race, has a better opportunity of enjoying the privileges of domestics; in other words, *is elevated* by the mixture of blood."[20] From the perspective of these elite white men, miscegenation was not to be condemned, since it did not threaten to upset the social identity of any of those involved and may, in fact, have affirmed their authority.

Senator J. H. Hammond, a South Carolina planter, evinced the acceptance of similar principles on a more personal level. In a letter to his son, Hammond addressed claims of ownership and fatherhood resulting from miscegenation:

In the last Will I made I left to you, over & above my other children, Sally Johnson the mother of Louisa and all the children of both. Sally says Henderson is my child. It is possible, but I do not believe it. Yet act on her's rather than my opinion. Louisa's first child *may* be mine. I think not. Her second I believe is mine. Take care of her and her children who are both of *your* blood if not of mine & of Henderson. The services of the rest will I think compensate for indulgence to these. I cannot free these people and send them North. It would be cruelty to them. Nor would I like that any but my own blood should own as slaves my own blood or Louisa. I leave them to your charge, believing that you will best appreciate & most independently carry out my wishes in regard to them. Do not let Louisa or any of my children or possible children be the slaves of strangers. Slavery in the family will be their happiest earthly condition.[21]

Hammond's words reveal the complicated relationships and attachments that existed within his own household. They also clearly reveal his patriarchal assumptions that as an elite white man in southern society he could order the world as he wished.

While Chancellor Harper characterized miscegenation as involving willing black women and hence protecting white females, women of neither race fully accepted such explanations. While many white southerners reassured themselves that black women purposefully enticed white men to gain the "privileges" of bearing their children, black women, in fact, were generally the victims of coercion, if not rape, rather than the sexual aggressors. Harriet Jacob's memoir of a life in slavery provides a vivid account of her own experiences of sexual abuse. Averring that "the degradation, the wrongs, the vices that grow out of slavery, are more than I can describe," she then does describe the repeated sexual advances of her master. Ultimately, she decides to become involved with another white man who could offer her a degree of protection from this master.[22]

Black women also faced potential abuse from white women who, unable to control their husbands, took out their ire on the object of their spouses' attention. Anti-slavery writer Kate Pickard suggested how anger over miscegenation could warp a white woman's personality and lead to the abuse of enslaved women. In her novel, a plantation owner named Mr. McKiernan used his position to force intercourse upon a number of enslaved women. In addition to this sexual abuse, "upon these unfortunate women fell the heavy hatred of their mistress; and year after year, as new instances of her husband's perfidy came to her knowledge, her jealousy ran higher, till at length reason seemed banished from her mind, and kindliness became a stranger to her heart."[23] While this was a semi-fictionalized account, it had resonance in the real experiences of some women. Fannie Kemble, for example, witnessed a scene on her husband's Georgia plantation of lashing-out by a white woman. Mr. K, the overseer, fathered children by a number of enslaved women at the same time. Kemble wrote that "it was not a month since any of them had been delivered, when Mrs. K—came to the hospital, had them all 3 severely flogged, a process which *she* personally superintended."[24] In Alabama, an enslaved woman accused of murdering her infant asserted that she had done so because her master had fathered the child and her mistress treated the infant cruelly. She explained that she killed the child to prevent further torture of both herself and the child by her mistress.[25] Such anger was futile against women who were themselves victims. Yet most white women ultimately chose to vent their rage in this way, rather than ask deeper questions about the system that, while it allowed white men to commit miscegenation, also provided these women with their own claims to a superior social and moral identity.

A few white women did feel compelled to turn their anger toward the white men involved, if only in their private writings. While southern society demanded the absolute purity of their white women, it seemingly let white men do as they pleased. Mary Chesnut confronted this double standard in her journal: "A man is supposed to confide his honor to his wife. If she misbehaves herself, his honor is tarnished. How can a man be disgraced by another person's doing what, if he did himself (that is, committed the same offense), he would not be hurt at all in public estimation?"[26] Gertrude Thomas followed a similar line, writing that "it is a shame that what is considered a venial thing in man should in a worldly point of view *damn a woman* and shut her out from every avenue of employment."[27] The social order depended on clear inheritances and the untainted reproduction of bloodlines, both of which relied on the purity of white women, while the honor code seemed to require no such purity from their male partners.

The journals of elite southern women bear witness to their knowledge of the existence of miscegenation in their midst. Sarah Gayle, for example, offered a stirring condemnation in her diary: "And those fathers whose beastly passions hurry to the bed of the slave do they feel no compunction when they see their blood sold, basely bartered like their horses? This sin is the leprosy of the earth nothing save the blood of the cross cleanses from it."[28] Keziah Brevard expressed relief that she had "never had a son to mix my blood with *negro* blood—Oh such sin would

[be] & is disheartening to Christian Mothers."[29] Her remarks imply that such transgressions were all too frequent.

Sometimes this written condemnation turned into a more direct confrontation. Mary Reynolds of Louisiana witnessed her mistress's reactions to evidence of miscegenation committed by her husband. When asked what was bothering her, Reynolds recalled that the white woman replied: "Since you asks me, I'm studyin' in my mind 'bout them white young'uns of that yaller nigger wench from Baton Rouge. . . . It look kind of funny they got the same kind of hair and eyes as my chillun and they got a nose looks like yours." Reynolds added that "Missus didn't never leave and Marster bought her a fine new span of surrey horses. But she don't never have no more chillun and since that time ain't so cordial with the Marster."[30] While this scene certainly represents the anger felt by many white women, most expressed their discontent less directly.

Some white women chose to focus on the activities of overseers or other lower-class men who did not have the same claims to honor as the elite men of their own families. Lizzie Neblett labeled one such offender a "detestable puke," adding that it was "no wonder he avoids decent ladies."[31] As with denigrating the morals of poor white women to explain illegitimacy, blaming miscegenation on poor white men offered the least upset to the southern social order. Yet if they looked, some elite women found evidence of miscegenation within their own households. Mary Chesnut suggested that "the mulattoes one sees in every family exactly resemble the white children—and every lady tells you who is the father of all the mulatto children in everybody's household, but those in her own she seems to think drop from the clouds, or pretends so to think." Some evidence suggests that Mary Chesnut's father-in-law sired mixed-race children, and Chesnut noted bitterly that "our men live all in one house with their wives and concubines[.]" Rosalie Calvert's husband, a scion of a prominent Maryland family, had a long-term affair with a black woman and sired several children by her. In Georgia, Gertrude Thomas' father almost certainly fathered mulatto children, and her husband may also have committed this offense.[32] On this subject, however, elite women remained largely mute. Patriarchal authority and feminine ideals of purity ordered this silence by assuring that, as Chesnut wrote, "there are certain subjects pure-minded ladies never touch upon, even in their thoughts."[33] Most elite southern women suffered (or seethed) in relative silence, aware of how the ideals of womanhood shaped their power in this society.

Perhaps those most affected by the unions between white men and black women were their mixed-race offspring, who sought to establish their own identity within the boundaries of antebellum race relations. A few of these offspring, as white social commentators such as Harper and Cobb predicted, felt that they had benefited from having a white father. Ella Johnson of Georgia, for example, recalled: "My father was a white man, who lived on the adjoining plantation. His name was Tom Glen, so you see my name was Ella Glen. My mother belonged to Dr. Lyles, so when I was born, Dr. Lyles took me in the 'big house' and I was treated just like one of his own children." The life of Amanda America Dickson provides another, and rather exceptional, example of the benefits accrued from having a white father. By the time of her death, Dickson had become one of the wealthiest women in Georgia.[34] Such examples, however, are rare.

Most children of miscegenation found that they were as likely to be victimized as privileged for their mixed blood. J. W. Terrill claimed that his father recognized his paternity and took him away from his mother to be raised by white relatives. According to Terrill, this father also "willed I must wear a bell till I was 21 years old, strapped 'round my shoulders with the bell 'bout 3 feet from my head in steel frame. That was for punishment for bein' born into the world a son of a white man and my mammy, a Negro slave."[35] Although the veracity of this story is suspect, it illustrates a belief among some slaves that white fathers might displace any guilt they felt about their transgressions by punishing the offspring of these unions. Masters/fathers might sell their mixed-race children if they felt guilty, if their wives objected, or if the child too closely resembled their white offspring. Former slave Ruth Allen recalled that she was sold when she was about three years old: "an' then when they saw I was goan 'a be much whiter and even better lookin' than his own chilern by his own wife, they sold me and my mammy, an' got rid of us for good."[36] Isiah Green told of the sale of his grandmother, Betsy Willis. Her father/master put her on the auction block and then, according to Green, said, "I wish to sell a slave who is also my daughter. Before anyone can purchase her, he must agree not to treat her as a slave but as a free person. She is a good midwife and can be of great service to you."[37] This seems an extraordinary public admission, but even if these words had been spoken, they had little power to protect Willis, any more than being his daughter protected her from sale.

On a personal level, issues of paternity may have been even more troubling to the identity formation of children of miscegenation than issues of race. Many white men who became fathers of enslaved children did not single their offspring out for either privilege or punishment. Rather, they claimed a paternal concern for all of those they held in slavery. One former slave spoke of her master, whom she believed had fathered a number of enslaved children. Those children had to work "just like the others. The mother would have a better time, but the children didn't. The only advantage they had was that Marster Gale wouldn't sell them."[38] Most children of miscegenation could not expect even this much consideration. They were apparently fatherless in a patriarchal society. While this cast a shadow on their own identity, it also raised questions about the paternalistic identities of white men.

Former slaves and anti-slavery activists alike linked miscegenation to a failure to meet the mandates of paternalistic fatherhood. Novelist Richard Hildreth questioned the morality of a system that allowed white men to (biologically) father enslaved children but not to act as fathers: "It is considered for instance, no crime whatever, for a master to be, if he chooses, the father of every infant slave born upon his plantation. Yet it is esteemed a very grave breach of propriety, indeed almost an unpardonable crime, for such a father ever, in any way, to acknowledge or take any notice, of any of his unfortunate children."[39] The narrator in Martha Griffith's *Autobiography of a Female Slave* noted that her father was a white man, adding, "I know nothing of him: for, with the most unpaternal feeling, he deserted me."[40] William Wells Brown made his indictment broader and more identifiable by writing in his novel, *Clotel*, that "sad to say, [Thomas] Jefferson is not the only American statesman who has spoken high-sounding words in favour of freedom, and then left his own children to die slaves."[41] In the eyes of these commentators, such lapses of paternal feelings and protection marked white men as derelict in their fatherhood role.

Ultimately, miscegenation represented a failure both of racial dichotomy and the paternal ideals that formed the foundations of most justifications of slavery. In the antebellum South, the social structure rested on hierarchical dualities of identity—men over women, rich over poor, free over slave, and white over black. In the ideal, champions of the South sought to justify this structure by defending the naturalness of these dualities; biology determined which side of the dyad one fell on, rendering one's social identity predetermined and immutable. Pro-slavery writers depended on the white/black dichotomy to defend the "natural" conditions of freedom and slavery. An article in the *Southern Literary Messenger* made this belief clear, proclaiming simply: "Here the slave is black, and the white man never is a slave."[42] Miscegenation, however, refuted the logic of this statement. While it proved white men's ultimate power over enslaved women (as well as their power over their own white wives, and the black men who could not protect their partners), the offspring of these unions complicated the South's dichotomous social relations. For individual southern men, it may also have raised questions about what it really meant to be a father in this society.

Although fatherhood did not dominate the public identity of southern men as motherhood did for southern women, it provided an important indicator of masculinity and the attainment of the ideals of manhood. In the immediate postwar years, Union officer John William DeForest observed the importance of manhood to southerners: "It seems to me that the central trait of the 'chivalrous Southron' is an intense respect for virility. He will forgive almost any vice in a man who is manly; he will admire vices, which are but exaggerations of the masculine . . . . if, in short, you show vigorous masculine attributes he will grant you his respect."[43] Fatherhood proved a man's virility and extended the dominion over which he held control. Mary Chesnut wrote of the desire for progeny among elite men: "These people take the old Hebrew pride in the number of children they have. True colonizing spirit. No danger of crowding here—inhabitants are wanted."[44] Antebellum southern fatherhood meant acting as head-of-household and providing for one's family. For elite white men, fatherhood also became a metaphor for their control over their slaves, the most subordinate "members of the family." For black men, claims to fatherhood, although less sanctified, were no less important to their identity as men. Both control and sentiment became part of the identity of southern fathers, providing an important facet of their personal identity and marking their position within the southern community.

Southern social mores taught white men to view their households as small kingdoms in which they themselves exercised "all the high functions of an unlimited monarch."[45] Control of the household allowed white men to regulate the behavior of both their white family and those they held in bondage, and to maintain the hierarchal order in broader society. While the increasing prevalence of companionate marriages may have softened husbands' claims of authority over their wives, the rhetorical ideal that made slaves part of the patriarchal family also allowed owners to claim reciprocity in these relationships, naturalizing authority and subordination. Ultimately, however, this society formally invested almost all of the power in the family's patriarch, giving white males a political interest in maintaining the social status quo.

Patriarchy was not a unique feature of antebellum southern society, yet a number of conditions of southern life during this period, particularly the household structure and the existence of racial slavery, made white southern men especially emphatic defenders of this ideology. In the industrializing North, ideologues increasingly associated the home with a woman's sphere, while the continuing agricultural basis of most households in the South kept southern men present and intimately involved in domestic decisions. White southern men, whether planters or yeomen, continued to claim authority over the household.[46] Mary Chesnut recalled such traits of control and authority in her father-in-law, whom she labeled "the last of the lordly planters who ruled this Southern world . . . he came of a race that would brook no interference with their own sweet will by man, woman, or devil." Chesnut viewed such traits as typical of elite southern men who "go blustering around—making everybody uncomfortable simply to show that they are masters—and we only women and children at their mercy." In her memoir, Mary Schoolcraft sought to justify this male authority over women to her readers by using religious imagery. She argued: "Eve, being made not as Adam was, in the image of God, but out of one of the small ribs of her husband, was entirely his inferior, and altogether subject to him."[47] Claims of male superiority, combined with a culture of honor, made clinging to the privileges of patriarchy an important element of white southern manhood. To sustain this authority, southern men first had to exert their claims as fathers within their own households.

Both the laws and social mores gave southern fathers ultimate dominion over their families. A sermon recorded in 1861 by Dolly Burge of Georgia portrayed the typical expectations of familial organization, which were in keeping with both religious and patriarchal ideals. Burge wrote that Bishop Andrew, the minister, "first proved that God had instituted families & had placed man over them that he & not woman should rule & that her assuming to do so was contrary to Divine Authority as he proved from Scripture." While this passage may have been meant to celebrate the passive ideal of southern womanhood, it also outlined a particular identity for male heads-of-household. The ideal of white fatherhood called for them to be providers and protectors, and this, in return, legitimized their claims to authority.[48]

Although few men offered hands-on childcare on a day-to-day basis, many took an active interest in raising their children. Southern fathers offered suggestions, and sometimes dictates, on matters from weaning, to education, to the right to name new additions. Kate Edmondston recorded a debate over the name of her newborn niece and concluded that "as the father seems to prefer Mary Livingston, Mary I suppose it will be." Men had the right to name their own children, and they could extend this right to name slaves, both of which were signs of ownership.[49] Men's involvement often began with decisions about conception. Most of the available methods of birth control, from abstinence to coitus interruptus to condom usage, required the knowledge and cooperation of the male partner. This cooperation did not always come easily, since it meant limiting the outward proof of a man's virility. Some men only accepted efforts to control fertility when they believed additional pregnancies would harm their wives' health.[50] Others were willing to accept their wives' desire. William Neblett responded to his wife's extreme fear of pregnancy by investigating contraceptive solutions. He wrote that "in regard to that one thing which gives you so much unhappiness you may make yourself easy. I think it not only possible but probable that we can live together and have no more children. I am willing to make sacrifices for your happiness or peace even if it results in unhappiness for me."[51] Other men expressed concern about their own role and their ability to provide for additional children. After the birth of what turned out to be their last child, David Harris wrote: "Eight children are as many as any poor man should have; and I am sure that I want no more. If I can do a good part by what I have got, I may congratulate myself."[52] While few particulars exist, some southern men clearly participated in decisions about family limitation, their acquiescence being essential for any possible successes.

Southern fathers also participated in the labor and delivery phase of the birth experience. Dr. Charles Hentz recorded one case in which a woman "delivered in her husband's lap." Hentz probably recorded this event because it was atypical in his experience, but a husband's presence would not have been so unusual, particularly in situations where other birth attendants were not readily available.[53] Women awaiting their delivery expressed the expectation and desire that their husbands would be nearby if possible. Nancy Kennedy's husband was away on a surveying trip when she was about to deliver their fifth child. She wrote to tell him "how much I need your beloved Society at this time to help to fortify me for my suffering."[54] Similarly, Varina Davis wrote to her husband, away on a speaking tour, just days before the birth of their first child: "really dear Husband, your wife's courage is giving out about your staying away at such a time—I feel the want of you every hour, though I try not to be so selfish."[55] Davis's reference to being "selfish" indicates her understanding that her husband ultimately made the decision about where he spent his time; yet her hopes for his presence at this event were clear.

After the birth of a child, a father's involvement in infant nurture showed elements of both care and control. Although gender-role expectations dictated that women should be the primary caregivers for infants, southern fathers frequently offered advice on tending to the health of the infant, and even on breastfeeding and weaning practices.[56] An 1850 article in the *Southern Planter* lamented that white men did not give enough of this input, and that men paid too little attention to issues of childcare. The author argued that "the mother is not the only person concerned in the management of children. The father has an equal interest in their welfare, and ought to assist in every thing that respects either the improvement of the body or mind."[57] The position of white men as head of the family led them to expect that women would follow the childcare advice that they gave. Yet the ideals of manhood taught men to view themselves as commanders and providers rather than nurturers. This distinction is particularly illustrated by widowed men with young children. It was not at all uncommon for these men to remarry quickly, so as to provide a caregiver for their children. For example, Thomas Chaplin of South Carolina, a father of four living children when his wife died in November 1851, became engaged to his wife's half-sister Sophy just five months later. He wrote in his diary: "My poor children, *you* have lost that which never, no, never can be replaced, a *mother's love, a mother's care*. Your dear aunt has promised to do all in her power to prevent your want of the latter, but alas! How can she replace the former."[58] Chaplin would not have been expected to attend to the physical needs of his children. But in providing such a caregiver, in this case through remarriage, he was fulfilling his primary role as a father in antebellum southern society.

If their public identity rested on being providers and authority figures, however, white men's personal identities embraced emotional ties to family and community.[59] These bonds of affection became apparent in the announcements men made of the new additions to their families. Thomas Kennedy, a surveyor and engineer, was away on a surveying trip when his fifth child was born in 1833. He wrote to his wife that on hearing of her safe delivery he "gave way to all the extravagancies of Joy." He admitted sheepishly that this celebration involved partaking "freely of egg nog" and getting "pretty well Fuddled."[60] Kennedy's emotional attachment to his children is evident in these actions and appears throughout his correspondence with his wife. Eleanor Lewis observed a similarly emotional reaction after her daughter gave birth. She wrote that her son-in-law was "so enchanted with his Son, that I suppose he has written *circulars* to every City in the Union."[61] Clearly, the birth of a child could be a source of joy for fathers, just as the ideal suggested it would be for mothers.

These emotional attachments often seemed to grow over time. George Southgate wrote to his wife Elizabeth in 1826: "My first thought[s] in the morning when I awake are for my dear wife and children, and they are they are [*sic*] the last at night, often I have offered fervent prayers for their happiness and preservation."[62] David Harris recorded all of the developments of his youngest child in his journal. In January 1862 he penned: "OUR BOY IS CRAWLING, just commenced. We consider him a *rara avis.* Every thing about him is so very interesting. We all think there is nothing to compare with him."[63] When Jefferson Davis wrote "[k]iss my dear Daughty and sweet little Boy for their old Tady who loves them 'too much,'" he seems far removed from the authoritative southern patriarch.[64] But while the role of doting father offered many rewards for southern men, it represented a personal choice. Southern ideals demanded emotional devotion of white mothers, insisting it was part of their nature, but no such expectations rested on white fathers. While individual men experienced an emotional connection as part of their personal identities, the social ideals of patriarchy required only that men rule over their households. For it was on their authoritarian identity, rather than on emotion, that family and household order, and ultimately the entire social structure, rested.

This is perhaps most apparent in the extension of white men's paternal identity and authority beyond their immediate family, encompassing the entire household, white and black. Many elite men adopted the family metaphor, with its contingent paternal interests and patriarchal control, to justify their slaveholdings. In 1823 Eleanor Lewis angrily decried a biography of her grandfather, George Washington, that claimed he called his slaves *"his children."*[65] As the antebellum period progressed, however, many slaveowners used just such language to describe their relationship with their slaves. The Reverend Benjamin Morgan Palmer, for example, wrote in 1860: "My servant, whether born in my house or bought with my money, stands to me in the relation of a child."[66] In 1854 novelist Caroline Hentz also used the father/child metaphor to create a model for her readers. She wrote that when her hero, an idealized example of southern manhood, was surrounded by those he held in bondage, he was "more like a father welcomed by his children than a king greeted by his subjects[.]"[67]

Such claims to fatherhood were not admissions of miscegenation; rather, they were assertions of patriarchal rights and power relations. William Holcombe wrote that "the management of negroes and the management of children should be based upon the same principle, and should be conducted by the same wise combination of unflinching firmness and tender humanity."[68] In claiming this familial structure, slaveowners sought to portray a relationship based more on mutuality than bondage, emphasizing the paternalism and beneficence of southern society. As one Virginia planter told Frederick Law Olmsted, "I can't help being attached to them, and I am sure they love us." Olmsted added that "in his own case at least, I did not doubt; his manner toward them was paternal—familiar and kind; and they came to him like children who have been given some task, and constantly wanting to be encouraged and guided, simply and confidently."[69] While such observations might not have reflected the views or experiences of those held in bondage, they demonstrate the attempt slaveholders made to justify their position under the guise of paternalism, assuring themselves of their patriarchal identity.

Black fatherhood suggested quite different meanings for the antebellum South and for individual black men, but it too was shaped by the patriarchal organization of society. From the standpoint of the white elite, enslaved fatherhood held little legitimate meaning. Although some slaveholders recognized black men as fathers within the confines of their own plantations, that identity had no legal standing and could be taken away at the whim of the white owner. The absence of legally sanctioned marriages reinforced the limits of enslaved fatherhood. Slaveowner and jurist Thomas R. R. Cobb asserted that "the marriage relation not being recognized among slaves, none of the relative rights and duties arising therefrom, belong strictly to the slave." French traveler Gustave de Beaumont observed that under such conditions "the slave cannot be invested with any paternal power over his children. He cannot own anything, because he is the possession of another."[70]

Plantation records listed the births of enslaved children as an assertion of ownership. William Wells Brown wrote that "the man who stole me as soon as I was born, recorded the births of all the infants which he claimed to be born his property, in a book which he kept for that purpose."[71] For slaveholding and selling, enslaved "families" generally meant only women and their children—in many plantation record books, men were listed as individual laborers rather than fathers with connections to a specific family. In the Manigault plantation records, for example, the births of children were recorded with only the mother's name listed, although many of the enslaved were bought as and lived in family units that included a father.[72] White southerners thus reduced enslaved fatherhood to a theoretical nonexistence, attempting to ensure the absoluteness of their own patriarchal authority over their household. Even when the plantation records included fathers in the family structure, these were private rather than legal recognitions.

Yet neither black men nor their community accepted black father-hood as meaningless.[73] Instead they created their own narrative of the meaning and experience of enslaved fatherhood. Despite limited resources, many still took on the role of provider, supplementing meager diets through hunting and fishing and providing material goods when possible. Kate Pickard's semi-fictionalized account of the Still family recounted that although Peter Still was kept on a different plantation, he took care of his wife by building her cabin and providing clothing and other material goods.[74] Enslaved men could also defy white perceptions and create their own identity as fathers through their emotional commitment to their children. Anti-slavery writers emphasized the "paternal affection and tenderness" experienced by enslaved fathers, asserting enslaved men's claims to at least the fatherhood norms of southern society. For example, Archy Moore, the title character in Richard Hildreth's 1836 novel, *The Slave*, recounts his feelings on the birth of his son: "[O]nly he who is a father, and as fond a husband too as I was, can know the feelings with which I pressed the little darling to my heart." Yet this passage also emphasizes the pain that accompanied the joys of fatherhood for en-slaved men when Moore adds

> No!—no one can know my feelings,—no one, alas, but he, who is, as I was, the father of a slave. The father of a slave!—and is it true then, that this child of my hopes and wishes, this pledge of mutual love, this dear, dear infant of whom I am the father, is it true he is not mine? Is it not my duty and my right, a right and duty dearer than life, to watch over his helpless infancy, and to rear him with all a father's tenderness and love, to manhood, . . . My duty it may be; but not my right. A slave can have no rights. His wife, his child, his toil, his blood, his life, and everything that gives his life value, they are not his; he holds them all but at his master's pleasure.[75]

Although a fictional account, this passage was intended to reflect the real fear of separation that hung over enslaved fathers. This threatened loss served as a constant reminder of black men's limited paternal rights under slavery, as well as the patriarchal control of white men.

Despite these fears, most enslaved men in the antebellum period formed families and fathered children. Although few enslaved men left accounts of their fatherhood, the actions of many enslaved fathers spoke of the emotional bonds, the desire to provide and protect, and occasionally the assertion of their role as head of the family following the patriarchal model.[76] Louis Hughes was unusual in that he did write a memoir of his life in, and escape from, bondage. As a slave he had watched helplessly when ill-treatment by his mistress led to the death of his infant twins. For Hughes, paternal responsibility and care became a mark of freedom: "My first effort as a freeman was to get something so to sustain myself and wife and a babe of a few months[.]"[77] His memoir suggests that opportunity rather than inclination limited an enslaved father's care for his children. In such narratives enslaved men claimed a paternal identity for themselves and at the same time built an identity for their children, linking them both to an immediate family and to broader community structures.

The importance of this paternal bond to enslaved children was often notable in its absence in the narratives of former slaves. Many of them asserted that not knowing one's father was typical. Easter Wells of Arkansas recalled: "I never saw my father; in fact, I never heard my mammy say anything about him and I don't guess I ever asked her anything about him for I never thought anything about not having a father."[78] White commentators attempted to justify the limited involvement of black fathers by claiming they were incapable of forming emotional bonds. Fannie Kemble, who expressed a degree of sympathy for enslaved mothers, wrote that an enslaved father, "having neither authority, power, responsibility, or charge in his children, is of course, as among brutes, the least attached to his offspring[.]"[79] In contrast, former slaves placed the blame for a lack of paternal involvement on the conditions of slavery and saw it as an indictment of the social system, rather than of individual fathers.

Some linked the absence of fathers to the existence of the breeding ethos. An interviewer asked former slave Jeff Rayford, born in 1840, "where his father came from. He immediately replied that he didn't know who his father was or anything about him. Said the colored people lived like stock in those days—they never married."[80] Others emphasized the separation from their fathers through sale. Hannah Scott, a former slave from Alabama, recalled: "I never knowed my own Pa, 'cause he belong to another man and was sold away 'fore I was old enough to know him. I guess I has see him, 'cause mamma has told me she has held me up to him when he had a pass to come see her, and I would jabber, habber to him, but I don't 'member nothing 'bout him, and mamma never see him no more after he was sold away."[81] The curtailments on enslaved fathers' involvement in their children's lives, as well as the limits on their paternal authority, symbolized the de-masculinization and patriarchal degradation of black men under slavery. Like narratives that lauded a master's paternalism, narratives of absence acknowledged the patriarchal control of white men but lamented its effects on enslaved men and children alike.

However, a contrasting set of narratives also emerged, in which some former slaves emphasized the activist role that their fathers took in providing care and protection. These recollections claimed manhood for the father and a sense of belonging for the child. Andrew Jackson Gill told his WPA interviewer: "My daddy, he was a fine man an' treated us chillun jus' dandy."[82] Another former slave recalled an enslaved father who provided hands-on care when the mother of his "teeny baby" ran away. He "would carry it to the field and keep a bottle of sweetened water in his shirt to keep it warm to give during the day."[83] Another interview subject recounted how his father exerted paternal influence by providing links to their heritage for his children with tales of "Africy."[84] In a society intent on denying enslaved men any fatherhood rights that might challenge the claims of the white patriarchy, each assertion of paternal influence and family connections challenged the identity assigned to black men by antebellum society.

The claims enslaved men made to take control over their families could result in punishment because of the potential disruption such claims offered to white authority structures. Sarah Ford recalled that when her father stepped in to prevent his pregnant wife from being whipped, he became the object of three days of torture.[85] Even when enslaved men tried to discipline their children, they could face opposition. Abe Livingston reported that "[w]hen my daddy beat me I'd go up to the big house and stay there with the boys and we'd git something to eat from the kitchen."[86] This defiance, perhaps more than any physical punishment, emphasized the limits on black men's claims to parental authority.

Within the confines of the plantation, owners might identify black men as family heads, but this position existed only at the convenience of the master and thus might be continually undermined. In this way, white men assured their own claims to absolute authority over everyone within their household.

In the antebellum period, the maintenance of white fatherhood supported, and was in turn supported by, the patriarchal structure. Black fatherhood also existed within this structure, and while elite society disputed their right to be fathers, individual black men's claims to the role challenged and defied assumptions about their manhood and their emotional commitment to their children and families. Fatherhood and control of the household provided a basic claim of authority for southern men, black and white, supplying the foundation upon which the broader political and social structures rested.

Men's perceptions of birth—linked to ideas about gender, race, and issues of authority and control—shaped both their personal identities and their understanding of their status in the wider community. As fathers and providers, white men claimed control of their households and, hence, of the right to contribute to decisions from conception to nurturing. This, in turn, lent legitimacy to their assertions of social power and dominance in economic and political arenas. The authority structures of the household became a microcosm for authority in southern society itself. Enslaved fathers also sought involvement in the lives of their children, despite interference from a culture that granted all paternal claims to white men. Each act of paternal care or authority made by an enslaved father challenged a social narrative that denied him such rights. Thus maintaining the patriarchal structure of southern society required sustaining the privileges of white manhood, honor, and authority while controlling or denigrating these claims for all other members in society. The actions and discussion associated with birth and parenting in southern society provided an important foundation for this patriarchal ordering.

CHAPTER SIX

Birth and Professional Identity in the Antebellum South

D R. D. WARREN BRICKELL, a noted New Orleans physician, com-
plained in 1856 that "we must condemn the almost universal practice, on the part of owners and overseers, of tampering with their sick
negroes for one, two, or more days before applying for medical aid." Increasingly, doctors such as Brickell included childbirth as one of the
"sicknesses" with which lay people ought not to tamper. Although agriculturalists did not necessarily desire to be as directly involved in the
delivery of a child, they too felt they had an interest in the events of
childbirth. The births of enslaved women, in particular, held a financial
interest for plantation owners. An author in the *Southern Quarterly Review* suggested that "prolific" enslaved women were a matter of some
concern, since "their increase is no small matter in the item of profits."
Southern jurist Thomas R. R. Cobb expressed a different but no less
pressing interest in birth from a legal perspective when he argued that
"from the principle of justice, the offspring, the increase of the womb,
belongs to the master of the womb." Although Cobb's particular interest
focused on the ownership of enslaved children, lawyers similarly were
concerned with the issue of custody, or "ownership," of white children.
Each of these professions—doctors, planters, and lawyers—addressed
the subject of birth, both to ascribe a social identity to the birthing
woman and her child and, equally importantly, to lay claim to their own
professional identity in antebellum society.[1]

Of the professions, physicians have been most clearly linked to childbirth. At least since the mid-twentieth century, medical discourse has

dominated discussions of pregnancy and childbirth in Western culture.[2] Such a perspective often obscures the struggle undertaken by physicians in the nineteenth century to establish their position as authoritative professionals. They were challenged in these aspirations by a democratic spirit and a system that allowed all manner of people to claim medical expertise. For example, Frederick Law Olmsted, in his travels through the South, stayed at the home of an illiterate man who styled himself "Doctor," and Olmsted observed that "the title of Doctor is often popularly given at the south to druggists and vendors of popular medicines." Charles Meigs, a professor of midwifery at Jefferson Medical College in Philadelphia, whose classes included a large percentage of students from the South, decried those "who, while they style themselves doctors, are really not members of the Scholar vocation, and of course not physicians." Yet Meigs found himself forced to admit that these individuals, rather than those he deemed appropriately trained, served the needs of a "major part" of the public.[3]

In their daily practice, physicians in the nineteenth-century South attempted to gain respect for their expertise and professional identity. Rather than relying purely on a neutral scientific authority to support them, southern doctors' claims to a professional identity were clearly shaped by the social and cultural expectations of their region. The medical narratives created by southern physicians exhibited the assumptions that they held about the physical needs of and acceptable treatments for women, based on their different races or classes.[4] Southern doctors took a particular interest in the reproduction of enslaved women. Many physicians sought to establish their professional reputations as "readers" of black women's bodies, dabbling in the mysterious world of fertility or helping planters determine the proper balancing of productive and reproductive labor. Access to enslaved bodies gave inexperienced doctors an opportunity to hone their skills on a largely uncomplaining clientele, and annual contracts with planters to attend to their enslaved populations' medical needs provided some doctors with a route to a steady income. Such arrangements meant that the doctor worked for the slaveowner rather than the slaves whom they attended. Thus most doctors remained firmly embedded in the hierarchy of the southern social system.[5]

While southern doctors managed to become increasingly professionalized in the late antebellum period, they still did not attend the majority of births in the South; they had not gained ascendency over the birth-ing room or over public discussions surrounding birth. Dr. William Dewees could suggest that the birthing woman should "yield implicit obedience to the directions of her medical attendant; she must have no opinions of her own, as regards her physical and medical treatment; submission is her duty," but this was more wishful thinking than reality when he wrote this in 1829.[6] The records of both southern doctors and their patients suggest that position and status within the birthing room was still being negotiated in the antebellum period.

The professional identity of doctors as medical authorities remained contentious, in large measure because many medical men could not agree among themselves about some of the key points of the reproductive ex-perience. Some disagreements resulted from doctors' own limited scien-tific knowledge. Issues of conception and the length of gestation remained matters of some speculation. In 1858 Dr. Charles Hentz astonishingly concluded that he had delivered a woman "eleven months pregnant ac-cording to best calculation." In the mid-1840s, New Orleans resident Madaline Edwards seemed to exhibit all of the symptoms of pregnancy, including a swollen abdomen. Although Edwards still had not delivered a child almost a year after experiencing what she had believed to be quickening, her doctor continued to assure her that he had delivered a woman pregnant for thirteen months. A midwife, in contrast, had in-formed Edwards that she was not pregnant, but instead suffered from some unnamed gynecological problem.[7] Edwards's intense desire for a child, and her reliance on this doctor's professional opinion, allowed her to continue to believe that her delivery was imminent. Such confusion over gestation periods was not surprising, since conception itself re-mained something of a mystery for physicians. Dr. William P. Dewees observed that "the ingenuity of physiologists has invented hundreds of hypotheses to account for impregnation in the human subject." His at-tempt to codify the "various notions" did not create a scientific certainty.[8] Rather than identifying doctors as the experts in these matters, most women continued to rely on their knowledge of their own bodies, and information passed on from mothers and other female kin, to determine if they were indeed pregnant.

Although medical schools often offered lectures on midwifery or ob-stetrics, antebellum medical education generally consisted of only one or two terms of lectures followed by an apprenticeship. With little regulation, some "doctors" received even less training. In 1856, Thomas Chaplin remarked on the perceived limits of a medical education. Noting the graduation from medical school of two of his acquaintances, he wrote in his journal: "Who is there that cannot get a diploma from the S.C. Medical College after this?" While Chaplin may have been making a jest at the expense of these fellows, serious questions could be raised about the efficacy of medical training in the mid-nineteenth century. In the case of obstetrics, few doctors would have witnessed a normal childbirth as part of their medical education.[9]

Even among well-trained physicians, debates raged about a doctor's proper role in childbirth. Early in the nineteenth century, the medical community debated the morality of a man even attending a woman in labor. Dr. Thomas Ewell of Virginia, for example, warned that men simply could not control themselves in such intimate circumstances. In his argument he referenced the case of "a physician in Charleston [who], infuriated with the sight of the woman he had just delivered, leaped into her bed before she was restored to a state of nature." Other physicians, however, defended their professionalism and warned that modesty should not keep women from seeking "proper care."[10]

But what that "proper care" should consist of became another source of debate in the medical community. Dr. William Dewees, a prominent physician and professor of obstetrics at the University of Pennsylvania, advocated assisting nature in its progress, arguing that "the sufferings of the patient" could be "much abridged, by the judicious interposition of skill." In contrast, Dr. John Gunn advised birth attendants "not to hurry Nature," warning that "hundreds of deaths and a long train of diseases" had been caused by precipitous interference by doctors or other birth attendants. He concluded that "long experience in my profession, in the obstetric art, has convinced me that patience is the great remedy in childbirth." Henry Miller, a medical professor in Louisville, staked out a middle position in the debate. While he asserted that "meddlesome midwifery is bad," he concluded that "a shilly-shallying midwifery is worse."[11] Similar debates emerged over the use of pain relief during labor, particularly after the introduction of anesthesia to the United States in 1847. Some doctors insisted that pain was a necessary part of the birth process, while others advocated the alleviation of suffering whenever possible.[12] The "heroic" medicine popular in the mid-nineteenth century dictated that physicians ought to do something at the patient's bedside, but what exactly constituted helpful assistance confounded many medical practitioners.

Assistance during childbirth formed only a small part of most doctors' practices. Many attended only five to eight births in a year. Even Charles Hentz, who seemed to specialize in such matters in his Florida practice, recorded only 178 obstetric cases between 1849 and 1865, or an average of less than twelve a year.[13] Thus most southern doctors were neither scientific nor experiential experts on matters of birth, and their narratives reflected these limits. Rather than offering scientific treatises, many doctors used medical narratives to gain professional status and to situate their experiences within a broader social understanding. The medical narratives created by these southern white men, usually of the elite or middling classes, reflected their acceptance of the social hierarchy. They valued elite white women over poorer white women, and both over women held in bondage. These physicians' approach to birth thus generally served to perpetuate and naturalize the identities ascribed by the southern social structure, while the doctors themselves sought to establish their own position within this hierarchy.[14]

Despite all of the medical debates surrounding birth, Professor Charles Meigs advocated properly trained men attending women's births, both because he believed in the science of obstetrics and because he saw this care as a means of obtaining professional respect. The practice of obstetrics, he counseled a class of medical students, "will make you rich men and respected men, if you learn it aright."[15] Given the patriarchal structure of southern society, male doctors sought to naturalize socially constructed ideas about gender through discussions of birth and biology. Some medical texts adopted the rhetoric of idealized womanhood in their expositions on women's reproductive functions. The discussion of menstrual discomfort in Dr. Gunn's popular medical guide even drifted toward religious imagery. "It is impossible to form a correct opinion of the mental and physical suffering frequently endured from her sexuality," Gunn told his readers, "and the affliction of her monthly period, which it had pleased her Heavenly Father to attach to woman—the mother of the world—the one who in soft endearments of love brings to us a vision of heaven." Other nineteenth-century physicians associated procreative abilities with problems ranging from hysteria to constitutional delicacy. An article in *Harper's* presented this latter view, labeling American girls and women "not generally strong in nerve and muscle, and too ready to fade before her true mid-summer has come." Antebellum physicians saw a woman, particularly a white woman, as "the product and prisoner of her reproductive system." Many American doctors, both northern and southern, were thus prepared to see birth as a pathology of the female gender over which they, as male professionals, should exercise control.[16]

Along with gender, class assumptions shaped physicians' perceptions of both their obstetric patients and their own professional identities. A wide range of people might claim to be "doctors" in the antebellum South, but those in the upper echelons of society created most of the public medical narratives, and these reflected both their subtle and overt class biases. The advice they gave birthing women on clean linens, attendants, and bed rest, while apparently neutral, assumed resources and the ability to control the circumstances of birth that were unavailable to poor women, black or white. Some medical authors directly attacked the failure of the poor to meet the standards they set. In 1817 James Ewell of Virginia told his readers to lament "that so many poor children should be made the innocent victims of their parents' laziness, and neglect of this sweet and healthful virtue, *cleanliness.*" John Gunn offered an equally harsh assessment in 1859: "The lower class are excessively ignorant, often superstitious and generally are far from being cleanly, or attentive to a variety of circumstances, affecting the comfort of their children."[17] Neither physician suggested that limited resources, rather than care, affected a woman's ability to provide adequately for her children.

Medical lecturers also made the suggestion that "ladies" suffered more in giving birth than poorer women.[18] In their records, doctors often noted the social status as well as the physical ailments of the women they treated. Dr. Charles Hentz, for example, recorded his attendance on a Mrs. Johnson, adding: "Poor woman—many children—drunken husband." Hentz's case notes also emphasized marital status when he wrote of attending a "Miss."[19] Hentz was clearly cognizant of the social position of these women, so different from his own. Elite doctors often treated such white women with contempt, even hatred. They felt free to practice their technique on these poor women, perhaps more so than on enslaved women, whose masters oversaw their care.[20] Medical treatments during birth thus reflected the larger patterns of hierarchy and control within southern society.

While the medical profession's gender and class biases undoubtedly existed to some degree throughout the United States, racial biases had a special intensity in the slave South. Northern doctors may have held racial assumptions, but in the South links between race, medicine, and biology took on political and social importance.[21] Many southern doctors believed that black men and women suffered medical problems that were different from those of their white counterparts. As James Ewell asserted, "[that] the constitution of the African is more firm than ours, and better fitted to sustain the toils of warm climates, is very certain, but it is equally true that his daily labors, with the sudden changes of weather, often puts his constitution, good as it may be, to trials, which loudly call for every aid that humanity can possibly afford him."[22] These sentiments thus justified the labor regime and called upon the controlling influence of the slaveowner to ensure proper health.

Such tenets also affected an enslaved woman's reproduction. The belief that black women gave birth more easily medically justified both work regimes during pregnancy and shortened recovery periods after birth. More enslaved women suffered complications or even death during childbirth than elite women did, but that did little to shake these assumptions.[23] Intent on believing that black women had healthy, even masculine, constitutions, slaveholders resorted to accusations of shamming to explain the debilities they observed. When Fannie Kemble intervened on behalf of a group of pregnant women who felt they were being overworked, the overseer reacted with anger: "He seemed evidently annoyed at their having appealed to me; said that their work was not a bit too much for them, and that constantly they were *shamming* themselves in the family-way in order to obtain a diminution of their labor."[24] Medical student M. D. McLeod suggested that slaves tended to be deceptive about illness; thus their complaints "demand at the hands of the Physician a more careful investigation than those of whites."[25] Such accusations corresponded to the identity assigned to slaves by their owners, who viewed them as lazy, disingenuous, and in need of constant regulation by whites. These beliefs also solidified the professional identity of southern doctors, who acted as "readers of slave bodies" and as mediators between the complaints of enslaved women and the suspicions of the slaveholder.[26] Medical discussions of birth put white men, and specifically male doctors, in a position to "scientifically" justify their control over black women's reproduction.

J. Marion Sims, originally from Alabama, used his access to the bodies of enslaved women to experiment with surgical treatments and establish his identity as the father of American gynecology. He performed multiple surgeries on several enslaved women, without anesthesia, before finding a successful technique for the treatment of vesico-vaginal fistulae, a tear that allowed urine to leak into the vagina. In the 1840s Simms carried out public surgeries on naked black women to demonstrate his medical techniques. These surgeries speak clearly of the selective privileges of modesty and privacy in the antebellum South. Enslaved women lacked the right to refuse this "care," whether benign or experimental.[27] Yet the experiments also suggest one of the paradoxes of antebellum southern society. Access to an enslaved woman's body emphasized the inaccessibility of a white woman's body, but in this case access proved valuable, precisely because of the shared physiology of black and white woman. Like birth itself, medical experimentation by southern doctors tested the limits of racial difference and gender commonality.

While the medical profession brought their social views and their own struggle for professional recognition—along with their medical knowledge—into the birthing room, they could not simply impose these ideas. They had to deal with real women who had their own concerns, primarily about their personal health and well-being. As discussed in chapter three, southern women who had a choice in selecting birth attendants generally sought out the individual with the most skill and experience. Practical considerations also shaped the options and decisions of many women, since limited numbers and rural distances often made retaining a doctor's services difficult. One estimate suggests that in 1850 Alabama had only 1 physician for every 610 residents, Georgia had 1 in 697, Louisiana had 1 in 567, and Mississippi had 1 in 498. Many of these physicians would be found in urban areas, far beyond the reach of plantation dwellers.[28]

Cost also deterred many people from seeking a physician's assistance, and again those living in rural areas faced greater obstacles, since doctors typically billed according to distance and difficulty. One practitioner, for example, charged "$1.00 per mile in the daytime, $2.00 per mile at night, and $2.00 per mile by water." The time involved in attending a birth also led doctors to charge more for their services. The ledger of North Carolina physician W. W. Watts usually recorded charges of $1 to $6 for daytime visits, but on at least two occasions he charged $20 "To Attend in Childbirth." In 1861, he recorded a night delivery of an enslaved woman named Dicey in which he used instruments. He charged the owner, Helen Slade, $40. Another doctor, Levi Smithwick Yates, also attended this birth and charged Slade another $25, a total of $65 for a single birth.[29] There is no clear evidence that doctors' fees varied according to the race of the patient, but it is probable that the plantation owners who would pay the doctor's bill assessed value differently, depending on who required assistance. Perhaps because of these cost considerations, or perhaps out of sheer necessity, those on remote plantations often managed healthcare themselves, reading medical manuals and collecting medicinal recipes and ingredients. According to his publishers, Dr. Gunn's popular manual for home healthcare sold over 100,000 copies in its first nine years, furnishing some indication of the demand for this sort of knowledge.[30] Given the limited training of many practicing physicians, laypeople may have felt perfectly justified in acting on their own behalf. But as southern doctors asserted their professionalism in the late antebellum period, they took particular aim at this "amateur" practice.

If a doctor's first struggle was simply to be called to the birthing room, the negotiation of their professional authority did not end there. Elite women who could afford to do so might hire both a physician and a female attendant to ensure at least one would be there for her delivery. Rosalie Calvert, a Belgian emigré who had married into a prominent Maryland family, wrote a letter to her sister after the birth of her fourth child. She reported that "an old negress" had been her primary attendant during this birth, but also added: "I had the doctor in the house in case of mishap."[31] Although enslaved women had far less control over whether a doctor would be called to their bedside, doctors still had to contend with the masters who paid the bill. Further, birthing women in the slave quarters would often find themselves assisted by other enslaved women, whether under the purview of the doctor (or master) or not. Thus, despite the growing professional status of physicians in the mid-nineteenth century, their occupational identity and authority remained a source of some debate within the birthing rooms of southern women.

Much of the historiography of birth has focused on its gradual medicalization, moving from a woman-centered birthing room to a hospital-centered medical event.[32] This type of critical examination of the adversarial relationship between midwives and doctors does not, however, fully reflect the attitudes of antebellum doctors, midwives, or birthing women. Some physicians certainly did evince a hostile attitude in their narratives. Charles Hentz, who attended nearly five hundred births during his career, often laid the blame on "an ignorant midwife" when things went wrong.[33] Nonetheless, many doctors recognized the value of working with midwives. If a female birth attendant was present, male physicians did not need to spend their time waiting at the home of a woman experiencing a normal delivery. Doctors gained the glory if a successful intervention occurred in a difficult delivery, but they had a scapegoat in the midwife if things went wrong. Further, doctors had few technological advantages over midwives—the effectiveness of forceps deliveries depended on the skill and experience of the doctor, and most other available instruments were useful only after the death of the baby or the mother. Thus the professional playing-field between doctors and midwives was relatively even in terms of the services they could offer.

In fact, most birthing women viewed cooperation between doctors and midwives as advantageous to their own well-being. As discussed above, some women had the financial resources to hire both physicians and female attendants, benefiting from the unique services that each could offer. The presence of a monthly nurse, for example, often proved an excellent substitute when a doctor did not arrive on time for the delivery.[34] More typically, a doctor was summoned only upon the advice of the midwife when the birth did not seem to be progressing as it ought. This was the case when David Harris called in a doctor in 1857 to attend the birth of Minerva, an enslaved woman, after the local midwife recommended that he do so.[35] These collaborations often occurred with the needs of the birthing woman as the central focus, and without overt professional rivalry.

Physicians had to recognize that they occupied a shared space in the birthing room. To sustain their professional identity and authority, they attempted to direct rather than thwart the activities of midwives. Dr. John Gunn addressed midwives specifically when he wrote: "The directions which I shall give, will impart such information as will enable a woman of good common sense and observation to manage almost any ordinary case of labor without the aid of a physician."[36] Written instructions, however, eluded most of the enslaved and poor white women who practiced midwifery throughout the South. So some doctors took a more direct approach in training them, ensuring a more interactive relationship. Former slave Clara Walker recalled that "when I was thirteen years old my ol' mistress put me wid a doctor who learned me how to be a midwife. Dat was cause so many women on de plantation was catchin' babies. I stayed wid dat doctor, Dr. McGill his name was, for five years. I got to be good. Got so he'd sit down an' I'd do all de work."[37] Her skills proved valuable both to the doctor who trained her and to her mistress, who hired her out. Racial and gender biases prevented most physicians from seeing midwives as equals or even as colleagues, but in training and working with these women they conceded the reality of their own negotiated position in the reproductive lives of southern women.

The regionally based social judgments that doctors made within the birthing room both reflected and shaped their positions in the broader world, particularly in the realm of politics. Doctors in the antebellum South linked their professional identity to their political stances, which, in the late antebellum period, were increasingly informed by a sense of regional difference. By the mid-nineteenth century, an extremist medical discourse was being advocated by doctors such as Samuel Cartwright and Josiah Nott. They were intent on providing a biological justification for slavery, and for the southern social structure, based on "scientific racism."[38] Physicians who were more moderate still claimed that the South's distinct climate affected the prevalence and symptoms of certain diseases for both blacks and whites. Some doctors believed that the southern climate affected childbirth, making both conception and delivery easier. Hence they argued that southern practitioners could best meet the needs of birthing southern women. As the sectional crisis intensified, they asserted that the South needed doctors with a distinctly southern medical education.[39]

By the late 1850s, southern students increasingly withdrew from northern medical schools. One New York newspaper responded to this exodus by insulting the "lantern-jawed" southern medical student who, "reared in the semi-savage solitude of a remote plantation, and deriving his ideas of morals, grammar and behavior from his negro nurse and picaninny playmates," would return "to his native wilds, to commence practice on a portentous stock of medical ignorance, calomel and quinine."[40] Southern journals cited this quotation as a Yankee insult to their honor. Increasingly, southern doctors took an active role in the political debate, "abandoning their pills" as one editorial noted in 1860, "to cure and eradicate the maladies of the body politic."[41] The professional identity that these doctors brought to the birthing room was clearly tied to a regional identity based on their southern heritage. Their actions in the birthing room are thus important to our understanding of antebellum southern society precisely because they were *not* based solely on neutral scientific treatises, but instead embraced the gender, class, and racial norms of the society in which they practiced. During the antebellum period, political considerations increasingly shaped their rhetoric.

Many of the doctors who practiced medicine in the South were plantation owners or had family connections to the planter class. But while physicians struggled with establishing their professional identity as medical experts in the antebellum period, the ownership of land and slaves provided the clearest avenue to social identity within southern society. Those who identified themselves as planters or plantation owners were making a claim to an elite social status (regardless of how successful they actually were at making their holdings profitable). Such claims were closely tied to the structures of patriarchy, and one of the ways in which planters exercised control was by managing all aspects of reproduction, speaking of it as agriculturalists desirous of improving their holdings. Planters' "professional" interest in, and open discussion of, the reproduction of enslaved women marked a great gulf in the status of black and white women. Such discourses also marked the identity of white men not only as planters, but masters.

Prior to the nineteenth century, the terms used to describe pregnancies and births of all women, black and white, drew on agricultural metaphors—"breeding," "teeming," or "fruitful" were all terms used to describe reproduction, signifying both the physicality and naturalness of this event.[42] Although southern society still welcomed abundant reproduction, by the antebellum period the fashions of language had altered, at least for upper-class women. Now southern opinion-makers considered it unseemly to make any public mention of an elite white woman's sexuality, or even physicality. In agricultural journals such discretion also extended to poorer white women. Although idealized narratives blamed poor women for any defiance of social norms, agricultural narratives maintained silence on the sexuality of all white woman, undoubtedly out of the same respect for their yeomen readership that suppressed references to poor white women's field work.[43] Articles involving white women in agricultural journals most often emulated the idealized rhetoric of advice literature and fiction. Sentimental essays and poems celebrated the duties and rewards of motherhood. A poem in the *Southern Planter* entitled "The Rights of Women" included among them "The right the little ones to guide" and "The right to live for those we love."[44] Agriculturists left discussions of the physical experiences of birth, at least of white women, to their medical counterparts. Silence around these issues marked a position of privilege for white women.[45]

However, little discretion was exercised in reference to the reproduction of black women. Just as the status of enslaved women made them subject to medical experimentation in a public forum, it allowed agricultural journals to openly discuss their bodies, health, and reproductive fitness. Planters exchanged letters and placed ads in newspapers that revealed an intimate physical knowledge of enslaved women. Robert Allston, for example, traded a series of letters with a law firm discussing the physical incapacities of an enslaved woman, apparently stemming "from her confinement some years ago." This exchange of letters between white men detailed doctors' examinations and other physical information pertinent to reproduction. Similarly, Frederick Law Olmsted overheard planters discussing the reproductive prospects of their female slaves in the public lobby of a Louisiana hotel.[46] Such discussions not only exposed black women to scrutiny, but amplified the silence surrounding elite white women, accentuating their relative power within society.

Southerners of all walks of life used agricultural metaphors to discuss their "peculiar institution." The comparison of slaves to animals was particularly common. William Holcombe, a doctor and social commentator, wrote that "the animal propensities very largely predominate in the negro." In his 1853 novel *Swallow Barn*, John Pendleton Kennedy conflated the characteristics of horses and slaves. He describes horses in the field as possessing the "power of sustaining fatigue, and fitness for the multiform uses . . . see how faithfully he drudges in the field, and wears away his life in quiet and indispensable services." Soon after, Kennedy uses similar terms of loyalty and servitude to characterize the slave population. Such comments seemed to have resonated with the attitudes of the southern reading public. For example, Mrs. Betty Bale, a white informant for the WPA, used an animal-based metaphor in describing her feelings toward her former slaves: "My sister and I cried when they were set free, not for the financial loss, but we regarded them as people of today regard dogs and livestock." Such metaphors suggest how white slaveowners, almost unconsciously, dehumanized those they held in bondage.[47]

Most enslaved men and women were themselves farm laborers, so agricultural metaphors resonated with them as they did with their white masters. Anti-slavery writers and former slaves asserted that white masters took the metaphor a step further, however, treating them like animals and ignoring their humanity. James Redpath, a northern newspaper editor writing of the condition of enslaved people, queried of his readers: "How can they respect themselves, when they know that their mothers are ranked with the beasts that perish—sold, exchanged, bought, forced to beget children, as cows and sheep are bartered and reared for breeding purposes?"[48] The narratives of a number of former slaves brought these links between agricultural metaphor, treatment as animals, and breeding to the fore.

Early in the eighteenth century, Americans had commonly used the term *breeding* to refer to pregnancy, but by the nineteenth century this term had become too closely associated with animal husbandry to suit the tastes of those aspiring to true womanhood and virtuous domesticity. Frederick Law Olmsted indicated that he occasionally encountered references to enslaved women as "breeding women" or "good breeders" as he traveled in the South, but in their private writings, and even in the literature specifically focused on the reproduction of enslaved women, southerners seemed to have assiduously avoided the term, possibly aware that abolitionists charged that they were breeding their slaves for profit.[49]

The existence of breeding has stirred much debate among historians and statisticians.[50] Demography, however, can only indicate the relative success of breeding endeavors, not the interest of the masters involved. Nor can it fully suggest the fear enslaved women experienced regarding potential intrusions into their reproduction. A statistical analysis only tells part of the story. While in some cases breeding might be used to describe personal experiences or observations, former slaves often used this term more broadly to indict a system that created, for all enslaved women, an element of dehumanization through the *possibility* of interference with their reproduction and their bodily integrity.[51]

The use of the language of breeding clearly tied reproduction to issues of status and identity. For example, former slave Ellen Cragin, from Mississippi, told her interviewer: "Mother was a breeder. While she did that weaving she had children fast." Willie McCullogh of South Carolina reported to a WPA interviewer what he had been told of slavery: "Some of the slave women were looked upon by the slave owners as a stock raiser looks upon his brood sows, that is from the stand point of production." His narrative illuminated his own familial connection to this attitude: "Grandmother said that several different men were put to her just about the same as if she had been a cow or sow. The slaveowners treated them as if they had been common animals in this respect." The statistical probability of such things happening was clearly less important than individual experiences and perceptions in shaping the identity of these women and their offspring.[52]

Former slaves' discussions of slave-breeding generally veered to one of two extremes. Some denied a personal knowledge of slave-breeding. They did not necessarily deny that breeding existed; they only refuted their personal involvement, as when Ella Daniels commented: "I don't know of any cases where slaves were compelled to breed but I have heard of them. I don't know the names of the people. Just remember hearing talk about them."[53] This choice of language indicated a reluctance to associate herself directly with an activity that was deemed immoral. Others, however, purposefully emphasized the sexual deviancy promoted by white masters. Their tales often involved the use of "stockmen" to impregnate numerous enslaved women, drawing a clear link to agricultural narratives of animal husbandry.[54] Former slave Laura Everett asserted the indecency of slavery in a narrative that combined breeding and voyeurism:

On this plantation were more than 100 slaves who were mated indiscriminately and without any regard for family unions. If their master thought that a certain man and woman might have strong, healthy offspring, he forced them to have sexual relations, even though they were married to other slaves. If there seemed to be any slight reluctance on the part of either of the unfortunate ones "Big Jim" would make them consummate the relationship in his presence. He used the same procedure if he thought a certain couple was not producing children fast enough.[55]

Besides her moral outrage, Everett suggested the hypocrisy of the family formation of slaves as advocated by the owning class, sacred only when it suited their agricultural purposes.

Ida Blackshear Hutchinson told another story of slave-breeding in which a master had ordered "all the fine looking boys and girls that was thirteen years old or older" stripped and put in a barn on Sunday nights. She reported that this method produced sixty babies, but then she added an unexpected twist. Unable to care for so many babies in the nursery, the planter ordered a trough built near the fields to contain the infants. But then a sudden storm filled the trough with water and drowned all sixty of them. "They never got nary a lick of labor and nary a red penny for any one of them babies," Hutchinson concluded.[56] While this tale is almost certainly apocryphal, in it this black woman expressed her vision of the proper fate for greedy masters who defied morality and forced the production of enslaved infants in the name of agricultural profit.

Other former slaves also dwelt on the financial elements of slave reproduction, suggesting implications that went beyond the individual victimization represented by forced breeding. Willie Williams, for example, drew a connection between raising slaves and agricultural profitability. According to Williams, his master took a particular interest in enslaved children, remarking "'Dat one be worth a t'ousand dollars.' Or 'Dat one be a whopper.' You see, 'twas jus' like raisin' young mules."[57] Mom Ryer Emmanuel's former mistress chose a different agricultural metaphor to describe raising slaves on her plantation: "Old Missus would say 'Ain' I got a pretty crop of little nigges comin on?'"[58] But whether compared to stock or crops, former slaves recognized that their owners valued them as agricultural assets rather than as human beings. These narratives of former slaves may be suspect in providing the details of any one specific event. But the frequent references to agricultural metaphors, and particularly to "breeding," suggest an overall sense that the slave system attempted to rob them of their most basic claims to identity, treating them as little better than livestock.

In telling their stories, a few former slaves sought to counter the dehumanized identity that had been ascribed to them. When former slave Henry Walson recalled that an enslaved woman "was in a delicate state," he challenged social assumptions that restricted claims of delicacy to white women. Walson's word choice also offered a poignant contrast with his statement that they took that woman in a "delicate" condition and "dug a hole and put her stomach down in it and whipped her till she could hardly walk."[59] Celeste Avery's account of her grandmother being in the "family way" also challenged the assumptions of a slave system that denied enslaved women any legal claim to the children they bore.[60] Such narratives contested the system and the perceptions that had made their enslaved ancestors merely part of the agricultural paradigm, obscuring their identity as human beings who applied their own meanings to reproduction.

During the antebellum period, however, planters rather than slaves dominated the public discourse, and elite white men's discussions of enslaved women's reproduction became part of the agricultural narrative, marking their own identity as successful planters. Professional agricultural journals, in contrast to the narratives of former slaves, generally avoided direct references to slaves as animals or stock and shied away from references to breeding.[61] Nonetheless, both the public and private writings of antebellum planters revealed an intense interest in the reproduction of enslaved women. These writers frequently focused on the profitability of slave increase, viewing it in terms of agricultural revenue. Thomas Jefferson evinced such an interest, remarking in an 1819 letter to his plantation manager, Joel Yancey: "I consider the labor of a breeding woman as no object, and that a child raised every 2 years is of more profit than the crop of the best laboring man. In this, as in all other cases, providence has made our interests & our duties coincide perfectly." William Trotter's *History and Defense of African Slavery* asserted that on large farms many enslaved women might be pregnant, "and this class of slaves, if properly taken care of, are the most profitable to their owners of any others." This profit, he claimed, was long term: "It is remarkable the number of slaves which may be raised from one woman in the course of forty or fifty years with the proper kind of attention." An 1857 article in the *Southern Cultivator* expressed similar sentiments, arguing that "raising a family of young negroes on a plantation is an important item of interest on our capital." But while both Jefferson and this author suggested that self-interest should ensure a beneficent treatment of enslaved women, the instructions they felt compelled to offer suggested that this treatment was not a foregone conclusion. The author of the *Southern Cultivator* article admitted that he had found many enslaved women to be barren, "rendered so by injudicious management at some period of their life—violating the laws of Physiology."[62]

Some slaveowners came to believe that an increase in enslaved property required not only interest but action, ranging from subtle encouragement to direct interference in the reproductive experience. The starting point for most plantation owners was promoting family formation. Although the legal system did not recognize slave marriages, those giving agricultural advice advocated a form of marriage as a means of achieving social stability and the reproduction of the enslaved workforce. Nathan Bass, in an essay for the Southern Central Agricultural Society of Georgia, advocated that "as far as practicable families of negroes should be kept together. In buying and selling this should be particularly observed, and as far as possible let all be provided with wives and husbands at home." Besides preventing runaways, "Negroes thus treated and managed are prolific, cheerful, industrious and happy."[63] A prolific and industrious workforce also meant greater productivity and profits for the plantation owner.

The ability to form strong emotional bonds was also intrinsic to the identity of the enslaved population. Some slaves viewed their ability to "marry" as a privilege, a recognition of their humanity, or a natural right. Others, however, experienced family formation as yet another interference by their masters. Former slave Henry Butler recalled that "the slaves were allowed to marry but were compelled to first obtain permission from the master. The main factor involved in securing the master's consent was his desire to rear negroes with perfect physiques."[64] Family formation represented an even greater violation for some, with their master selecting their mates. Lizzie Grant recalled her own wedding: "No shoes as I was barefooted the day I was married to that boy and Maser made me marry him as we were going to raise him some more slaves. Maser said it was cheaper to raise slaves than it was to buy them, and I guess it was for they did not lose so much when we was free by the government." Annie Row of Texas resorted back to animal imagery when she told her interviewer: "Weddin's on dat place, mos'ly was lake de weddin' 'tween de cows an' de bulls. You see, dey wants bigger niggers an' dey mates 'em to suits demse'ves. Dat's de way deys 'spect mai'iage on dat place. Dem poor niggers warnt 'lowed to larn any thing nor 'lowed to do right."[65] Although family bonds played an important role in the lives of most slaves, they knew that the identity they gained from these ties did not have the same value or meaning to white slaveowners.

A plantation owner's involvement in enslaved reproduction did not end with family formation, or with the encouragement of conception implied in accusations of "breeding." Slaveowners in the antebellum period increasingly understood that prenatal treatment affected the well-being of both women and infants. But what constituted "proper" treatment became a focus of some discussion in agricultural journals and reports. Nathan Bass, for example, suggested in 1851 that "females during a state of pregnancy should be exempt from all labour that would have a tendency to injure them, such as lifting heavy burdens, fencing, plowing, and &c., and for several weeks previous to confinement they should be required to perform no out-door labor."[66] An 1830 report out of North Carolina suggested that planters give pregnant women some consideration, although perhaps not to the extent recommended by Bass. The authors of the report noted: "Women are generally shown some little indulgence for three or four weeks previous to childbirth; they are at such times not often punished if they do not finish the task assigned to them."[67] Such discussions, however, demonstrated a concern about good agricultural management rather than any solicitude for individual women; planters viewed their treatment of these women during pregnancy through the lens of their own professional interests.

Planters' attention to and involvement in enslaved women's reproduction extended beyond conception and pregnancy through the birth and recovery period. Agricultural journals offered suggestions of appropriate behavior for all involved during recovery from childbirth. The contract P. C. Weston of South Carolina provided for his overseer, and subsequently published in *DeBow's Review*, gave explicit instructions:

> Lying-in women are to be attended by the midwife as long as is necessary, and by a woman put to nurse them for a fortnight. They will remain at the negro houses for four weeks, and will then work two weeks on the high-land. In some cases, however, it is necessary to allow them to lie up longer. The health of many women has been entirely ruined by want of care in this particular.[68]

Instructions on another plantation recommended that "after *childbirth* women should be kept quietly in bed from 10 days to two weeks—and kept quiet in their houses for one month before going to work again[.]"[69] These recommendations represented the planters' agricultural interests and stemmed from an attempt to balance their short- and long-term goals, production and reproduction.

But while a large number of southerners shared an interest in agricultural matters, not all agreed on what that ideal balance of production and reproduction should be. Commercial interests altered a planter's or farmer's priorities. While some southern agriculturalists encouraged enslaved women to reproduce, others viewed the pregnancy of enslaved women, which limited their ability to help grow cash crops, as, in Landon Carter's words, "that plague to all farmers."[70] Edmund Covington of Mississippi had land ill-suited to growing cotton and thus relied on, and encouraged, the reproduction of enslaved women to increase his assets. The Manigault family, in contrast, exhibited a willingness to forgo reproduction in favor of the immediate production of rice.[71] Intensive labor needs on the South's western frontier, and particularly on sugar plantations, discouraged reproduction; the limited yields of worn-out soil in the eastern regions may have led some slaveowners to encourage childbearing.[72]

Class identity also played an important role in the way those who managed agricultural production viewed reproduction. This class distinction became particularly evident in the conflicting interests of plantation owners and overseers. Planters hired overseers to ensure crop success and profitability on a yearly basis, while the planters themselves looked to the long term. An article in the *Southern Agriculturalist* outlined the potential disparity. The overseer "presses everything at the end of the lash; pays no attention to the sick, except to keep them in the field as long as possible, and drives them out again at the first moment, and forces sucklers and breeders to the utmost. He has no other interest than to make a big cotton crop." The letter from Thomas Jefferson to plantation manager Joel Yancey, quoted earlier in this chapter, also placed the blame for poor reproductive outcomes at the feet of overseers, stating that "the loss of 5 little ones in 4 years induces me to fear that the overseers do not permit the women to devote as much time as is necessary to the care of their children." Jefferson then instructs that in regard to reproducing women, Yancey must "inculcate upon the overseers that it is not their labor, but their increase which is the first consideration with us." M. W. Phillips, a planter from Jackson, Mississippi, suggested that a change in overall policy was necessary, since "overseers are not interested in raising children, or meat, in improving land, or improving productive qualities of seed, or animals." The issue of slave reproduction was central to this debate, pitting a focus on short-term profit against the long-term prosperity of the planter.[73]

A letter to James Polk in 1838 from his overseer George Bratton indicated how reproduction interfered with Bratton's purpose: "[M]y force is too weak for the place at best—as one of the women will be of little or no service in April and May if you can in any way send your waiting boy here I have no doubt but he will make a good hand." Bratton, his workforce decreased by pregnancy, believed that Polk should sacrifice his own comfort and the use of a "waiting boy" for the good of the crop. Another overseer employed by Polk, William Bobbitt, wrote of a "pregnant woman who has been *grunting* some time."[74] Bobbitt could not say that the woman was laboring, since that held a different meaning in the context of the relationship between overseer and enslaved woman. While "grunting" might have provided an accurate description of the woman's mien, it also conveyed information about her status and the limited respect of the man who labeled her thus. The ideals of southern womanhood would never have allowed such a corporal reference to a white woman; only enslaved women's bodies were open to such descriptions. But this language choice also suggested the overseer's own identity within southern society. When elites with education and pretensions to sophistication mentioned the physical aspects of birth at all, they tended to use "polite" language that reflected their own manners as much as the status of the parturient women they discussed.

Agricultural interests were shared by a large portion of the southern population. A majority of southerners derived their livelihood from the land, and even urban dwellers were not far removed from the region's agrarian economy. Historian Drew Faust suggests that agriculture "offered symbols with which Americans apprehended their world in social and moral as well as economic terms." This imagery existed in both the North and the South, but it was also "section specific; it expressed the particular response of the society in which it was articulated."[75] Although southerners from all walks of life recognized and used agrarian metaphors, white men of the elite or middling classes produced most of the published agricultural commentaries. Here they detailed their own concerns with production, reproduction, and profitability. The language of agriculture allowed these authors to focus on rational economic decisions, turning away from the physical experience or humanity of those held in bondage. Agricultural narratives thus served to justify a white master's interference in the reproductive lives of enslaved women, to perpetuate the dichotomous view of black and white women, and specifically to suggest black women's debased position in the social structure. While their discussion shaped the public identity of enslaved women and their offspring, they also created an identity for themselves as professional agriculturists within a specifically southern frame.

Legislators, judges, and legal commentators, unlike physicians or agriculturists, did not include involvement with birthing women among their professional duties. Yet because legal commentaries and opinions attempted to shore up social ideals and ensure social order by regulating and explaining discrepancies between ideals and reality, reproductive issues became a part of their professional dialogue. Their narratives represented an intellectual interpretation of birth and motherhood and its place within southern society. Legal discussions of birth, whether addressing status, custody, or illegitimacy, focused on ownership and power, seeking to affirm and regulate the social hierarchy and each southerner's place within it. They thus shaped the social identity of both parents and infants, as well as the legal community's own professional identity as arbiters of social standards.

While laws cannot tell us how people actually behaved, statutes can indicate expectations of what was appropriate and the social values generally embraced by the elites who controlled the legal system.[76] Legal discourse, like the scientific language of medicine, may seem to be neutral at first glance. One advocate for legal education in the South expressed a belief in this impartiality of the law, arguing that "the spirit of true law is all equity and justice," and concluding, "none are high enough to offend it with impunity, none so low that it scorns to protect them." In practice, however, laws, and more particularly the application of these laws, reflected assumptions and concerns about class, race, and gender relations in southern society. Legislators and legal commentators laid out both social ideals and the punishments for failing to conform. Variations in laws among southern states, among courts, and over time represented attempts to adapt the law to the social circumstances and beliefs of specific places and times. Such adaptations belied the abstract application of "justice." Rather, the law—both statutes and court decisions—became a compass of social morality and a tool to maintain the social hierarchy and values of those who held power.[77] While social commentators penned advice and fiction to influence the behavior of individual women, legal commentators sought to influence the institutional structures of society; the former used the private power of social shame to enforce compliance with social ideals, and the latter called on the public power of the state to enforce an individual's position and identity within antebellum southern society.

Laws regulating slavery have often been the focus of studies of southern jurisprudence, raising important questions about property, personal liberty, and the fundamental differences between the North and the South. Nineteenth-century laws throughout the United States, for example, placed a premium on the protection of property, but slavery added a unique challenge for southern legal commentators. Ideas about birth became intertwined with legal decisions about status and ownership within southern society. Cases of disputed inheritance, particularly conflicts over the offspring of enslaved women, reinforced the view of slaves as property. Yet the birth of a slave child also asserted his or her humanity in a way that property laws could only address imperfectly. The decisions and narratives of southern jurists indicated a struggle to balance the existence of slaves as persons with the depiction of slaves as a form of property.[78]

Most southern states adopted the principle of *partus sequitur ventrem*, making the status of slavery inheritable, based on the condition of the mother, and tying one's social identity directly to the circumstances of one's birth. Virginia enacted the first statute asserting this principle in 1662, establishing that "all children borne in this country shall be held bond or free only according to the condition of the mother." By the time Thomas R. R. Cobb codified the laws of slavery in 1858, he could argue that "[t]he rule *partus sequitur ventrem* has been adopted in all the States." While this may not have been strictly true, this principle guided the decisions of judges throughout the slaveholding states with only a few exceptions, so that rulings cited it as "the general rule."[79]

Although the demarcation of status was made clear by the principle of *partus sequitur ventrem*, on a daily basis antebellum southern society operated instead on a caste system in which visible racial indicators marked status and identity; it was simply easier to ascertain skin color than the status of a person's mother or the conditions of his or her birth. Legal status, however, did not always follow this easy demarcation. Free blacks existed in all southern states, and some enslaved persons could appear to be white. This led to what now seems to be quite tortured reasoning, in an attempt to maintain a clear aura of authority for the judicial system. Courts at times allowed the testimony of "experts" who claimed to be able to unequivocally identify the race of an individual. A witness before the Arkansas Supreme Court in 1863, for example, was permitted to testify: "No one who is familiar with the peculiar formations of the *negro foot* can doubt but that an inspection of that member would ordinarily afford some indication of race." Southern courts also developed a definition of race based on percentages of blood; one black grandparent made an individual "a person of color." Such references to birth, blood, or physical attributes gave legal decisions about status and identity a veneer of impartiality.[80]

Legal commentators could also argue that the principle of *partus sequitur ventrem*, designed to assign the ultimate in inequality, was applied equally and was thus natural, fair, and just. Although lawyers and judges generally considered the principle in relation to enslaved mothers and infants, it applied equally to the offspring of free women. Thomas R. R. Cobb, a leading legal commentator from Georgia, made this dual application clear when he asserted that "a free mother cannot have children who are slaves. Such a birth would be monstrous, both in the eye of reason and of law."[81] Cobb's remarks suggest how southerners defined status and identity in relation to the "other." The law linked the meaning of slavery and freedom; allowing birth to lay the foundation for one's status in southern society apparently kept it as much beyond the control of the elites as those they held in bondage.

Custody of children became another area of concern for lawyers and legal commentators. In essence, *custody* meant the ownership of children. The Tennessee courts made this meaning explicit in *State v. Paine* (1843), ruling that under English common law children were "as the property of the husband and the father, having no will of their own, no rights in contradiction to his power and authority, and only considered *through him* as a portion of the community in which they lived."[82] While enslaved and free children had different social destinies, the legal identities of both placed them firmly under the control of the white head-of-household. Decisions of custody generally followed the race and gender ideals embedded in the southern social hierarchy. This meant that the law tended to privilege the rights of white fathers. In contrast, enslaved fathers had no legal claim to the custody or ownership of their children in the antebellum period. Moreover, the law allowed white men to claim the ownership of enslaved children for themselves. Thus, for example, the colonial birth register of King William Parish, Virginia, recorded the births of enslaved children under the name of the owner, rather than the child's father or even the mother.[83]

Custody claims for white children proved slightly more challenging for southern jurists. Such claims only emerged when the "natural" order of families and households had begun to crumble. Although divorce and custody proceedings were civil matters, and did not officially reflect the interests of the state, jurists still felt the responsibility of shoring up the social order and sustaining gender roles. When families remained intact, the father, as head-of-household, held ultimate legal authority. The Alabama Supreme Court acknowledged this authority in 1858: "The law regards the father as the head of the family, obliges him to provide for its wants, and commits the children to his charge, in preference to the claims of the mother or any other person."[84] This ruling corresponded with common law, as recorded by Blackstone, which entitled mothers to "no power, but only reverence and respect."[85] "Reverence" for a mother's wishes might prove sufficient in a loving marriage, but the breakdown of the family challenged normal boundaries of appropriate behavior.

The common-law tradition that had favored the father's custody rights to his children came under increasing scrutiny by the mid-nineteenth century. The idealization of maternal feelings began to challenge the authority of the male patriarch when these identities came into conflict as a result of acrimonious custody disputes. Further, a new concept of "the best interest of the child" offered the possibility of judicial discretion in custody hearings. Increasingly, jurists across the nation struggled with contentious custody cases. Judges made rulings based on their own perceptions of both the laws and the mores of their own state. In making their decisions they established new boundaries in family relations and made themselves the arbiters of these social boundaries.[86]

Some courts continued to accept the common-law assertion that a father's right to custody of his children was as absolute as a master's right to his slaves. A South Carolina court granted custody to a father in 1833, although he had been convicted of cruelty by a lower court; his fatherhood rights overrode any other transgressions.[87] The Alabama courts made a similar decision in 1859. Frances Bryan had sued her husband for divorce, claiming he was a drunkard. The judge denied her both the divorce and custody of their children, aged two and seven. In his decision he wrote that

> the defendant is not shown to be of such character, or to have such habits as would necessarily contaminate the children, or render them unsafe in his custody, and the *strong favor with which the law regards the father's prior right to the custody of his children* . . . and also that the children have passed the age when the mother's care though valuable and desirable, is not indispensable.[88]

Frances Bryan lost, but the judge's words suggest a growing belief that the interest of the child should be considered, and that for the very young such an interest lay with the mother.

An 1842 discussion in the *Southern Quarterly Review* attempted to balance the rights of both parents, as well as the needs of the children. Although admitting that the father had certain claims to the children who bore his name, the author added that "the mother has an equal right to the person of the infant, for she brings it into the world."

> The true position is, that the rights of neither party should be regarded, for nature declares them equal. The advantage, prosperity, and happiness of the children, should be alone consulted: and wherever it appears that one or the other parent will be the better custodian of the children, to that parent they should be given. The notion that the father is the natural guardian of the children, in preference to the mother, is a remnant of barbarism.[89]

Such ideas acknowledged the sentimental motherhood of the nineteenth century, a change from the colonial advocacy for custody decisions based on the rights to labor.[90] This shift in judicial attitudes, however, did not occur quickly or consistently. The 1830s had witnessed something of a conservative backlash in legal decisions, but by the 1840s a number of southern states ruled that the best interest of the child would be of "paramount consideration."[91] As the 1859 Frances Bryan case indicated, however, judges made their rulings based on their own beliefs and assessments of how best to maintain the social order. In rendering such decisions, these lawmakers shored up their own identities as guardians of southern social values.

Custody cases also often reflected broader social mores. In the case of *JFC v. ME* (LA, 1843), JFC had abused his wife and killed a man he believed to be her lover. Although the judge conceded that JFC's actions had been "cruel and unmanly," and that his wife's behavior had previously been "ladylike and above reproach," he awarded custody to JFC, apparently deeming a woman's adultery worse than a man's murdering in defense of his honor.[92] Other members of the judiciary, in contrast, attempted to balance the ideals of motherhood with the rights of the father. In *Cornelius v. Cornelius* (AL, 1858), the judge granted temporary custody of a three-year-old boy to the mother but emphasized the impermanence of this solution. He noted that "there would be much difficulty in laying down an absolute rule, fixing a period when custody of a male child should be taken away from the mother and given to the father." The judge ultimately ruled that "the child should remain with her until he has reached an age when he can dispense with those tender offices only a mother can bestow."[93] Court cases in the antebellum South rendered legal decisions that struggled to balance a white woman's motherhood identity with white men's identification with patriarchal manhood. The inconsistent outcomes suggest both the difficulty of this task and the importance lawmakers believed these matters had in defining social values.

The southern legal system was also called upon to address questions of *legitimacy*, the word itself implying status and identity within southern society. Idealized narratives offered a moral and emotional punishment for illegitimate birth, usually resulting in the death of the mother, the infant, or both. In real life, social order was not so easily restored. While southern jurists may have shared the moral outrage expressed by social commentators, legal narratives focused on issues of property. A primary duty of the antebellum father was to provide materially for his children; courts fretted that children without legal fathers would become dependent on the community's resources. Early laws aimed at ensuring support either by identifying the father or by giving the state the right to apprentice the child.[94] The fear of children becoming a financial burden may also have inspired the court's decision in *Jeter v. Jeter* (AL, 1860). The judge awarded the couple's only child more than half of the estate because Mr. Jeter had denied paternity and "wrongly disowned" the child.[95] For those without marital assets, local southern courts enacted "bastardy bonds" in an attempt to ensure that a local government would not become liable for the material care of children born out of wedlock.[96] If the courts could not prevent the actual breakdown of the family and household structure, they could at least try to ensure the social responsibilities embedded in these relationships. Those white children who fell outside of the traditional, or legitimate, family structure had to be provided for in a manner that prevented the complete abdication of social roles.

If the support of illegitimate children born to white women caused concern among jurists, the illegitimate children of enslaved women evoked no such worry. The former threatened the social structure; the latter only boosted the assets of the head-of-household. Because enslaved couples lacked the legal right to marry, all children from these unions were, by legal definition, illegitimate. But legal commentators saw no threat to the social structure from this illegitimacy. Since the principle of *partus sequitur ventrem* established the legal status and identity of enslaved children, and the slave owner held all custody claims, the absence of a father carried no legal import.[97] Whatever moral meanings "illegitimate" births had in the enslaved community, in the eyes of the white legal system concern for the circumstances of such births extended only to the condition of the mother as free or enslaved.

The children produced by interracial couplings of black women and white men also technically involved illegitimacy, but like other children born to enslaved women, this illegitimacy did not seem to trouble legal commentators. Further, although these unions often involved an unwilling woman, legal commentators eliminated the possibility of rape as a prosecutable offense. The white man's right to "use" his property superseded any right the enslaved woman might have to her body.[98] The principle of *partus sequitur ventrem* and the custody rights of the white owner assured the legal status of children born of black mothers and white fathers. Yet the presence of mixed-race children complicated the legal definitions of race, forcing courts to rule on a matter that social ideals sought to portray as "natural" and immutable.[99] The children produced in unions between white women and black men more immediately challenged the social structure, for these children were born free and thus exposed the fictions embodied in boundaries of race and status created by the legal narratives of birth.[100]

Social ideals and hierarchy clearly affected the neutrality and due-diligence of the legal system and the narratives it produced around issues of birth and parenting. The law's ability to interfere in these "private" household matters in itself became both an indication of imperiled status and an attempt to set things right through legal ministrations.[101] Jurists sought to maintain social order when confronted with behavior that clearly defied gender, racial, and familial ideals. This book does not seek to present an exhaustive listing of all judicial decisions touching upon mothers, children, or status as derived from birth, nor does it seek to explain the intricacies of the southern legal system. But it does suggest how legal commentators, legislators, and judges created narratives around the issues of birth and motherhood that sought to ensure the maintenance of the social structure. Laws and judicial opinions presented ideals ascribing the "limits of morally tolerable behavior."[102]

Court cases created a narrative between the enforcers of the law and those who had defied social standards, usually those marginalized by race, class, or gender. Legal decisions created fictive social boundaries, attempting, not always successfully, to provide guidelines that balanced competing ideals, eliminated uncertainties, and based status on the "natural" event of one's birth. The legal status bestowed by conditions of birth set the path of the individual—whether slave or free—within antebellum southern society. Legal narratives demonstrated how closely birth was tied to the public and politically volatile issues of authority, property, and status in southern society. In controlling these narratives, southern lawyers and jurists also assured their own position as protectors and beneficiaries of the southern patriarchy.

James Henry Hammond, a United States senator and one of the largest plantation owners in South Carolina, struggled over the issue of health-care regarding the slaves on his own plantation. Although he sought to exercise control by threatening severe punishment to the enslaved physicians and their patients, his slaves developed a system of care independent of his oversight.[103] Despite the patriarchal authority Hammond undeniably held over his household, his claims of professional authority did not go unchallenged. Many others who made comparable assertions in the antebellum South faced similar challenges that shaped the identity of both the objects of this authority and the professionals themselves. The professional ambitions of antebellum southern doctors, planters, and lawyers became intertwined with ideas about reproduction because birth and motherhood provided a particularly rich arena for negotiating status and identity in the antebellum South. Each profession focused on birth and motherhood (or parenthood) in a way that incorporated its particular concerns: physical, economic, or ideological. These public discussions of birth by professional elites both mirrored and shaped the mores of broader society. Through their discourses on birth they expressed their vision of this society, reflecting and reaffirming gender, class, and racial identities.

CHAPTER SEVEN

Birth, Motherhood, and the Sectional Crisis

IN THE WAKE OF John Brown's 1859 raid on Harpers Ferry, Virginia native Mrs. M. J. C. Mason and anti-slavery writer Lydia Maria Child began an exchange of letters. Among the issues they discussed, the treatment of birthing women became a key indication of the moral well-being of their respective societies. Mason began the exchange by querying of Child: "Do *you* soften the pangs of maternity in those around you by all the care and comfort you can give?" White southern women, Mason asserted, did this and "more for our servants, and why? Because we endeavor *to do our duty in that state of life it has pleased God to place us.*" Mason thus both lauded the assistance offered during childbirth to enslaved women and justified the status white women derived from their own births in the South. In reply, Child assured Mason that women in the North did indeed assist at childbirth: "I have never known an instance where the 'pangs of maternity' did not meet with requisite assistance." But then, in a clear condemnation of the slave system, Child added, "here in the North, after we have helped the mothers, *we do not sell the babies.*"[1] The exchange between these two women was representative of the ongoing debate between abolitionists and defenders of the slave system, in which birth and mothering became symbolic of broader social and political differences. Birth and motherhood claimed a symbolic role as new political loyalties became part of the southern identity.

Politics, or the negotiation of power and status within a society, existed in many forms in the antebellum South. Just as birth could serve to shape southerners' understanding of their place within their families, households, and communities, so birth became an important element in the creation of regional and political identities as the sectional crisis intensified. As these divisions hardened, birth became a means of attempting to unite people within the region, drawing on preexisting identities and loyalties. The language of birth functioned in political rhetoric as a metaphor to reinforce gender and race-based hierarchies and regional allegiances. Southern elites engaged in constructing a nationalistic sentiment actively used this symbolism to defend their values and positions and link "southerners" together. Southern blood and a southern birth, according to pro-southern commentators, meant a common character and a common political loyalty. And, as sectional tensions turned into warring nationalism, motherhood became part of the symbolism of the nascent nation, evoking familial loyalty and the need to fight and protect both the "motherland" and the archetypal southern mother. While many born in the South rejected the Confederate enterprise, the use of birth and motherhood symbols in political rhetoric suggested the salience these ideas held for many southerners.

In the antebellum period, slavery, and the social structures that supported it, increasingly came under attack by abolitionist writers and politicians. Although never a large movement, the charges of abolitionists, and the southern response to them, created a dialogue that provided great insight into the values and social identity of the slaveholders and abolitionists alike. "Who," asked one anti-slavery writer upon observing the sale of an énslaved mother at a New Orleans slave auction, "can think of his own mother, and not drop a tear of sympathy for this mother—so young, so interesting, and yet so degraded?" Similarly, William Wells Brown inquired of his anti-slavery audience, "Shall not the wail of the mother as she surrenders her only child to the grasp of the ruthless kidnapper, or the trader in human blood, animate our devotions?"[2] But while abolitionists focused on the maternal suffering of enslaved women, pro-slavery advocates emphasized the southern ideals of birth and motherhood—and their superiority in fulfilling these ideals. Both sides used discussions of these issues in hopes of garnering support for their cause. In this context, birth and motherhood became symbolic either of the perniciousness of southern society or of its moral superiority compared to the radicalism of the North.

Harriet Beecher Stowe's novel, *Uncle Tom's Cabin*, became the most widely discussed anti-slavery novel in contemporary America. Motherhood provided both the impetus for writing the novel and a major set of symbols within the story. "I remember many a night weeping over you as you lay sleeping beside me," Stowe wrote to one of her children, "and I thought of the slave mothers whose babies were torn from them."[3] She thus felt compelled to write this novel to expose such travails and evoke sympathy for those enslaved mothers. She also intended to convince white mothers that they must become the saviors of the enslaved. She made her appeal explicit at the novel's conclusion, addressing female readers directly:

> And you, mothers of America,—you who have learned, by the cradles
> of your own children, to love and feel for all mankind,—by the sacred
> love you bear your child; by the joy in his beautiful, spotless infancy;
> by the motherly pity and tenderness with which you guide his growing
> years; by the anxieties of his education; by the prayers you breathe
> for his soul's eternal good;—I beseech you, pity the mother who has
> all your affections, and not one legal right to protect, guide, or
> educate, the child of her bosom![4]

For Stowe, the superior morality embodied in maternal love became the ultimate political weapon in overcoming the evils of slavery.

Stowe was not alone in appealing to the maternal empathy of white mothers to inspire opposition to slavery. Fredrika Bremer, a Swedish woman who journeyed through the South in the 1850s, made a clear link between maternal values and abolition. In her travelogue, she wrote of anti-slavery sentiments:

> I can not understand why, in particular, noble-minded American
> women, American *mothers* who have hearts and genius, do not take
> up the subject, and treat it with a power which should pierce through
> bone and marrow, should reduce all the prudential maxims of states-
> men to dust and ashes, and produce a revolution even in the old
> widely-praised Constitution itself. It is the privilege of the woman
> and the mother which suffers most severely through slavery. And if
> the heart of the women, and the women would heave warmly and
> strongly with maternal life's blood, I am convinced that the earth,

the spiritual earth of the United States, must quake thereby and overthrow slavery![5]

William Wells Brown, a black man, also called on the activism of white women. In a lecture he delivered to the Female Anti-Slavery Society of Salem in 1847, Brown counseled: "A million of women are in Slavery, and as long as a single woman is in Slavery, every woman in the community should raise her voice against that sin, that crying evil [that] is degrading her sex."[6] Although relatively few white women actually answered this call, in either the North or the South, the possibility of such an uprising would have struck fear in the hearts of many southern politicians and social commentators.

To further support their appeal to white women, anti-slavery writers emphasized a slavemaster's interference in the mother/child relationship. They wrote of the limited time and resources enslaved women were allowed so they could fulfill their maternal duties and of the constant threat of separation through sale. Kate Pickard's 1856 book, *The Kidnapped and the Ransomed*, caught the bitter irony that some enslaved mothers must have felt in a society which condemned them as bad mothers while at the same time creating the barriers and burdens which impeded their ability to meet the ideals of motherhood. A slave infant in this semi-fictional novel contracts whooping cough, and when his mother "sought her mistress, who had seen four of her own little ones laid in the grave, the lady sharply bade her 'Go out to work.' 'It's no use,' said she, 'for you to stay in—you don't know how to take care of children—if you did, your baby never would have been so bad.'"[7] The death of this mistress's four children did not make her a bad mother in the eyes of society, but she felt free to condemn the enslaved mother for her child's illness.

For many abolitionists, the separation of an enslaved mother from her infant represented one of the worst horrors of the slave system. Heart-wrenching separations became an anti-slavery trope. In one of the most famous scenes from *Uncle Tom's Cabin*, the enslaved Eliza risks her life crossing the Ohio River on an ice floe to prevent the sale of her son to a trader. Another anti-slavery writer, G. W. Henry, told of an enslaved couple forced to "surrender their first born" over "to the unfeeling keepers of the slave nursery, a kind of pig pen, to be fed on slops, or suck a bacon rind, to be fitted for a Legree's or Haley's slave market."[8] For abolitionists, such separations meant the rending of the social fabric at its most basic level, and they became symbolic of the South's moral decay. For example, the heroine of Martha Griffith's 1857 novel, *Autobiography of a Female Slave*, lamented her separation from her mother:

> Surely I was to take my mother with me! No mortal power would dare to sever *us*. Why, I remember that when master sold the gray mare, the colt went also. Who could, who would, who dared, separate the parent from her offspring? Alas! I had yet to learn that the white man dared do all that his avarice might suggest; and there was no human tribunal where the outcast African could pray for 'right'![9]

According to abolitionists, this disregard for maternal feelings, and the failure of southern white women to intervene, defied the ideals of motherhood embraced by civilized societies. Abolitionists linked the emotions of losing a child through death to the loss of an enslaved mother's children through sale, emphasizing that the loss was not an act of God, but of a greedy slaveowner. Some even suggested that such manmade separations were more painful, since, as one enslaved woman told James Redpath, "When they're dead, it seems as if we knowed they was gone; but when they're sold down South uh!—ah!"[10]

For many abolitionists, the trials of enslaved motherhood began well before the threat of sale, with the sexual abuse that could lead to an unwelcome pregnancy. This abuse included accusations of forced breeding. Social critic G. W. Henry identified Maryland and Virginia as "the hotbed and nursery in furnishing slaves for the more tropical regions of the South."[11] Abolitionist tracts cited advertisements for enslaved women that highlighted their "generating qualities" and promised "a rare opportunity to any one who wishes to raise a strong and healthy lot of servants for their own use."[12] The Reverend William Goodell argued that a "prominent use of slave property, in the case of females capable of being mothers, is that of *breeders* of slaves." He cited a speech by a Virginia legislator named Gholson that claimed enslaved women's "increase" as a major source of wealth.[13] For abolitionists, even the potential existence of "breeding" signified the licentiousness of southern society, a moral corruption both resulting from and contributing to the excesses of slavery.

Harriet Jacobs referenced her own experiences of sexual abuse in averring that "the degradation, the wrongs, the vices that grow out of slavery, are more than I can describe."[14] Theodore Weld denounced "the hardened brutality with which slaveholders regard their slaves, the shameless and apparently unconscious indecency with which they speak of their female slaves," demonstrating an inappropriate familiarity with their bodies.[15] The sexual impropriety of enforced reproduction indicated to them that the South was a society in moral decay, unworthy of the American ideals of domesticity.

But while exposing the moral failings and lasciviousness of the slave system could compel outrage, it also repelled potential supporters. Many middle-class readers deemed the sexual aspects of reproduction, even if presented as a result of forced breeding and abuse, as improper topics, particularly for female readers.[16] Abolitionists faced the danger of being considered immoral themselves for discussing such subjects. So while the sexual abuse of enslaved women and the specter of breeding never disappeared from the anti-slavery lexicon, other aspects of childbearing and motherhood evoked a more symbolic resonance and thus became more politically important.

A number of informants for Theodore Weld's 1839 publication, *American Slavery As It Is*, reported assaults on pregnant women resulting in miscarriage, and sometimes death, for the expectant mother. The Reverend Horace Moulton, a seven-year resident of Georgia, wrote of the slaveholders' practice where

> whipping the women when in delicate circumstances, as they sometimes do, without any regard to their entreaties or the entreaties of their nearest friends, is truly barbarous. If negroes could testify, they would tell you of instances of women being whipped until they have miscarried at the whipping-post. I hear of such things at the south— they are undoubtedly facts.[17]

Facts or not, such narratives could evoke horror and sympathy from northern readers, which might be transformed into action. Abolitionists presented the abuse of pregnant women as evidence of the slaveholders' willingness to attack even the most vulnerable members of society. Such abuses indicated to these abolitionists that slaveowners were willing to sacrifice their moral and fiscal interests to satisfy their immediate passions and anger, another sign of a deteriorating value system. The maltreatments of pregnant women, as outlined by abolitionists, ranged from overwork to physical violence. Anti-slavery writer Kate Pickard wrote of two incidents in which pregnant women toiled until the moment of delivery, with tragic consequences. The enslaved woman Delphia told the overseer that she was in labor. He denied her knowledge of her condition but gave her two hours to rest, in which time she delivered the baby. The story ends sadly, for "before night, poor Delphia lay still and cold in death, with her dead baby by her side." In the other incident a woman named Leah went into labor in the field. In response to her repeated requests to return to her cabin, her master "gave her a few cuts with his cowhide, in token of what she might expect if she repeated her request[.]" The child, delivered a short time later, suffered a week before dying.[18] Pickard undoubtedly hoped that female readers who had themselves given birth would react with horror to such treatment. Thus birth narratives evincing abuse became a means for abolitionists to garner support for their political initiatives, while reiterating their own identities as protectors of the most vulnerable members of society.

If incidents of abuse could evoke the sympathy of female readers, threats of separation or a mother's loss of a child could stimulate a more direct empathy. High infant mortality rates, in both the North and the South, meant that most mothers had lost, or feared the loss of, a child of their own. Abolitionists used separation as a symbolic indictment, but for enslaved mothers and their children it was a continuous, painful possibility. Separation became part of George Johnson's family history. He told his interviewer that each of his grandmother's twenty-one children had been sold to a different slaveholder. "My mother said almost all the time 'round my grandmother's cabin there was weeping and wailing everyday or so when they'd come to buy some of 'em; 'Course as I say, I never saw it but it must a been awful." Carter Jackson, in contrast, himself witnessed such a sale and sadly concluded, "Crying didn't stop them from selling the mammy away from her chil'ren."[19] Fredrika Bremer decried the limited hold these enslaved mothers had on their offspring:

> These children do not belong to their parents; their mother, who
> brought them into the world with suffering, who nourished them at
> her breast, who watched over them, she whose flesh and blood they

are, has no right over them. They are not hers; they are the property of her possessor, of the person who bought her, and with her all the children she may have, with his money; and who can sell them away whenever he pleases.[20]

Nineteenth-century white women also had few legal claims to their children, yet they generally expected to have their maternal claims recognized by society. Abolitionists highlighted the disregard of slaveholders for these "ties that an elevated, free Christian country holds sacred," thus condemning southern society's immorality and suggesting that white women had both a religious and a maternal duty to intervene.[21]

If, as these abolitionists contended, white women could become the saviors of American society, why did the cruelties of slavery persist? Abolitionists explained this failure by arguing that as much as slavery affected enslaved motherhood, it also corrupted the white mothers of the South. Angelina Grimké, a southerner by birth, called directly on southern women to end "this horrible system of oppression and cruelty, licentiousness and wrong."[22] But few white southern women, themselves invested in the hierarchy of southern society that defined their own status and identity, heeded this appeal. Abolitionists viewed these women as both victims and perpetrators of the moral corruption of slavery.

To make the point of their victimhood, the journalist James Redpath quoted a Mrs. Douglas of Virginia, who lamented the existence of miscegenation, claiming "the white mothers and daughters of the South have suffered under it for years—have seen their dearest affections trampled upon—their hopes of domestic happiness destroyed, and their future lives embittered, even in agony, by those who should be all to them, as husbands, sons, and brothers."[23] But victim is replaced by collaborator in William Goodell's presentation of a "well-authenticated account of a respectable Christian lady at the South, who kept a handsome mulatto female for the use of her genteel son, as a method of deterring him, as she said, from more indiscriminate and vulgar indulgences."[24] Kate Pickard condemned the image of southern women, those "frail, delicate ladies, whom one would instinctively shield from a rude breath of the fresh air, [who] can strip and tie their slaves, both men and women, and beat them with the zest of a base-born overseer."[25] Similarly, Kentucky-born anti-slavery author Martha Griffith remarked on the limits of white women's nurturing through the words of her black heroine:

> Oh, I have often marveled how the white mother, who knows, in such perfection, the binding beauty of maternal love, can look unsympathizingly on, and see the poor black parent torn away from her children. I once saw a white lady, of conceded *refinement*, sitting in the portico of her own house, with her youngest born, a babe of some seven months, sallying on her knee, and she toying with the pretty gold threads of its silken hair, whilst her husband was in the kitchen, with a whip in his hand severely lashing a negro woman, whom he had sold to a trader—lashing her because she refused to go *cheerfully* and leave her infant behind.[26]

Abolitionists intended not just to show the depravity of a few women, but to suggest the degeneracy of the entire social structure that corrupted the ideals and identity of womanhood. Such accusations were weapons in the political war of words, which made gender ideals an indicator of the moral well-being of society as a whole.

Abolitionists further suggested that living in a slave society diminished southern white women's maternal feelings—not only did they lack empathy for the suffering of slave mothers but, abolitionists suggested, elite southern women also lacked a bond with their own children. Turning children over to the care of a mammy seemed to indicate a lack of maternal love and responsibility. Harriet Beecher Stowe's portrayal of Marie St. Clair embodied this maternal corruption. A pampered southern belle, she was wholly selfish, lacking all affection. Her husband expressed the fear that their daughter would "fall a sacrifice to her mother's inefficiency" and sought a northern cousin to care for the child.[27] In this fictional account, an elite woman of the South proved unfit for her sacred duty of motherhood and, Stowe suggests, she had to be rescued by a more capable northern woman.

Abolitionists used the corruption of birth and motherhood for both black and white women in the South to support their campaign to convert others to the anti-slavery cause. Their female readers, who were themselves defined by their motherhood role, could relate to the trials of childcare and the fears of separation. Abolitionist literature called on men to act politically, but it also created an activist role for white women as the potential saviors of American society. At the same time, anti-slavery writers questioned the ability of white southern women, defiled by slavery, to fulfill the ideals of womanhood, specifically the mothering role. This condemnation extended from individual southern women to the nation as a whole, which allowed the abuses of slavery to continue. If America was "the 'cradle of liberty,'" William Wells Brown told an audience of female anti-slavery activists, using a maternal metaphor, "they have rocked the child to death."[28]

As sectional tensions increased in the political arena, pro-southern writers and commentators began to defend the slave system, southern culture, and their entire way of life. In their speeches and writings they frequently responded to abolitionist attacks that indicted the ideals of southern birth and motherhood. Such defensiveness stemmed in part from their own social and political investment in these symbols. The identity of southern elites, and the maintenance of the social order, placed great value on the ideals and behaviors surrounding birth. Just as internal deviations had to be controlled or explained away, external attacks had to be vehemently rebutted.

An 1845 article in the *Southern Quarterly Review* claimed: "the people of the Southern States have never formally vindicated, until lately, the rightfulness, advantages, and necessity of slavery, as established among us." The author, however, avowed that this was about to change, for "the perpetual din of the Northern and European press, has roused the attention of our people."[29] Novelists such as Caroline Hentz and Caroline Gilman began to celebrate a southern social structure that enabled white women to fulfill their maternal destiny and be glorified for it. A minister from Alabama addressed the Presbyterian General Assembly meeting in Buffalo in 1853. He averred that if slavery allowed "the exquisite delicacy and heavenly integrity and love to southern maid and matron, it has then a glorious blessing with its curse."[30] As the sectional debate intensified, southern politicians ignored the "curse" and focused their attention on the positive benefits of their social structure. The image of ideal white womanhood, happily fulfilling her "natural" mothering role, proved the justness of southern society and its "peculiar institution."

In response to abolitionist attacks, southern politicians and writers claimed benefits for black as well as white women. They proclaimed that the conditions of slavery affected enslaved mothers and their children positively. They based such assertions on assumptions that the African ancestors of their slaves had lived in a state of barbarism. Slaveowners viewed themselves as "missionaries appointed to civilize and christianize the sons and daughters of Africa."[31] Under their influence, elite southerners believed that relationships between enslaved peoples, including mother and child, would emulate their own "civilized" ideal. Further, elite southerners noted that the enslaved mother need not worry about providing for her offspring, because slaveowners took on this duty themselves.[32] Mary Eastman assured her readers that such provisions would always be more than adequate, explaining that "it is the interest of a master to make his slaves happy, even were he not actuated by better motives."[33]

Eastman, like other pro-southern writers and politicians, also refuted accusations that slavery separated mothers from their children. Some denied that such separations ever occurred, while others attributed these acts to evil individuals who received condemnation, not just from abolitionists, but also from their fellow southerners. Eastman told the story of Lucy, whose master had sold away all of her seven children. The white character hearing this tale responds that she had never "known children to be sold away from their mother, and I look upon the crime with as great a horror as you do."[34] Eastman thus attributed responsibility to a single master rather than the slave system. Pro-southern authors were compelled to write these passages by the charges of anti-slavery writers, who portrayed rampant family separations in the slave South. Clearly motherhood, and the bond between women and their infants, became a political symbol for both pro- and anti-slavery authors.

Besides denying such partings, pro-slavery authors further claimed that a white mistress "universally takes more care of her little negro property, than a black mother ever does of her children," thus intimating that it was not a great loss for the child or mother if separation did occur.[35] Southern author John Pendleton Kennedy took a more conciliatory tone, arguing that the law should forbid the "coercive separation of children from the mother—at least during that period when the one requires the care of the other." He reasoned that "[a] disregard of these attachments has brought more odium upon the conditions of servitude than all the rest of its imputed hardships."[36]

Pro-southern writers took pains to emphasize that slavery not only made black women better mothers to their own children, but it also created a bond of devotion between black women and their white "family." Caroline Gilman articulated this belief: "none but those who live under our peculiar institutions can imagine the strong bond existing between faithful servants and the families with whom they are connected."[37] Whether in denial about the discontent of those held in bondage, or misrepresenting this relationship expressly for political purposes, southern social commentators countered abolitionist charges of abuse and alienation with portrayals of a harmonious society in which mothers, black and white, could strive for and attain the maternal ideal.

Pro-southern politicians did not merely fend off abolitionist attacks; they also made a proactive defense of their society and chastised their northern critics for failings of their own. Southern elites used links between birth and status to justify and naturalize the social hierarchy to those living within their region; they made similar arguments to defend themselves from external critics. But while the former emphasized family metaphors, the latter focused upon the familiar political phrase "all men are created equal." An 1851 article in the *Southern Quarterly Review* boldly defended slavery by asserting that "the Declaration of Independence was, then, a great and noble act; but never was a greater or more mischievous fallacy contained in six unlucky words, than in the blundering sentence, '*all men are born free and equal.*' *No man is born free.*" Although birth was clearly a metaphor for an inherited condition, the author makes a link to real birth and infancy, querying "Will any man contend that the infant 'meuling and puking in the nurse's arms' is a free agent?"[38] The conditions and treatment of the reproduction of real women in the South perpetuated social differences; here, these conditions became proof for political assertions. The links between birth, status, and social experience provided a platform from which southern politicians could increasingly express their dissent from "American" political tropes.

Southern politicians emphasized their intention of maintaining what they saw as "natural" social distinctions. In their view, they simply sought to rectify the rhetorical excesses of the Revolution and the slide away from the founding values that had been occurring ever since. They particularly emphasized their conservatism in their attacks on northern womanhood, birth, and mothering. If southern society nurtured the ideal woman, content in bearing and nurturing her family, northern radicalism, they argued, created bad women and bad mothers. Commentators did not, of course, restrict their critique of radicalism to mothers or women. The Reverend J. H. Thornwell asserted in 1850 that "the parties in this conflict are not merely abolitionists and slaveholders—they are atheists, socialists, communists, red republicans, jacobins, on the one side, and the friends of order and regulated freedom on the other."[39] But attacks on womanhood and motherhood had a particular symbolic value in this war of words, representing society's morality at its very foundations.

In 1857, an article in *DeBow's Review* decried northern women who, although married, "forego the duties of domestic life, bestow their minds upon dress and equipage, and refuse to no inconsiderable extent to undergo the pains of child-bearing."[40] If these fashionable women garnered reproach, activist women inspired vitriolic condemnation. Such attacks emerged most vocally in response to the female authorship of *Uncle Tom's Cabin*. In George Holmes's review of this work for the *Southern Literary Messenger*, he critiqued "the land of Mrs. Stowe's nativity" that "would place woman on a footing of political equality with man, and causing her to look beyond the office for which she was created—the high and holy office of maternity—would engage her in the administration of public affairs; thus handing over the state to the perilous protection of diaper diplomatists and wet-nurse politicians."[41] By 1860, such attacks had become more broadly aimed—and more virulent. The author of "Northern Mind and Character" in the *Southern Literary Messenger* denounced the "unsexed wives, mothers and daughters" of the North. He condemned women who,

> abjuring the delicate offices of their sex, and deserting their nurseries, stroll over the country as politico-moral reformers, delivering lewd lectures upon the beauties of free-love and spiritualism, or writeing [*sic*] yellow back literature, so degraded in taste, so prurient in passion, so false in fact, so wretched in execution, and so vitiating to the morals

of mothers in the land, as almost to force them to bring daughters without virtue and sons without bravery.[42]

While directing his remarks specifically at reformers and abolitionists, the author hinted that all northern women might be tainted by this atmosphere. He extended his condemnation to northern men and to the entire social system in words which articulated the southern values of patriarchy and order, concluding, "there are no *masters* there."[43]

As southern social commentators fended off outside attacks from abolitionists, they also sought to form a sense of regional identity amongst themselves, with birth and motherhood playing an important role in its formation. As an author for the *Southern Literary Messenger* intoned in 1839, "[t]he love of country is but the love of home, expanded and enlarged." Southern birth, some contended, linked people of the region together and made them different from their northern compatriots. According to popular beliefs, people carried the seeds of their character and of their political loyalties from infancy, all tied to their birthplace. Rosalie Calvert, herself born in Belgium, wrote of her Maryland-born daughter in 1819: "She is American to the bottom of her soul and declares she is determined to marry only an American."[44] In the antebellum period, the identity of "American" proved insufficiently specific for many southerners, who chose instead to identify themselves with the state or region of their birth. Edmund Kirke, traveling through the South during the secession crisis, related an incident that portrayed this specificity to a comical extreme. Kirke encountered a poor white man who proudly claimed *not* to be a South Carolinian. This North Carolinian explained that he had missed that fate "by several miles" because his mother had "moved over the line to born me a decent individual."[45]

In her 1854 novel *The Planter's Northern Bride*, Caroline Hentz attempted to ameliorate tensions based on birth in one region or the other by uniting a southern planter, Moreland, and a northern woman, Eulalia, in marriage. That such a union could form a major plot line reveals in itself the depth of perceived differences linked to birthplace. "What a sweet, lovely creature she is!" Eulalia's new southern sister-in-law observes. "Who would believe that the North gave birth to such an angel?"

Later, a minister hails the offspring of this union: "The blood of the North and the South is blended in its veins, and may he be a representative of the reunion of these now too divided parties!" Yet as the southern father celebrates his son as a future plantation master, birthplace seems to outweigh other considerations in determining his destiny.[46]

Those not actually born in the South, but tied to it by sentiment, could alter the metaphor to express their own loyalty. Thus Sarah Wadley wrote that fighting for the Confederacy gave her New England-born father the opportunity to "protect and aid the country which has been his foster mother."[47] But the loyalty of those not born in the South became a source of suspicion for some, who increasingly associated northern birth with suspect political and moral views. Some commentators went so far as to suggest that people from the northern United States constituted an entirely different breed, with distinct bloodlines contributing to their different character.[48] During the Civil War, Eliza Andrews of Georgia expressed her distress at imminent defeat through assertions of immutable difference. Stating her hatred for a "little Yankee preacher," whom the family had once welcomed into their home, she pondered in her diary: "What is it, I wonder, that makes them so different from us, even when they mean to be good Southerners! You can't even make one of them look like us, not if you were to dress him up in a full suit of Georgia jeans."[49] Although southerners like Andrews often had numerous connections to northerners in the antebellum period, regional distinctions based on birth now became identifiable and exaggerated in an attempt to construct the last best reason for the southern fight.

Those opposed to southern slave society did not necessarily deny the significance of one's place of birth, but they did refute the valorous character attributed to that birth having occurred in the South. African American author William Wells Brown proposed that sectional differences, and specifically the moral inferiority of the southern slave system, stemmed from the parent state:

> Behold the May-flower anchored at Plymouth Rock, the slave-ship in James River. Each a parent, one of the prosperous, labour-honouring, law-sustaining institutions of the North; the other the mother of slavery idleness, lynch-law, ignorance, unpaid labour,

poverty, and duelling, despotism, the ceaseless swing of the whip, and the peculiar institutions of the South. These ships are the representation of good and evil in the New World, even to our day.[50]

Northern journalist James Redpath acknowledged that he had met a number of noble southerners in his travels and claimed his hatred had turned to pity. He decried the "demoralizing pro-slavery influences" inflicted on southerners "from their cradle to their tomb."[51] Thus, according to commentators in both the North and the South, inherited character, passed through blood and birth, created the traits and values that differentiated their regions, although who benefited from these differences remained a source of debate.

Perceived regional differences based on birthplace had serious consequences, fueling some of the disputes that led to secession. An 1860 article in the *Southern Literary Messenger* that suggested people in the North and the South emerged from different bloodlines asked readers to ponder "how then is the South to remain in a Union of equality with a people who differ so widely in race, in interest and latitude?"[52] Confederate poetry called on "Sons of the South" and "ye braves of Southern birth" to take up arms in defense of their birthplace.[53] Even Caroline Seabury, a northern-born schoolteacher stranded in the South by the war, identified the link between place of birth and a willingness to fight: "were it my native soil 'nil desperandum' would be my watchword—I feel every hour how natural is the strength of love which one has for a birth-place."[54] Both before and during the war, one's place of birth became a foundation of loyalty in antebellum America, with many southerners discovering an inborn sense of regional identity.

As the "South" became the "Confederacy," birth and motherhood took on an intensified metaphorical meaning for those advocating a southern political identity. Drew Faust, in her study of Confederate nationalism, suggests that southerners drew on "existing systems of meaning, [and] long-cherished bodies of thought and legitimation." Thus "the language Civil War southerners used to explicate their social world stressed concepts like harmony, reciprocity, duty, and dependence, alongside metaphors of family and of organic unity."[55] Antebellum southerners made the behavior of mothers a symbol of social order and well-being; Confederates used motherhood's symbolic links to origins, nurture, and loyalty to create an attachment to the nascent nation.

After an unsuccessful bid for a South Carolina senate seat early in his career, Francis Pickens adopted a symbolic rhetoric that identified the state as his mother. He wrote of South Carolina: "She is my mother, and although repelled and repudiated by her: yet I will proudly lay my head upon her bosom, even though her heart never beat for me." The papers reporting Pickens's defeat similarly adopted mothering metaphors, praising Pickens for his "dutiful devotion to his Mother State and deep concern for her welfare and honor." Similar language propelled Pickens to the governorship in 1860. "I come as a son to lay my head upon the bosom of my mother," he reportedly said, "to hear her heart beat—beat with glorious and noble accents worthy of her past and glorious future."[56] This rhetoric of a mother/child relationship was not limited to officeseekers. As the sectional crisis deepened, politicians and poets alike reminded ordinary citizens that the southern nation was a mother to every southerner, and as such they owed "her" their loyalty.

Building on the identity of birthplace, Confederate politicians and writers used the imagery of motherhood to mark their distinct origins from their northern foes. They made both individual states, and the Confederacy as a whole, the metaphorical mother of southern citizens. Poets celebrated the South's "maternal love" and urged that "sons of the South arise" in defense of their "mother state." Maryland became a particular focus of poets because of secession's failure there. Poems such as John Collins M'Cabe's "Maryland, Our Mother," and James Randall's "My Maryland" poured out the feelings of pro-southern citizens as sons in exile with their mother held a hostage to hostile interests. Addressing "O, Maryland, sweet Mother!" M'Cabe wrote, "And we Swear, O Mother dear, we swear to be true to thee, / To make thy smiters bite the dust, and thou, O Mother free!" A poem entitled "Prosopopeia" reminded all southern "sons" of their duty to the mother who speaks the words:

'Tis I, my sons, no other;
'Tis I, my sons, no other;
I am your common mother,
For I have borne you all.

That mother, look upon her;
Will you desert her now,
And suffer foul dishonor.
To brand her sacred brow?

These poets took the idealized attachment and loyalty between mother and child and made it a symbol of southern citizens' obligation to the new Confederate nation.[57]

Politicians also used these metaphors in their speeches to rally support for secession. Jefferson Davis gave an address before the United States Senate in January 1861, entitled "Pulling Down the Political Temple," that used a number of birth metaphors to explain a previous example of "secession": "Tennessee, born of secession, rocked in the cradle of revolution, taking her position before she was matured, and claiming to be a state because she had violently severed her connection with North Carolina, and through an act of secession and revolution to have become a state. I honor her for it."[58] This speech used the violent rendering of ties between child and mother state to validate secession. Most political narratives and speeches, however, emphasized the strong bond between Mother state and citizen Child. The southern code of honor, they argued, dictated that white men should take up arms to defend their "political mother" against perceived insults. President Davis, speaking to a Richmond audience in June 1861, stated: "there is not one true son of the South who is not ready to shoulder his musket, to bleed, to die, or to conquer in the cause of liberty here."[59] The violent rhetoric remained, but here Davis's purpose was to unite men with a common bond of birth. "Sons of the South" would fight for their mother state.

Besides defending their metaphorical mother, Confederate politicians also urged southern men to defend the archetypal southern mother against northern aggressors. Again, such appeals referred less to protecting real mothers, many of whom would suffer greatly in the war, and more to protecting what narratives proclaimed as the ideals of motherhood and domestic order.[60] When the former governor of Virginia, Henry Wise, claimed that northerners "have invaded the sanctity of your home and firesides, and endeavored to play master, father, and husband for you in your household," he did not refer to literal invasions, but to an encroachment on the concept of these things, an upsetting of the south-

ern social structure.[61] Gertrude Thomas recorded that General Beauregard expressed similar outrage after General Butler issued his General
Order #28 in New Orleans. Beauregard reportedly declaimed: "Men of
the South! Shall our Mothers, our wives, our daughters and sisters, be
thus outraged by the ruffianly soldiers of the North, to whom is given the
right to treat at their pleasure the ladies of the South as common har-
lots? Arouse friends, and drive back from our homes the disturbers of
our family ties."[62] Although southerners had some reason to dread actual home invasions, the war's impact on domestic order garnered equal
dread. The Reverend James Thornwell wrote that southerners would
fight fiercely for "our wives, our children, and our sacred honor."[63] Ideals
and experiences could not be separated in this call to arms.

Lurking beneath the antebellum ideals of childbirth and motherhood were fears that the behavior of individual women could upset these
paradigms and challenge existing social structures. Similarly, those who
used symbols of motherhood to articulate a political loyalty to the Confederacy relied on the complicity of white southern women not to under-
mine the tenuous claims to loyalty. Their political words lost their meaning if real women refused to accept the mantle of the ideal or to sacrifice
their husbands and sons in its defense. Motherhood metaphors were politically valuable because white women embraced and perpetuated the
symbolic and political meanings of their role.

In her writings, Louisa McCord urged women to demonstrate their
loyalty by willingly offering their sons and husbands to "the cause."[64] A
Texan named John Shropshire iterated the same sentiments in a private
letter, suggesting that if a female acquaintance "had the pluck of our
ancient mothers" then "she would hen-peck Ben like the——if he did not
leave soon for the wars."[65] Virginia Clay wrote in her memoir that such
sacrifices and prodding were not difficult for most women, because "no
Roman matron, no Spartan mother, ever thrilled more to the task of
supporting her warriors, than did we women of the South land!" She
quoted, approvingly, a soldier who wrote that if "only one woman was
left, and she should bear a child, that child would be a secessionist."[66]
The poet Ellen Moriarty begins "My Only Boy" with a mother weeping
as she sends her son off to war, but by the end of the poem, when her son
lies dead on the field of battle, she celebrates her "patriot boy" and resolves
not to cry over his glorious death in fighting for the cause.[67] Similarly,

Caroline Merrick recorded a letter she received from one mother during the war who struggled with sacrificing her sons but then concluded, "I cannot keep them, not say a word to stay them from defending their country."[68] Many women might never have entirely accepted this sacrifice, but the public rhetoric sought to convince them of their proper role by insisting that in bearing and raising citizens, and ultimately sacrificing them to the southern cause, women gained a claim to their own Confederate identity. Southern politicians and their supporters knew that real sacrifices would be necessary in their pursuit of victory and used this symbolic glorification to ensure a lasting loyalty of both mothers and soldiers.

Yet the rhetorical appeals made for loyalty to the new southern nation—with birth and motherhood providing just one set of symbols—suggest that this loyalty was not necessarily a given. And indeed, for many the southern identity formed by their birth, one that tied them to kin and community, did not extend to an identification with the Confederate cause. The prominent Charleston lawyer and noted unionist James L. Petigru argued that it was a love for the South of his birth that compelled him to speak out against secession. After the war, his family, who themselves had been divided in their loyalties, erected a gravestone to their fallen patriarch that included the inscription "In the great Civil War / He withstood his People for his Country," evincing the coexistence of an American political loyalty with a southern identity that tied him to "his People."[69] Many less-noted southerners shared the sentiments of Petigru. Southerners by birth, they were tied to the land, their families, and their communities, but they did not extend that loyalty to a political allegiance to the Confederacy (particularly if it meant that they would be forced to fight to defend it). The hegemonic narrative's appeals to birth and motherhood might fall on deaf ears, despite the resonance that these ideas had in the formation of the personal identities of white southerners.

That most black southerners felt no compelling loyalty to the Confederate cause was surprising to perhaps only a few of their erstwhile masters. Yet this did not mean that they did not identify as southerners or feel a connection to the region in which they were born. Frederick Douglass, a former slave and noted black abolitionist, clearly articulated the ties, and the limits, that a southern birth created for a slave. In a letter he wrote to his former master, and subsequently published in the *Liberator* in September 1848, Douglass wrote: "You will be surprised to learn that people at the North labor under the strange delusion that if the slaves were emancipated at the South, they would flock to the North. So far from this being the case, in that event, you would see many old and familiar faces back again to the South." Douglass's explanation was founded on an identity shaped by birth and family ties: "The fact is, there are few here who would not return to the South in the event of emancipation. We want to live in the land of our birth, and to lay our bones by the side of our fathers'; and nothing short of an intense love of personal freedom keeps us from the South."[70] For Douglass, Petigru, and many others, their sense of being southern ultimately came not from political structures and loyalties, but from a deeper, inborn sense of identity.

Southern political elites saw birth and motherhood as powerful political symbols, not only because they were concepts that glorified women and naturalized social status, but also because these leaders understood that a subversion or rejection of the childbearing mandate by women had the potential to upset the structures of southern society. In making birth and motherhood political symbols, these politicians attempted to harness them for their own purposes, complementing the ideals of womanhood, patriarchy, domesticity, and social order. In responding to external attacks, pro-southern politicians countered abolitionist charges of the abuses of southern childbearing and motherhood by attacking these same elements within northern society. Birth and motherhood did not cause these conflicts, but they became a powerful symbolic weapon in assertions of sectional difference and superiority by both sides. One's place of birth became a mark of character and loyalty. Narratives of birth and bloodlines could naturalize status and social hierarchy, justifying claims to political power and authority.

Childbearing and motherhood acted as an organic political symbol in the nascent Confederate nation. Universally recognized and apparently natural, birth and motherhood carried symbolic values in their links to family, domesticity, loyalty, and hope. Confederate politicians encouraged soldiers and women alike to embrace these symbols and metaphors as part of their Confederate nationalism—for birth pointed toward continuity and endurance in the future. While not everyone accepted this political manifestation of the southern identity, a Confederate loyalty did become part of the hegemonic narrative closely tied to meanings of southernness. And some, like Sally Perry of Dallas County, Alabama, continued to cling to the birth metaphor long after the mother state had been lost, writing that "the country that gave birth to such Patriots will surely rise again, Phoenix-like, purified from the ashes of the Past."[71] But this cause would not rise once more, and the political meanings of southern birth and motherhood had been forever altered.

Conclusion

IN 1860, the Reverend Benjamin Morgan Palmer of South Carolina asserted his loyalty to an emerging southern nation, writing that "born upon her soil, of a father thus born before me—from an ancestry that occupied it while yet it was a part of England's possessions—she is in every sense my mother." Nearly four decades later, Victoria Clayton of Alabama made a similar link between her birth and her sense of southern identity. In her memoir of life in the Old South, Clayton suggested that "our thoughts, our morals, our most fixed beliefs, are consequences of our place of birth."[1] Although the South's political experiment in nation-building had failed, for many southerners, black and white, the belief that the land of their nativity shaped their identities remained. The foundations laid in the antebellum period, in which birth and motherhood provided individuals with a sense of personal identity and linked them to broader social networks, remained a salient part of what it meant to be southern in the postbellum world.

While the Civil War left basic family structures intact, both small and at times radical shifts had occurred in how people lived within these structures. Newly freed black mothers looked forward, with aspirations of bettering the condition of both their children and their race; white mothers looked backward to memorialize the past. The possibility of recognizing commonalities in birth and mothering experiences seemed to dissipate in the late nineteenth century.[2] Elite white women increasingly had their children in hospitals, abandoning both the racially integrated and gender-segregated birthing room. Black women, too, moved away from integrated birthing rooms, although the gendered space of their birthing room remained much longer because of their continued reliance on black midwives.[3] But while these experiences gradually changed to reflect the social and political realities of a racially segregated South, birth itself remained essential to southerners—black *and* white—in defining their identity within this society.

Emancipation transformed the family life of freedmen; it also changed the meaning of "family" for many white southerners. Birth and motherhood remained important social symbols for southerners of both races, but the meanings embedded in these symbols had altered for everyone. No longer did birth determine the legal status that a person held in southern society. For black southerners, emancipation entailed, among other things, the legal recognition of their family ties—no one could now take away their infants and treat them as commodities. For white southerners, absent the enslaved labor force, emancipation meant that they had to reformulate their understanding of household structures.

Just as the separation of mothers and children had symbolized the abuses of the slave system, the claim to ownership of their own children became a mark of freedom for formerly enslaved mothers and fathers. As early as 1864, newly freed father Spotswood Rice wrote to his children still held in bondage: "Don't be uneasy my children[,] I expect to have you. If Diggs dont give you up this Government will and I feel confident that I will get you. Your Miss Kaitty said that I tried to steal you. But I'll let her know that god never intended for man to steal his own flesh and blood." Rice also wrote to Kitty Diggs, the white woman who held his children, with a warning:

> now I want you to understand that mary is my Child and is a God
> given rite of my own[,] and you may hold on to her as long as you can
> but I want you to remembor this one thing that the longor you keep
> my Child from me the longor you will have to burn in hell and the
> qwicker youll get their. . . . now you call my children your pro[per]ty
> not so with me my Children is my own and I expect to get them . . . .[4]

Rice, who had been denied a claim to his own personhood as a slave, now insisted on the identity and rights of fatherhood for himself and freedom for his children.

Even when formerly enslaved couples did not wish to remain married to each other after emancipation, a desire to claim their children did not necessarily diminish. Madison Day and Maria Richard of Florida, for example, sought not just to gain possession of their children from white owners, but from each other after they had separated. Such custody fights were something new for black southerners. In October 1866, First Lieutenant F. E. Grossmann, who had been called on to settle this dispute, wrote to the acting assistant adjunct general. He expressed surprise that although they had been "married" for seven years and had three children, Day and Richard had no desire "to legallize [*sic*] their relation." But although they wished to live apart, they "both appear to have an affectionate regard for the children and each loudly demands them."[5] These newly freed parents could now fight, even with each other, against being separated from their children. In the case of Day and Richard, the governmental authorities to whom they appealed ruled that the father had a right to the children.[6] During slavery, the principal of *partus sequitur ventrem* had linked enslaved children only to their mothers; now, in the legal arena, this principle had been replaced by common-law traditions that privileged the rights of the father. Thus, for black men, emancipation meant a new authority over, and responsibility for, their wives and children.[7]

Within the freedmen's households, the ideal of the sole, male breadwinner was paired with that of the stay-at-home black mother. Just as antebellum ideals had sanctified white motherhood as the inculcator of social values, the emerging black middle class in the postbellum era celebrated black motherhood as the foundation of morality, respectability, and racial progress.[8] Under slavery, black mothers struggled to ensure the physical and emotional survival of their children. In freedom they became, in the ideal, the "mothers of the race." While economic realities frequently confounded attempts to meet these ideals, few freedmen left the South in the immediate postbellum era to seek opportunities elsewhere. Long-standing ties to kin and community linked black southerners to the land of their birth.

Emancipation also affected white southerners' perceptions of family, belying the notion of the "family, black and white." Many former slaveowners reacted with bitterness as they were purposefully excluded from the families created by their former slaves. In July 1865, Eliza Andrews of Georgia noted in her diary that freed slaves almost always rejected the family name of their former masters when selecting a surname and added that "they have their notions of family pride. All of these changes are very sad to me, in spite of their comic side. There will soon be no more old mammies and daddies, no more old uncles and aunties." Yet if Andrews seemed to feel rejected and betrayed in her loyalties, only a month earlier she had issued her own partial rejection of the black "members of the family," justifying her father's financial abandonment of the freedmen: "Of course, now that they are no longer his property, he can't afford to spend money bringing up families of little negro children like he used to, but humanity, and the natural affection that every right-minded man feels for his own people, will make him do all that he can to keep them from suffering." The image of the paternalistic master met with the reality of economic interests here—if black infants were no longer commodities, then they no longer deserved the attention or resources of white plantation owners.[9]

White southerners tended to believe that withdrawing their care in the postwar era would mean harm to black infants. They recorded reports of black mothers allegedly "throwing away their babies in their mad haste to run away from their homes and follow the Northern deliverers."[10] Some white mothers took a personal interest in the fate of black infants, a fate they presumed would be negative without their guidance. Their belief, established in the antebellum period, of the inadequacy of black women's nurturing and their own superior mothering skills contributed to these perceptions. One such white woman, Nancy Robinson, bemoaned the behavior of her former slaves: "[M]any I have raised from infancy, watched over their orphan childhood, and reared them to manhood. Now, regardless of my feelings for them, they seemed pleased with the chance of going."[11] Claiming the identity of "mother" of these black children for herself, Robinson apparently could not grasp why this relationship had been rejected by those she had held in bondage.

Tryphena Fox of Louisiana commented on the fate of her former slaves in 1864: "I have heard that Susan went to Memphis & one of her children is dead—they needed 'Mistress nursing and care.'"[12] In May 1865, Gertrude Thomas of Georgia noted that her former slave Sarah had come to take away her daughter Betsey. Expressing her own "interest" in the child's well-being, Thomas wrote that Betsey "was a bright quick child and raised in our family would have become a good servant. As it is she will be under her mother's influence and run wild in the street."[13] Clinging to the antebellum identity of idealized white motherhood, both

Fox and Thomas believed that the care of a black mother was inferior to that which they themselves could offer.

The development of a system of apprenticeship represented an attempt by former slaveholders to cling to old patterns and identities. This labor system, which bound children and young adults to a white master, often their former slaveowner, reflected white southerners' need for labor and their belief in the natural dependency of the African American population.[14] In 1867 Tryphena Fox, who lamented the departure of her former enslaved women, had a twelve-year-old black girl, Emily, bound to her for five years. Although she would clearly benefit from the child's labor, Fox framed her actions in terms of care, responsibility, and instruction—in other words, as a sort of mother figure.[15] At the same time that they predicated the apprenticeship relationship on claims of paternal (or maternal) concern, white southerners used this system as a means of maintaining their illusion of control and ownership, at least over black children. Some unscrupulous whites even told their adult slaves that they were free, but that their children had to remain under the supervision of the white master until they too had reached adulthood, creating their own extralegal form of apprenticeship. Most, however, did not feel the needed to resort to such subterfuge. Southern laws allowed whites to gain apprenticeship rights to black children who were orphaned or whose parents were deemed materially or morally unstable.[16] This system continued the pattern, not only of white control of black children, but also of making black parenthood a conditional identity. These ongoing challenges to the claims of black parenthood made the assertions of the rights and responsibilities of these roles resonate with meaning in the postbellum South.

If the Civil War and emancipation changed white southerners' relationships with freedmen and their newly formed families, it also changed the structures of their own households. The white southern household underwent a process of nuclearization in the immediate postwar period. Within this context, elite women had to face the illusions of their idealized motherhood identity directly. For poor and yeoman women, who had always tended their own children, the war affected their material resources but not their maternal responsibilities. But elite women, particularly those who had relied on the unspoken assistance of enslaved women even as their own mothering skills were lauded, found that the war, and particularly emancipation, had greatly increased their responsibilities as mothers. While their husbands were away, a number of elite women had taken on the full burden of household management. Many discovered, to their chagrin, that the men who returned would not or could not resume their roles as providers and heads-of-household. In 1870, Gertrude Thomas fretted about how her family's financial resources, limited since the war, affected her newborn infant. She wrote that this child "has come since our change of fortune, since Mr. Thomas has thought we had children enough. The little baby who in my great anxiety to avoid adding to Mr. Thomas' expense I scarcely provide clothing enough for a change."[17] As a privileged woman in the antebellum period, Thomas had been able to supply her children with everything they might need, including enslaved nursemaids; now maintaining this entitled identity had become a struggle. Yet despite diminished resources and the loss of household help, motherhood remained the central identity of white southern women, and they continued to face expectations that they would fulfill the ideals of this role.

Another significant shift in the meanings attached to white motherhood occurred in the postbellum period. Elite southern society continued to celebrate the ideal of the white mother as the teacher of social values, but rather than focusing on the future, these mothers found their role in instilling memories of the Confederacy and the "Lost Cause" in their children. The process of imbuing children with "Confederate values" began on an individual level as the war was ending. In May 1865 Gertrude Thomas's son Jefferson, named for his father, had "Davis" added to his name—honoring the Confederate president.[18] In August of the same year, Tryphena Fox wrote of her young son Georgy: "'I'm a rebby'—being his first *sentence*—he has always gone by the name 'the little rebel' ever since his birth[.]"[19] In these narratives, women expressed their own loyalty, as well as the allegiances they hoped to instill in their children. Hannah Rawlings of Virginia made a broader call for white southern mothers to exhibit defiance in defeat: "Mothers will teach their young children to abhor the slayers of their fathers and brothers, they will teach it to them from their earliest infancy. Had I sons, this is the religion that I would inculcate from the time they could lisp: *'Fear God, love the South, and live to avenge her!'* That is short and easily remembered."[20]

As time passed, these individualized expressions of memorialization and defiance would become codified into a new ideal of "Confederate motherhood."

In the years immediately following the Civil War, elite women began to form memorial associations that engaged in organizing and fundraising to build cemeteries where these women acted as "surrogate mothers (and thus mourners) for boys and men who had died beyond the reach of their families."[21] Memorializing the Confederate past gained new momentum in the late nineteenth century with the founding of the United Daughters of the Confederacy (UDC). As it had been for women before and during the war, motherhood continued to be an important symbol of loyalty, evoking family, kin, and social networks. Adelia Dunovant, chair of the UDC's Historical Committee in 1901, told the "Mothers of the Southland" that their role was the preservation of the ideals of liberty as embodied in the aims of the Confederacy. This goal could be met by mothers "instilling its principles into the minds and souls of your children."[22] Well into the twentieth century, white southern mothers would continue to have a political purpose in constructing a usable past that could unite white southerners in a common cause.

Like so much else in the postbellum South, the meanings of birth and motherhood had undergone some fundamental changes. Perhaps most importantly, birth no longer determined legal status. For black mothers, this meant that they no longer passed their enslaved status on to their children. Further, black parents now had a legal claim to their offspring and to recognition of their family ties. They could look forward, working to secure the well-being of their kin and community. In contrast, many white southerners experienced the postbellum era as a period of loss. While their own families remained largely intact, the illusions of an organic social structure in which they held a superior position by right of birth had been damaged, if not entirely destroyed. Yet for both black and white southerners—whether mothers, fathers, children, or professionals—birth and motherhood remained salient pieces of their identity. And the ideals and experiences of the antebellum period continued to form the foundation of these identities in the postbellum world.

All southerners were born, and birth helped create and shape the identity of them all. Whether black or white, male or female, South Carolinian or Virginian, birth tied people together even as it divided them. Black and white southerners often lived under distinctly different conditions, yet they also shared many common experiences. Together they negotiated their own and each others' identities. Giving birth and being born tied women, children, and ultimately all southerners to networks of family, kinship, and community. The myriad discussions of birth that occurred in this region encompassed complex understandings of gender, class, and status. Negotiating between ideals and personal realities, these narratives were put to work in defining the meaning of southern identity for all involved. Antebellum southerners, both black and white, used birth to define themselves and their place within society. This, in turn, laid the foundation for the development of a sense of regional identity. Long before the Civil War forced the adoption of clear political loyalties, birth and motherhood, and the connections they drew to family and social networks, provided a sense of personal identity and an understanding of what it meant to be "born southern."

Abbreviations

DAS	Documenting the American South Project at the University of North Carolina at Chapel Hill (digitization of many primary sources)
DU	Manuscript Department of the William R. Perkins Library at Duke University
LC	Library of Congress
SCHS	South Carolina Historical Society
SHC	Southern Historical Collection at the University of North Carolina at Chapel Hill
TU	Special Collections at the Howard-Tilton Memorial Library, Tulane University

Introduction

1. Mahala P. H. Roach Diaries, especially 3 July 1856 and 16 Sept. 1855, Roach-Eggleston Family Papers, #2614, SHC.

2. Robert Manson Myers, ed., *The Children of Pride: A True Story of Georgia and the Civil War* (New Haven, CT: Yale University Press, 1972), 528, 532–533.

3. The best of this historiography examines how power relations between birthing women and doctors, shaped by gender expectations, gradually moved birth from the home to the hospital. These include Catherine Scholten, *Childbearing in American Society: 1650–1850* (New York: New York University Press, 1985); Judith Walzer Leavitt, *Brought to Bed: Childbearing in America, 1750–1950* (New York: Oxford University Press, 1986); and Richard Wertz and Dorothy Wertz, *Lying-In: A History of Childbirth in America* (New Haven, CT: Yale University Press, 1989).

4. Sally McMillen, *Motherhood in the Old South: Pregnancy, Childbirth, and Infant Rearing* (Baton Rouge: Louisiana State University Press, 1990); Sylvia D. Hoffert, *Private Matters: Attitudes toward Childbearing and Infant Nurture in the Urban North* (Urbana: University of Illinois Press, 1989); and Stephanie

Shaw, "Mothering under Slavery in the Antebellum South," in *Mothers and Motherhood: Readings in American History*, ed. Rima Apple and Janet Golden (Columbus: Ohio State University Press, 1997), all provide excellent examples of the birth and motherhood experience discussed within a specific historical context. Sociologists and anthropologists have offered valuable cultural studies of birth, including Robbie E. Davis-Floyd and Carolyn F. Sargent, eds., *Childbirth and Authoritative Knowledge: Cross-Cultural Perspectives* (Berkeley: University of California Press, 1997); and Barbara Katz Rothman, *In Labor: Women and Power in the Birthplace* (New York: W. W. Norton, 1982).

5. "The Negro," *DeBow's Review* (May 1847): 421.

6. This book tends to focus on the narratives of elite and enslaved southerners, because these groups offer a richer historical record. Poor, and often illiterate, whites left few reports of their birth experiences. Wherever possible, however, class comparisons are included because they provide an important counternarrative in the construction of southern identity. A few useful studies of poor and yeomen southerners do exist, including Victoria E. Bynum, *Unruly Women: The Politics of Social and Sexual Control in the Old South* (Chapel Hill: University of North Carolina Press, 1992); Stephanie McCurry, *Masters of Small Worlds: Yeoman Households, Gender Relations, and the Political Culture of the Antebellum South Carolina Low Country* (New York: Oxford University Press, 1995); and Bill Cecil-Fronsman, *Common Whites: Class and Culture in Antebellum North Carolina* (Lexington: University Press of Kentucky, 1992), but this is an area that requires further exploration.

7. "The Duty of Southern Authors," *Southern Literary Messenger* 23 (Oct. 1856): 243.

8. Peter W. Bardaglio, *Reconstructing the Household: Families, Sex, and the Law in the Nineteenth-Century South* (Chapel Hill: University of North Carolina Press, 1995); Orville Vernon Burton, *In My Father's House Are Many Mansions: Family and Community in Edgefield, South Carolina* (Chapel Hill: University of North Carolina Press, 1985); and Steven M. Stowe, *Intimacy and Power in the Old South: Ritual in the Lives of the Planters* (Baltimore: Johns Hopkins University Press, 1987).

9. C. Vann Woodward, "The Search for Southern Identity," in *The Burden of Southern History* (Baton Rouge: Louisiana State University Press, 1968); David Goldfield, *Still Fighting the Civil War: The American South and Southern History* (Baton Rouge: Louisiana State University Press, 2002); W. Fitzhugh Brundage, *The Southern Past: A Clash of Race and Memory* (Cambridge, MA: Harvard University Press, 2005); Drew Gilpin Faust, *The Creation of*

Confederate Nationalism: Ideology and Identity in the Civil War South (Baton Rouge: Louisiana State University Press, 1988); and Anne Sarah Rubin, *A Shattered Nation: The Rise and Fall of the Confederacy, 1861–1868* (Chapel Hill: University of North Carolina Press, 2005). For an overview of southern identity formation at various points in history, see James C. Cobb, *Away Down South: A History of Southern Identity* (New York: Oxford University Press, 2005).

10. Anne Firor Scott, *The Southern Lady: From Pedestal to Politics, 1830–1930* (Chicago: University of Chicago Press, 1970); Catherine Clinton, *The Plantation Mistress: Woman's World in the Old South* (New York: Pantheon Books, 1982); Elizabeth Fox-Genovese, *Within the Plantation Household: Black and White Women of the Old South* (Chapel Hill: University of North Carolina Press, 1988); Marli Weiner, *Mistresses and Slaves: Plantation Women in South Carolina, 1830–80* (Urbana: University of Illinois Press, 1998); Suzanne Lebsock, *The Free Women of Petersburg: Status and Culture in a Southern Town, 1784–1860* (New York: W. W. Norton, 1984); Laura F. Edwards, *Scarlett Doesn't Live Here Anymore: Southern Women in the Civil War Era* (Urbana: University of Illinois Press, 2000); and Drew Gilpin Faust, *Mothers of Invention: Women of the Slaveholding South in the American Civil War* (Chapel Hill: University of North Carolina Press, 1996).

11. Deborah Gray White, *Ar'n't I a Woman?: Female Slaves in the Plantation South* (New York: W. W. Norton, 1999); David Barry Gaspar and Darlene Clark Hine, *More than Chattel: Black Women and Slavery in the Americas* (Bloomington: Indiana University Press, 1996); and Jacqueline Jones, *Labor of Love, Labor of Sorrow: Black Women, Work, and the Family from Slavery to the Present* (New York: Basic Books, 1985).

Chapter One: Idealizing Birth and Motherhood in the Antebellum South

1. Thomas R. Dew, "Dissertation: On the Differences between the Sexes, and on the Position and Influence of Women in Society," *Southern Literary Messenger* 1 (May 1835): 503–504; "A Mother's Love," Copy Book of Mary Ezell, Folder 18, Edward Conigland Papers, #859, SHC; and Robert Manson Myers, ed., *The Children of Pride: A True Story of Georgia and the Civil War* (New Haven: Yale University Press, 1972), 698.

2. Arbor Vitae, "Advice to Young Ladies," *Southern Literary Messenger* 15 (May 1849): 249, 253; and "Woman," *Southern Literary Journal* (Nov. 1836): 181. On the southern belle, see also Anya Jabour, *Scarlett's Sisters: Young Women in the Old South* (Chapel Hill: University of North Carolina Press, 2007); and Christie Anne Farnham, *The Education of the Southern Belle: Higher Education*

and Student Socialization in the Antebellum South (New York: New York University Press, 1994).

3. "Why is Celibacy so Prevalent in Charleston?" *Southern Literary Journal* (Sept. 1836): 80. See also "Good—Virtue," *Southern Literary Messenger* 17 (Feb. 1851): 80.

4. Lydia Sigourney, *Letters to Mothers* (Hartford, CT: Hudson & Skinner, 1838), 2, 47. Although Sigourney was a northerner, the editors of the *Southern Literary Messenger* fully endorsed the sentiments of her work for their southern readers. "Review of *Letters to Mothers* by L. H. Sigourney," *Southern Literary Messenger* 5 (Apr. 1839): 257–262.

5. "Female Education," *Southern Literary Messenger* 6 (June 1840): 453.

6. John C. Gunn, M.D., *Gunn's New Domestic Physician; or, Home Book of Health* (Cincinnati: Moore, Wilstach, Keys, 1859), 126. See also "Review: *Women Physiologically Considered* by Alexander Walker," *Southern Quarterly Review* 2 (Oct. 1842): 310.

7. "To Our Youngest Readers; God is Our Father," *Rose Bud* (Oct. 20, 1832). See also Nancy Schrom Dye and Daniel Blake Smith, "Mother Love and Infant Death, 1750–1920," *Journal of American History* 73 (Sept. 1986): 332, 338.

8. Penelope Eliza Howard Alderman Diary, 13 Oct. 1851, Alderman Family Papers, #4479, SHC. See also Diary of Frances Woolfolk Wallace, 28 Apr. 1864, DAS.

9. Cynthia Eagle Russett, *Sexual Science: The Victorian Construction of Womanhood* (Cambridge, MA: Harvard University Press, 1989), 7; Stephanie McCurry, "The Two Faces of Republicanism: Gender and Proslavery Politics in Antebellum South Carolina," *Journal of American History* 78 (Mar. 1992): 1258–1259; and Jan Lewis, *The Pursuit of Happiness: Family and Values in Jefferson's Virginia* (Cambridge: Cambridge University Press, 1983), 222.

10. "Introduction," *Southern Ladies' Book* 1 (Jan. 1840): 1; and "The Duty of Southern Authors," *Southern Literary Messenger* 23 (Oct. 1856): 243.

11. John Pendleton Kennedy, *Swallow Barn; or, A Sojourn in the Old Dominion*, 2nd ed. (1853; reprint, New York: Hafner, 1962), 40. See also George Tucker, *The Valley of the Shenandoah; or, Memoirs of the Graysons* (1824; reprint, Chapel Hill: University of North Carolina Press, 1970), vol. 1, 13, on Mrs. Grayson's reproductive history.

12. Caroline Lee Hentz, *The Planter's Northern Bride* (1854; reprint, Chapel Hill: University of North Carolina Press, 1970), 501–502.

13. Mary H. Eastman, *Aunt Phillis's Cabin; or, Southern Life As It Is* (Philadelphia: Lippincott, Grambo, 1852), 258.

14. Kate E. R. Pickard, *The Kidnapped and the Ransomed: Being the Personal Recollections of Peter Still and His Wife 'Vina,' after Forty Years of Slavery* (1856; reprint, New York: Negro Universities Press, 1968), 121; and William Wells Brown, *Clotel; or, The President's Daughter: A Narrative of Slave Life in the United States* (London: Partridge & Oakey, 1853), 162. See also Brenda E. Stevenson, "Gender Convention, Ideals, and Identity among Antebellum Virginia Slave Women," in *More than Chattel: Black Women and Slavery in the Americas*, ed. David Barry Gaspar and Darlene Clark Hine (Bloomington: Indiana University Press, 1996), 169.

15. Pickard, *Kidnapped and the Ransomed*, 90.

16. Dew, "Dissertation: On the Differences," 493. For the imperative to reproduce heirs, see Catherine Clinton, *The Plantation Mistress: Woman's World in the Old South* (New York: Pantheon Books, 1982), 8; and Laura F. Edwards, *Scarlett Doesn't Live Here Anymore: Southern Women in the Civil War Era* (Urbana: University of Illinois Press, 2000), 25.

17. Quoted in Peter W. Bardaglio, *Reconstructing the Household: Families, Sex, and the Law in the Nineteenth-Century South* (Chapel Hill: University of North Carolina Press, 1995), 4. See also Russett, *Sexual Science*, 12; and Nancy M. Theriot, *The Biosocial Construction of Femininity: Mothers and Daughters in Nineteenth-Century America* (New York: Greenwood Press, 1988), 25.

18. According to the author's statistics, the population had grown from 2,833,585 to 4,635,637. Review of "Lecture on the North and the South, Delivered Before the Young Men's Mercantile Library Association of Cincinnati, Ohio, 16th January 1849, by Elwood Fisher," *Southern Quarterly Review* (July 1849): 286, 287. See also Richard Keith Call, "Letter to John S. Littell" (1861), reprinted in *Southern Pamphlets on Secession, November 1860–April 1861*, ed. Jon L. Wakelyn (Chapel Hill: University of North Carolina Press, 1996), 182.

19. Frederick Law Olmsted, *Journeys and Explorations in the Cotton Kingdom: A Traveller's Observation on Cotton and Slavery in the American Slave States* (London: Sampson Low, Son, 1861), vol. 1, 59 and vol. 2, 80, 209; Mrs. Henry Rowe Schoolcraft, *Plantation Life: The Narratives of Mrs. Henry Rowe Schoolcraft* (1852–1860; reprint, New York: Negro Universities Press, 1969), 111; and Duncan Clinch Heyward, *Seed of Madagascar* (Chapel Hill: University of North Carolina Press, 1937), 75.

20. The national birthrate fell from 7.04 births in 1800 to 5.42 births in 1850. These figures do not include miscarriages and stillbirths, which many women also experienced as pregnancies. Nineteenth-century American women reproduced at rates greater than their European counterparts, and southern

women at rates higher than women in New England (30 percent higher in 1810, and approximately 60 percent higher by 1860). By 1850 enslaved women's rate of increase surpassed the average rate of increase for the white population of the United States. Trussell and Steckel place the age for first births among enslaved women at approximately 21 years, and for white southern women at 22.7 years. White southern women married younger (age 20 versus 22 or 23) and had higher fertility (7–8 versus 4–5 surviving children) than their northern counterparts, but they also suffered from higher mortality rates during childbirth. Michael R. Haines, "The White Population of the United States, 1790–1920," in *A Population History of North America*, ed. Michael R. Haines and Richard H. Steckel (Cambridge: Cambridge University Press, 2000), 307, 323; Joan E. Cashin, ed., *Our Common Affairs: Texts from Women in the Old South* (Baltimore: Johns Hopkins University Press, 1996), 14–15; and James Trussell and Richard H. Steckel, "The Age of Slaves at Menarche and Their First Birth," in *Without Consent or Contract: The Rise and Fall of American Slavery*, ed. Robert W. Fogel and Stanley L. Engerman (New York: W. W. Norton, 1992), vol. 2, 445. See also Janet Farrell Brodie, *Contraception and Abortion in Nineteenth-Century America* (Ithaca, NY: Cornell University Press, 1994), 2; Herbert S. Klein and Stanley L. Engerman, "Fertility Differentials between Slaves in the United States and the British West Indies: A Note on Lactation Practices and Their Possible Implications," *William and Mary Quarterly* 35 (Apr. 1978): 367; Margaret Marsh, "Motherhood Denied: Women and Infertility in Historical Perspective," in *Mothers and Motherhood*, ed. Rima Apple and Janet Golden (Columbus: Ohio State University Press, 1997), 217, 221; Yasukichi Yasuba, *Birth Rates of the White Population in the United States, 1800–1860: An Economic Study* (Baltimore: Johns Hopkins University Press, 1962), 54; Michael Tadman, "The Demographic Cost of Sugar: Debates on Slave Societies and Natural Increase in the Americas," *American Historical Review* 105 (Dec. 2000): 1534; Richard H. Steckel, "A Peculiar Population: The Nutrition, Health, and Mortality of American Slaves from Childhood to Maturity," *Journal of Economic History* 46 (Sept. 1986): 721–741; and Richard H. Steckel, "Antebellum Southern White Fertility: A Demographic and Economic Analysis," *Journal of Economic History* (June 1980): 331–350.

21. Linda Kerber, "The Republican Mother," in *Women's America*, ed. Kerber and De Hart, 93; Ruth Bloch, "American Feminine Ideals in Transition: The Rise of the Moral Mother, 1785–1815," *Feminist Studies* (June 1978): 101, 109–115; and Patricia Brady, ed., *George Washington's Beautiful Nelly: The Letters of Eleanor Parke Custis Lewis to Elizabeth Bordley Gibson, 1794–1851* (Columbia: University of South Carolina Press, 1991), 62.

22. Dye and Smith, "Mother Love," 330, 343; Jacqueline S. Reiner, *From Virtue to Character: American Childhood, 1775–1850* (New York: Twayne Publishers, 1996), 22; and Mary P. Ryan, *The Empire of the Mother: American Writing about Domesticity, 1830–1860* (New York: Haworth Press, 1982), 46.

23. "The Mother," *Ladies' Repository* 21 (Oct. 1861): 623. See also Barbara Welter, "The Cult of True Womanhood: 1820–1860," *American Quarterly* 18 (1966): 151–174; and Sylvia D. Hoffert, *Private Matters: Attitudes toward Childbearing and Infant Nurture in the Urban North* (Urbana: University of Illinois Press, 1989), 2.

24. See, for example, "The New Constitution," *Southern Literary Messenger* (Feb. 1852): 121.

25. Quoted in Jane H. Pease and William H. Pease, *A Family of Women: The Carolina Petigrus in Peace and War* (Chapel Hill: University of North Carolina Press, 1999), 27.

26. Elizabeth F. Perry Diary, 28 Mar. 1838, #1642-z, SHC.

27. "Mother," Writing Book of Madaline Selima Edwards, 23 Feb. 1846 (pp. 98–100), Folder 15, Charles William Bradbury Papers, #3011, SHC. Both Clinton, *Plantation Mistress*, 39, and Burton, *In My Father's House*, 106, comment on the "extreme" devotion of southern sons.

28. Laura Cole Smith Diary, 1 Oct. 1833, Folder 2, Brumby and Smith Family Papers, #2780, SHC.

29. Allie Bayne Windham Webb, ed., *Mistress of Evergreen Plantation: Rachel O'Connor's Legacy of Letters, 1823–1845* (Albany: State University of New York Press, 1983), 167.

30. George Rawick, ed., *The American Slave: A Composite Autobiography* (Westport, CT: Greenwood Press, 1972), vol. 13.4, 206.

31. Frances Anne Kemble, *Journal of a Residence on a Georgia Plantation in 1838–1839* (1863; reprint, Chicago: Afro-American Press, 1969), 60.

32. "Management of a Southern Plantation; Rules Enforced on the Rice Estate of P. C. Weston Esq. of South Carolina," *DeBow's Review* 22 (Jan. 1857): 44; and Rawick, vol. 13.4, 38; suppl. 1, vol. 8, 809; and vol. 17, 257. See also Marie Jenkins Schwartz, *Born in Bondage: Growing Up Enslaved in the Antebellum South* (Cambridge, MA: Harvard University Press, 2000), 20.

33. D. R. Hundley, *Social Relations in Our Southern States* (1860; reprint, New York: Arno Press, 1975), 27; Bertram Wyatt-Brown, *Southern Honor: Ethics and Behavior in the Old South* (New York: Oxford University Press, 1982), 119–123; and Robert Criswell, *"Uncle Tom's Cabin" Contrasted with Buckingham Hall, the Planter's Home; or, A Fair View of Both Sides of the Slavery Question* (New York: D. Fanshaw, 1852), 10. See also Gustave de Beaumont, *Marie; or, Slavery in the United States; A Novel of Jacksonian America*, trans. Barbara

Chapman (Stanford, CA: Stanford University Press, 1958), 228. In the postbellum period, formerly elite southerners continued to recite their ancestry as a claim to their own nobility. See, for example, Caroline Merrick, *Old Times in Dixie Land: A Southern Matron's Memories* (New York: Grafton Press, 1901), 5; and Susan Dabney Smedes, *A Southern Planter*, 4th ed. (New York: James Pott, 1890), 47.

34. Tucker, *Valley of the Shenandoah*, vol. 2, 223–236, 316–318.

35. William Gilmore Simms, *Charlemont; or The Pride of the Village; A Tale of Kentucky* (1855; reprint, New York: AMS Press, 1970), 405–433.

36. "The Fatherless Daughter," *Southern Literary Messenger* 7 (July 1841): 462, 468.

37. Eastman, *Aunt Phillis's Cabin*, 35–36.

38. L. S. M., "Woman and Her Needs," *DeBow's Review* 13 (Sept. 1852): 273. See also Carroll Smith-Rosenberg, "Beauty, the Beast, and the Militant Woman: A Case Study in the Sex Roles and Social Stress in Jacksonian America," *American Quarterly* 23 (Oct. 1971): 562–584; and Susan Newcomer, "Out of Wedlock Childbearing in an Ante-Bellum Southern Community," *Journal of Family History* 15, no. 3 (1990): 357–368.

39. The Pickens incident is recorded in Burton, *In My Father's House*, 141; Virginia Ingraham Burr, ed., *The Secret Eye: The Journal of Ella Gertrude Clanton Thomas, 1848–1889* (Chapel Hill: University of North Carolina Press, 1990), 127; and Margaret Law Callcott, ed., *Mistress of Riversdale: The Plantation Letters of Rosalie Stier Calvert, 1795–1821* (Baltimore: Johns Hopkins University Press, 1991), 132.

40. Hentz, *Planter's Northern Bride*, 203; and Olmsted, *Journeys and Explorations*, 509. See also Martha Hodes, *White Women, Black Men: Illicit Sex in the Nineteenth-Century South* (New Haven, CT: Yale University Press, 1997). For a discussion of miscegenation between white men and black women, see chapter 5.

41. Eliza Cope Harrison, ed., *Best Companions: Letters of Eliza Middleton Fisher and Her Mother, Mary Hering Middleton, from Charleston, Philadelphia, and Newport, 1839–1846* (Columbia: University of South Carolina Press, 2001), 269.

42. Brady, *George Washington's Beautiful Nelly*, 107.

43. Moses Moore to John Moore, 24 July 1849, Folder 9, Kennedy, Moore, and Southgate Papers, SHC. Ironically, almost fifteen years earlier Newton Moore wrote to his brother John that he had chosen to marry this woman because of *her* property. See Newton Moore to John Moore, 25 Jan. 1835, Folder 7.

44. "Good—Virtue," *Southern Literary Messenger*, 79.

45. Thomas R. R. Cobb, *An Inquiry into the Law of Negro Slavery in the United States of America* (1858; reprint, New York: Negro Universities Press, 1968), ccxx; and Frederick Law Olmsted, *A Journey in the Seaboard Slave States* (New York: Dix and Edwards, 1856), 508. See also Victoria E. Bynum, *Unruly Women: The Politics of Social and Sexual Control in the Old South* (Chapel Hill: University of North Carolina Press, 1992), 7.

46. Journal of Sarah Ann Gayle, 7 Mar. 1828, Denegre Papers, #662, TU.

47. Susan Klepp, "Revolutionary Bodies: Women and the Fertility Transition in the Mid-Atlantic Region, 1760–1820," *Journal of American History* 85 (Dec. 1998): 939.

48. Kennedy, *Swallow Barn*, 270, 293; Olmsted, *Journey in the Seaboard Slave States*, 508; Burton, *In My Father's House*, 112; and Richard H. Steckel, "Children and Choice: A Comparative Analysis of Slave and White Fertility in the Antebellum South," in *Without Consent or Contract*, ed. Fogel and Engerman, vol. 2, 389.

49. For example, one-third of the white women in Savannah between the ages of twenty and fifty-nine were listed with occupations in 1860. Timothy Lockley, "Spheres of Influence: Working White and Black Women in Antebellum Savannah," in *Neither Lady Nor Slave: Working Women of the Old South*, ed. Susanna Delfino and Michele Gillespie (Chapel Hill: University of North Carolina Press, 2002), 104.

50. Edwards, *Scarlett*, 34.

51. Victoria Bynum, "Mothers, Lovers, and Wives: Images of Poor White Women in Edward Isham's Autobiography," in *The Confessions of Edward Isham: A Poor White Life of the Old South*, ed. Charles C. Bolton and Scott P. Culclasure (Athens: University of Georgia Press, 1998), 93; Laura F. Edwards, *Gendered Strife and Confusion: The Political Culture of Reconstruction* (Urbana: University of Illinois Press, 1997), 20, 61; Edwards, *Scarlett*, 157; and Bynum, *Unruly Women*, chapter 4.

52. Cobb, *Inquiry into the Law*, ccixi. See also Kimberly Wallace-Sanders, ed., introduction to *Skin Deep, Spirit Strong: The Black Female Body in the American Culture* (Ann Arbor: University of Michigan Press, 2002), 2–3.

53. William Holcombe, "Characteristics and Capabilities of the Negro Race," *Southern Literary Messenger* 33 (Dec. 1861): 405–406. See also Dr. Collins, *Practical Rules for the Management and Medical Treatment of Negro Slaves, in the Sugar Colonies; By a Professional Planter* (1811; reprint, Freeport, NY: Books for Libraries Press, 1971), 133.

54. [Nathaniel Beverley Tucker], "An Essay on the Moral and Political Effect of the Relation between the Caucasian Master and the African Slave," *Southern Literary Messenger* 10 (June 1844): 336.

55. John Hammond Moore, ed., *The Plantation Mistress on the Eve of the Civil War: The Diary of Keziah Goodwyn Hopkins Brevard, 1860–1861* (Columbia: University of South Carolina Press, 1993), 39.

56. Eliza Frances Andrews, *The War-Time Journal of a Georgia Girl, 1864–1865* (New York: D. Appleton, 1908), 293.

57. John R. McKivigan, ed., *The Roving Editor; or, Talks with Slaves in the Southern States, by James Redpath* (1859; reprint, University Park: Pennsylvania State University Press, 1996), 222.

58. Carey Pettigrew to Charles Pettigrew, 19 June 1854, Box 8, Folder 172, Pettigrew Family Papers, #592, SHC.

59. Mahala P. H. Roach Diary, 28 Oct. 1858, Roach-Eggleston Family Papers, #2614, SHC.

60. Todd L. Savitt, *Medicine and Slavery: The Diseases and Health Care of Blacks in Antebellum Virginia* (Urbana: University of Illinois Press, 1978), 126; and Zenah Preston, Plantation Diary, Louisiana, 11 May 1845, LC. Medical historians have convincingly argued that most of the deaths attributed to overlaying may have been caused by Sudden Infant Death Syndrome. Todd L. Savitt, "Smothering and Overlaying of Virginia Slave Children: A Suggested Explanation," *Bulletin of the History of Medicine* 49 (1975): 400–404; and Michael Johnson, "Smothered Slave Infants: Were Slave Mothers at Fault?" *Journal of Southern History* 47 (Nov. 1981): 493–520.

61. Theodore Rosengarten, ed., *Tombee: Portrait of a Cotton Planter; with The Journal of Thomas B. Chaplin* (New York: William Morrow, 1986), 622.

62. Andrews, *War-Time Journal*, 277.

63. "Inhuman," *Rose Bud* (May 18, 1833).

64. William Wells Brown, *The Narrative of William Wells Brown, a Fugitive Slave; and A Lecture Delivered before the Female Anti-Slavery Society of Salem* (1848; reprint, Reading, MA: Addison-Wesley, 1969), 84; and Stephanie Shaw, "Mothering under Slavery in the Antebellum South," in *Mothers and Motherhood*, ed. Apple and Golden, 308, 313.

65. Harriet A. Jacobs, *Incidents in the Life of a Slave Girl*, ed. and with an intro. by Jean Fagan Yellin (Cambridge, MA: Harvard University Press, 1987), 115.

66. Brown, *Narrative of William Wells Brown*, 14. See also Louis Hughes, *Thirty Years a Slave: From Bondage to Freedom; The Institution of Slavery as Seen on the Plantation and in the Home of the Planter* (Milwaukee: South Side Printing, 1897), 79.

67. Eastman, *Aunt Phillis's Cabin*, 103.

68. Kennedy, *Swallow Barn*, 466.

69. Kennedy, *Swallow Barn*, 468–469; and Copy Book of Mary Ezell, Folder 18, Edward Conigland Papers, #859, SHC.

70. Eastman, *Aunt Phillis's Cabin*, 112, 258, 253. See also "To My Nurse," *Rose Bud* (Dec. 15, 1832).

71. "A Southern Scene from Life," in *War Songs of the South*, ed. William G. Shepperson, (Richmond: West and Johnson, 1862), Documenting the American South Collection, University of North Carolina at Chapel Hill, 180–182.

72. Historians who examine the mammy figure have frequently focused on the mythic elements of this role, a postbellum fantasy of racial harmony; others describe her multifaceted duties within the household. Few have offered a sustained analysis of the mammy's maternal role, although her significance within both the black and white communities rested on her mothering capacity. Patricia Morton provides a good overview of mammy historiography, ranging from U. B. Phillips to historians writing in the late 1980s. She argues that political concerns have rendered the mammy figure "largely invisible," and "when she figures at all she is quickly dismissed as a racist and sexist stereotype and myth." Patricia Morton, " 'My Ol' Black Mammy' in American Historiography," in *Southern Women*, ed. Caroline Matheny Dillman (New York: Hemisphere, 1988), 35–36. Jessie Parkhurst, in "The Role of the Black Mammy in the Plantation Household," *Journal of Negro History* 23 (July 1938): 349–369, provides an early but interesting analysis of the mammy role. See also Cheryl Thurber, "The Development of the Mammy Image and Mythology," in *Southern Women: Histories and Identities*, ed. Virginia Bernhard, Betty Brandon, Elizabeth Fox-Genovese, and Theda Perdue (Columbia: University of Missouri Press, 1982), 87–108. Additional sources include Eugene D. Genovese, *Roll, Jordan, Roll: The World the Slaves Made* (New York: Vintage Books, 1976), 355–61; Clinton, *Plantation Mistress*, 202; and White, *Ar'n't I a Woman?*, 46–61.

73. L. H. Sigourney, "On Health: To Mothers," *Southern Literary Messenger* 4 (July 1838): 476; and A. G. M., "The Condition of Woman: A Review of *Woman in the Nineteenth Century* by S. Margaret Fuller," *Southern Quarterly Review* (July 1846): 149.

74. Charles E. Rosenberg, "Sexuality, Class, and Role in 19th-Century America," *American Quarterly* 25 (May 1973): 133.

Chapter Two: Conception and Pregnancy

1. M[ary] L[ydia] Hauser to Julia Conrad Jones, 2 Apr. 1854, Folder 7, Jones Family Papers, #2884, SHC.

2. Thomas Ewell, *Letters to Ladies, Detailing Important Information, Concerning Themselves and Infants* (Philadelphia: printed by the author, 1817), 23. Ewell (1785–1828) was a physician from an established Virginia family. He was also the father of four daughters and five sons.

3. Charles East, ed. *The Civil War Diary of Sarah Morgan* (Athens: University of Georgia Press, 1991), 82–83.

4. Beth G. Crabtree and James W. Patton, eds., *"Journal of a Secesh Lady": The Diary of Catherine Ann Devereux Edmondston, 1860-1866* (Raleigh: North Carolina Division of Archives and History, 1979), 214.

5. Carol Bleser, ed., *Tokens of Affection: The Letters of a Planter's Daughter in the Old South* (Athens: University of Georgia Press, 1996), xxvii.

6. Quoted in Jane H. Pease and William H. Pease, *A Family of Women: The Carolina Petigrus in Peace and War* (Chapel Hill: University of North Carolina Press, 1999), 52–53.

7. C. Vann Woodward, ed., *Mary Chesnut's Civil War* (New Haven, CT: Yale University Press, 1981), 32, 28. In her own diary, Chesnut listed other women who remained childless, an activity apparently directed more toward comforting herself than to reproaching the other women. See also Elisabeth Muhlenfeld, *Mary Boykin Chesnut: A Biography* (Baton Rouge: Louisiana State University Press, 1981), 62–63. Margaret Marsh, "Motherhood Denied: Women and Infertility in Historical Perspective," in *Mothers and Motherhood: Readings in American History*, ed. Rima Apple and Janet Golden (Columbus: Ohio State University Press, 1997), traces the social patterns which could make childlessness a "tragedy" for women in antebellum America.

8. Quoted in Jan Lewis and Kenneth A. Lockridge, "'Sally Has Been Sick': Pregnancy and Family Limitation among Virginia Gentry Women, 1780–1830," *Journal of Social History* 22 (Fall 1988): 8 (my emphasis).

9. Patricia Brady, ed., *George Washington's Beautiful Nelly: The Letters of Eleanor Parke Custis Lewis to Elizabeth Bordley Gibson, 1794–1851* (Columbia: University of South Carolina Press, 1991), 263; see also pp. 68, 147, 173. In addition, see Jenny Carter and Thérèse Duriez, *With Child: Birth through the Ages* (Edinburgh: Mainstream, 1986), 19.

10. George Tucker, *The Valley of the Shenandoah; or, Memoirs of the Graysons* (1824; reprint, Chapel Hill: University of North Carolina Press, 1970), vol. 1, 137. See also Helen Waite Papashvily, *All the Happy Endings: A Study of the Domestic Novel in America, the Women Who Wrote It, the Women Who Read It, in the Nineteenth Century* (New York: Harper & Brothers, 1956), 90.

11. Mary H. Eastman, *Aunt Phillis's Cabin; or, Southern Life As It Is* (Philadelphia: Lippincott, Grambo, 1852), 247.

12. Woodward, *Mary Chesnut's Civil War*, 101; and John Hammond Moore, ed., *The Plantation Mistress on the Eve of the Civil War: The Diary of Keziah Goodwyn Hopkins Brevard, 1860–1861* (Columbia: University of South Carolina Press, 1993), 55. See also Christine Jacobson Carter, "Indispensable Spinsters: Maiden Aunts in the Elite Families of Savannah and Charleston," in *Negotiating Boundaries of Southern Womanhood: Dealing with the Powers That Be*, ed. Janet L. Coryell, Thomas H. Appleton Jr., Anastatia Sims, and Sandra Gioia Treadway (Columbia: University of Missouri Press, 2000), 111.

13. Deborah Gray White, *Ar'n't I a Woman?: Female Slaves in the Plantation South* (New York: W. W. Norton, 1999), 106. Barbara Bush, "Hard Labor: Women, Childbirth, and Resistance in British Caribbean Slave Societies," in *More than Chattel: Black Women and Slavery in the Americas*, ed. David Barry Gaspar and Darlene Clark Hine (Bloomington: Indiana University Press, 1996), 204, suggests that "in African cultures sterility in mature women is regarded as a terrible stigma and social identity for women comes solely through motherhood."

14. George Rawick, ed., *The American Slave: A Composite Autobiography* (Westport, CT: Greenwood Press, 1972), vol. 12.1, 191 and vol. 8.1, 105; see also vol. 7.1, 73 and 345; vol. 11.8, 303; vol. 12.1, 197; vol. 12.2, 50; and suppl. 1, vol. 3.1, 180.

15. Frederick Law Olmsted, *Journeys and Explorations in the Cotton Kingdom: A Traveller's Observation on Cotton and Slavery in the American Slave States* (London: Sampson Low, Son, 1861), 57.

16. James Trussell and Richard H. Steckel, "The Age of Slaves at Menarche and Their First Birth," in *Without Consent or Contract: The Rise and Fall of American Slavery*, ed. Robert W. Fogel and Stanley L. Engerman (New York: W. W. Norton, 1992), vol. 2, 445; Michael R. Haines, "The White Population of the United States, 1790–1920," in *A Population History of North America*, ed. Michael R. Haines and Richard H. Steckel (Cambridge: Cambridge University Press, 2000), 321; and Daniel Scott Smith, "The Long Cycle of Illegitimacy and Prenuptial Pregnancy," in *Bastardy and Its Comparative History: Studies in the History of Illegitimacy and Marital Nonconformism in Britain, France, Germany, Sweden, North America, Jamaica, and Japan*, ed. Peter Laslett, Karla Oosterveen, and Richard M. Smith (London: Edward Arnold, 1980), 373.

17. "Advertisement for Sir James Clarke's Celebrated Female Pills," *American Cotton Planter & Soil of the South* 3 (Apr. 1859): Advertisement Section, 2; and "Advertisement for Holloway's Pills," *Semi-Weekly Raleigh Register*, Jan. 9, 1856. See also Janet Farrell Brodie, *Contraception and Abortion in Nineteenth-Century America* (Ithaca, NY: Cornell University Press, 1994), 3–4, 224–225.

18. Mahala P. H. Roach Diaries, 27 Feb. 1855, 13 Oct. 1855, and 3 July 1856, Roach-Eggleston Family Papers #2614, SHC. Nancy M. Theriot argues that

"[f]or a woman to use abstinence as an effective means of birth control she had to avoid sexual intercourse as much as possible. This required that she deny or re-define whatever physical desire she might feel, that she distance herself from her body." Theriot, *The Biosocial Construction of Femininity: Mothers and Daughters in Nineteenth-Century America* (New York: Greenwood Press, 1988), 53. See also Nancy F. Cott, "Passionless: An Interpretation of Victorian Sexual Ideology, 1790–1850," *Signs* (Winter 1978): 219–236.

19. Anne Firor Scott, "Women's Perspective on the Patriarchy in the 1850s," *Journal of American History* 61 (June 1974): 57.

20. Herbert S. Klein and Stanley L. Engerman, "Fertility Differentials between Slaves in the United States and the British West Indies: A Note on Lactation Practices and Their Possible Implications," *William and Mary Quarterly* 35 (Apr. 1978): 368, 371.

21. Sally McMillen, "Mothers' Sacred Duty: Breast-Feeding Patterns among Middle- and Upper-Class Women in the Antebellum South," *Journal of Southern History* 51 (Aug. 1985): 347; Paula A. Treckel, "Breastfeeding and Maternal Sexuality in Colonial America," *Journal of Interdisciplinary History* 20 (Summer 1989): 38; Anita Dwyer Withers Diary, 25 Feb. 1864, DAS; and Margaret Law Callcott, ed., *Mistress of Riversdale: The Plantation Letters of Rosalie Stier Calvert, 1795–1821* (Baltimore: Johns Hopkins University Press, 1991), 111.

22. Virginia Ingraham Burr, ed., *The Secret Eye: The Journal of Ella Gertrude Clanton Thomas, 1848–1889* (Chapel Hill: University of North Carolina Press, 1990), 148.

23. Callcott, *Mistress of Riversdale*, 21, 176, 233 n. 2, 240, 340–341.

24. Erika L. Murr, ed., *A Rebel Wife in Texas: The Diary and Letters of Elizabeth Scott Neblett, 1852–1864* (Baton Rouge: Louisiana State University Press, 2001), 12, 230, 363, 416, 426–427. Richard H. Steckel's statistical analysis of fertility suggests that "contraception was relatively unimportant or ineffective among Southern whites." Neblett's narrative clearly suggests that these adjectives were not interchangeable in a woman's experience. Rather, the more ineffective the methods to control conception, the more contraception became an important issue for her. Steckel, "Antebellum Southern White Fertility: A Demographic and Economic Analysis," *Journal of Economic History* (June 1980): 339.

25. Murr, *Rebel Wife in Texas*, 134.

26. Bush, "Hard Labor," 204. In contrast, Richard H. Steckel—in his "A Peculiar Population: The Nutrition, Health, and Mortality of American Slaves from Childhood to Maturity," *Journal of Economic History* 46 (Sept. 1986): 726; and his "Children and Choice: A Comparative Analysis of Slave and White Fertility in the Antebellum South," in *Without Consent or Contract*, ed. Fogel

and Engerman, vol. 2, 370—argues that enslaved women did not attempt to limit their fertility.

27. Rawick, suppl. 2, vol. 10, 4295–4296.

28. Rawick, suppl. 2, vol. 6, 2299.

29. Rawick, suppl. 2, vol. 6, 2284; a nearly identical account is given by Dave L. Byrd of Texas, suppl. 2, vol. 3, 568.

30. Rawick, suppl. 2, vol. 5, 1453.

31. Elizabeth Keckley, *Behind the Scenes: Thirty Years a Slave and Four Years in the White House* (New York: Arno Press and New York Times, 1968), 46.

32. Stephanie J. Shaw, "Mothering under Slavery in the Antebellum South," in *Mothers and Motherhood*, ed. Apple and Golden, 309; and Jennifer L. Morgan, *Laboring Women: Reproduction and Gender in New World Slavery* (Philadelphia: University of Pennsylvania Press, 2004).

33. Quoted in George C. Rable, *Civil Wars: Women and the Crisis of Southern Nationalism* (Urbana: University of Illinois Press, 1989), 9.

34. The average birth interval of enslaved women was calculated at just 1.87 years (22.4 months), while white women had an average interval of 2.28 years (27.4 months). Steckel, "Children and Choice," 391 n. 8.

35. Calvert's children were born in 1800, 1803, 1804, 1806, 1808, 1810, 1812, 1814, and 1816. She also experienced a miscarriage between the births of her first child and her second. Perry's reproductive life began with a stillbirth in 1838. She had living children in 1839, 1841, 1843, 1847, 1851, 1854, and 1856. Her sixth child was stillborn some time between 1851 and 1854. Roach's children were born in 1845, 1847, 1849, 1851, 1856, and 1859. The lifestyle of these women as members of the elite may not have been typical of the southern experience, but their reproductive patterns mirrored both statistical patterns and the dictates of the ideal. Perhaps they are most atypical in leaving a complete record of their reproductive history in their own words. Callcott, *Mistress of Riversdale*, xi; Elizabeth F. Perry Diary, 6 May 1868, #1642-z, SHC; and Roach Diaries, Folders 8–15, SHC. Tracing these birth patterns is largely dependent on the records of individual women, since most states did not begin to register births until 1933.

36. Perry Diary, 6 May 1868; see also 6 Apr. 1843 and 6 June 1848, SHC. See also Mary Jefferys Bethell Diary, 26 June 1861, DAS.

37. Woodward, *Mary Chesnut's Civil War*, 32; James Petigru Carson, *Life, Letters, and Speeches of James Louis Petigru, the Union Man of South Carolina* (Washington, DC: W. H. Lowdermilk, 1920), 441; and Susan Dabney Smedes, *A Southern Planter* (New York: James Pott, 1890), 101.

38. Meta Morris Grimball Diary, 9 June 1861, DAS; Callcott, *Mistress of Riversdale*, 169, 299; Edward Conigland to Mary Wyatt Conigland, 16 Sept.

1855, Folder 4, Edward Conigland Papers, #859, SHC; and Roach Diary, 6 Aug. 1858SHC.

39. Journal of Sarah Ann Gayle, 13 Apr. 1828 and 5 Mar. 1834, Degenre Papers, TU.

40. Allie Bayne Windham Webb, *Mistress of Evergreen Plantation: Rachel O'Connor's Legacy of Letters, 1823–1845* (Albany: State University of New York Press, 1983), 9; and letter dated 13 May 1852, Folder 4, Webb Family Papers, #1900, SHC.

41. Brady, *George Washington's Beautiful Nelly*, 183; Perry Diary, 6 Apr. 1843, SHC. See also Burr, *Secret Eye*, 130. The capitalization of "Mother" further shows the importance of this ongoing role that began with birth.

42. Wilma King, ed., *A Northern Woman in the Plantation South: Letters of Tryphena Blanche Holder Fox, 1856–1876* (Columbia: University of South Carolina Press, 1993), 57; and Withers Diary, 1 Jan. 1863, DAS.

43. Callcott, *Mistress of Riversdale*, 82; Gayle Journal, July 1834, TU; and Burr, *Secret Eye*, 130, 212, 258. Dr. William P. Dewees wrote: "What happens to almost every woman very soon after impregnation has taken place? Nausea and vomiting." Dewees, *A Treatise on the Physical and Medical Treatment of Children* (Philadelphia: Carey, Lea, & Carey, 1829), 23.

44. Steven M. Stowe, "Obstetrics and the Work of Doctoring in the Mid-Nineteenth-Century American South," *Bulletin of the History of Medicine* 64 (Winter 1990): 552; and "Management of a Southern Plantation; Rules Enforced on the Rice Estate of P. C. Weston, Esq. of South Carolina," *DeBow's Review* 22 (Jan. 1857): 41. On the diverse forms and purposes of personal birth narratives, see Della Pollack, *Telling Bodies Performing Birth: Everyday Narratives of Childbirth* (New York: Columbia University Press, 1999), 5–7; and Carole H. Carpenter, "Tales Women Tell: The Function of Birth Experience Narratives," *Canadian Folklore* 7, nos. 1–2 (1985): 32–33.

45. Anthropologists have studied how different cultures determine pregnancy. Some signs are shared across many cultures, while others may be culture specific. An emphasis on a medical diagnosis obscures an appreciation of these cultural distinctions. Hormonal tests did not come into general clinical use until the mid-twentieth century. Interestingly, a study conducted by medical anthropologist Brigitte Jordan found that a significant majority of women could predict their condition without the benefit of a medical test, although doctors now refuse to recognize pregnancy until it is confirmed by testing. John C. Gunn, M.D., *Gunn's New Domestic Physician; or, Home Book of Health* (Cincinnati: Moore, Wilstach, Keys, 1859), 431, 434; Wendy Mitchinson, *Giving Birth in Canada, 1900–1950* (Toronto: University of Toronto

Press, 2002), 124; and Brigitte Jordan, "The Self-Diagnosis of Early Pregnancy: An Investigation of Lay Competence," *Medical Anthropology* 1 (Spring 1977): 2, 8, 21.

46. Withers Diary, 11 Nov. 1862, 11 Dec. 1862, 1 Jan. 1863, 7 Jan. 1863, 18 Feb. 1863, and 13 Apr. 1863, DAS.

47. Callcott, *Mistress of Riversdale*, 131. In 1850 Dolly Burge also recorded definitively that she was not pregnant, based on the appearance of her monthly flow. Christine Jacobson Carter, ed., *The Diary of Dolly Lunt Burge, 1848-1879* (Athens: University of Georgia Press, 1997), 57.

48. With the advent of medical tests, quickening now occurs long after the diagnosis of pregnancy for most women and is no longer considered a sign of conception. Roach Diaries, 17 Nov. 1858, 28 Nov. 1858, and 2 May 1859, SHC; and Madaline Selima Edwards Diary, 15 Apr. 1844, 25 Apr. 1844, 13 Jan. 1845, and 9 Apr. 1845, Charles William Bradbury Papers, #3011, SHC. For some of the cultural meanings assigned to quickening, see Sheila Kitzinger, *Rediscovering Birth* (New York: Pocket Books, 2000), 20.

49. Marie Jenkins Schwartz, *Born in Bondage: Growing Up Enslaved in the Antebellum South* (Cambridge, MA: Harvard University Press, 2000), 33, 39; and Theodore Rosengarten, ed., *Tombee: Portrait of a Cotton Planter; with The Journal of Thomas B. Chaplin* (New York: William Morrow, 1986), 589. See also John Spencer Bassett, *The Southern Plantation Overseer: As Revealed in His Letters* (Northampton, MA: Smith College, 1925), 141.

50. Brady, *George Washington's Beautiful Nelly*, 184; Webb, *Mistress of Evergreen Plantation*, 228–232; Eliza Cope Harrison, ed., *Best Companions: Letters of Eliza Middleton Fisher and Her Mother, Mary Hering Middleton, from Charleston, Philadelphia, and Newport, 1839-1846* (Columbia: University of South Carolina Press, 2001), 208; and Gayle Journal, 4 Jan. 1835, 20 Jan. 1835, 6 Feb. 1835, and 7 Apr. 1835, TU.

51. Rosengarten, *Tombee*, 383–384.

52. Burr, *Secret Eye*, 154.

53. Harrison, *Best Companions*, 109.

54. Roach Diaries, 2–3 July 1856 and 23 Apr. to 2 May 1859, SHC; and Ishbel Ross, ed., *First Lady of the South: The Life of Mrs. Jefferson Davis* (Westport, CT: Greenwood Press, 1958), 66, 94. See also Withers Diary, Jan. to July 1863, DAS. Elite southern women's freedom to set limits on their activities was shared by elite women in England and in the northern United States during the antebellum period. See Judith Schneid Lewis, *In the Family Way: Childbearing in the British Aristocracy, 1760-1860* (New Brunswick, NJ: Rutgers University Press, 1986), 124–127; and Sylvia D. Hoffert, *Private Matters: Attitudes toward*

Childbearing and Infant Nurture in the Urban North (Urbana: University of Illinois Press, 1989), 26.

55. The example of the Sloan family of Spartanburg, SC is given in Stephanie McCurry, "Producing Dependence: Women, Work, and Yeoman Households in Low-Country South Carolina," in *Neither Lady nor Slave: Working Women of the Old South*, ed. Susanna Delfino and Michele Gillespie (Chapel Hill: University of North Carolina Press, 2002), 63–64.

56. Sally McMillen, *Southern Women: Black and White in the Old South* (Arlington Heights, IL: Harlan Davidson, 1992), 55. Margaret Hagood found that these conditions still existed for many poor white women well into the twentieth century. She wrote of one interview subject: "The mother did almost full-time field work in addition to household duties up to the last minute of her 'ever' two years' pregnancies and was back in the field again before the baby was a month old." Hagood, *Mothers of the South: Portraiture of the White Tenant Farm Woman* (1939; reprint, New York: Greenwood Press, 1969), 42; see also pp. 22–23.

57. John Campbell, "Work, Pregnancy, and Infant Mortality among Southern Slaves," *Journal of Interdisciplinary History*, 14, no. 4 (Spring 1984): 793–812. See also Jacqueline Jones, *Labor of Love, Labor of Sorrow: Black Women, Work, and the Family from Slavery to the Present* (New York: Basic Books, 1985), 19.

58. Cheryll Ann Cody, "Cycles of Work and of Childbearing and Seasonality in Women's Lives on Low Country Plantations," in *More than Chattel*, ed. Gaspar and Hine, 71.

59. Philip N. Racine, ed., *Piedmont Farmer: The Journals of David Golightly Harris, 1855–1870* (Knoxville: University of Tennessee Press, 1990), 296, 301.

60. Webb, *Mistress of Evergreen Plantation*, 37.

61. Nathan Bass, "Essay on the Treatment and Management of Slaves," reprinted in James O. Breeden, ed., *Advice among Masters: The Ideal in Slave Management in the Old South* (Westport, CT: Greenwood Press, 1980), 13.

62. Rawick, vol. 3.3, 3.

63. Rawick, suppl. 1, vol. 5.2, 422; vol. 11.8, 255; and vol. 17, 129.

64. Ariela Gross, *Double Character: Slavery and Mastery in the Antebellum Southern Courtroom* (Princeton, NJ: Princeton University Press, 2000), 116–117.

65. Rawick, vol. 5.4, 169.

66. See, for example, Rawick, vol. 4.1, 224; vol. 6.1, 66; vol. 6.2, 200; vol. 9.3, 9; vol. 11.7, 16; suppl. 1, vol. 1, 89; and suppl. 2, vol. 6.2, 2299.

67. Racine, *Piedmont Farmer*, 321.

68. Rawick, vol. 6.1, 90.

69. Rawick, vol. 14.1, 312.

70. Rawick, vol. 9.3, 231; see also suppl. 2, vol. 8, 3100.

71. Withers Diary, 11 Dec. 1862 and 1 Jan. 1863, DAS; and Stowe, "Obstetrics and the Work of Doctoring," 549.

72. Wilma King, "'Suffer with Them Till Death': Slave Women and Their Children in Nineteenth-Century America," in *More than Chattel*, ed. Gaspar and Hine, 148, offers a critique of the limited prenatal care offered to enslaved women. White, *Ar'n't I a Woman?*, 119–141, suggests the sharing of knowledge among enslaved women.

73. Roach Diary, 27 June 1856, SHC; when expecting her sixth child, on 6 Dec. 1858 Roach again expressed a reluctance to sew for the coming child: "I sat down to work, and *meant* to begin some *little* clothes, which I dread making." Tryphena Fox, removed from close family, attributed her lack of preparation for her expected first child to her lack of knowledge about how things should be made. King, *Northern Woman*, 53.

74. Hudson Strode, ed., *Jefferson Davis, Private Letters, 1823–1889* (New York: Harcourt, Brace & World, 1966), 66.

75. Plantation Records, 1833–1855, Folder 2, Manigault Family Papers, #484, SHC; Roach Diary, 30 Aug. 1858, SHC; and Smedes, *Southern Planter*, 74–75.

76. Burr, *Secret Eye*, 149.

77. Frances Anne Kemble, *Journal of a Residence on a Georgia Plantation in 1838–1839* (Chicago: Afro-American Press, 1969), 41.

Chapter Three: Childbirth

1. Jane North to Adèle Allston, Apr. 1853, Folder 12/13/13, R. F. W. Allston Papers, SCHS.

2. Sheila Kitzinger, *Rediscovering Birth* (New York: Pocket Books, 2000), 101.

3. Eleanor Parke Lewis to Mary Pinckney, 3 Jan. 1802, Custis-Lee Family Papers, LC; Ishbel Ross, *First Lady of the South: The Life of Mrs. Jefferson Davis* (Westport, CT: Greenwood Press, 1958), 67; Allie Bayne Windham Webb, ed., *Mistress of Evergreen Plantation: Rachel O'Connor's Legacy of Letters, 1823–1845* (Albany: State University of New York Press, 1983), 32. See also Elizabeth Fox-Genovese, "Family and Female Identity in the Antebellum South: Sarah Gayle and Her Family," in *In Joy and in Sorrow: Women, Family, and Marriage in the Victorian South, 1830–1900*, ed. Carol Bleser (New York: Oxford University Press, 1991), 24.

4. Mary Jones to Charles C. Jones Jr., 15 Sept. 1859, in Robert Manson Myers, ed., *The Children of Pride: A True Story of Georgia and the Civil War* (New Haven, CT: Yale University Press, 1972), 410, 516. See also Judith Walzer Leavitt, "Under the Shadow of Maternity: American Women's Responses to Death and Debility Fears in Nineteenth-Century Childbirth," *Feminist Studies* 12 (Spring 1986): 143.

5. Eliza Cope Harrison, ed., *Best Companions: Letters of Eliza Middleton Fisher and Her Mother, Mary Hering Middleton, from Charleston, Philadelphia, and Newport, 1839–1846* (Columbia: University of South Carolina Press, 2001), 139, 383–391.

6. Patricia Brady, ed., *George Washington's Beautiful Nelly: The Letters of Eleanor Parke Custis Lewis to Elizabeth Bordley Gibson, 1794–1851* (Columbia: University of South Carolina Press, 1991), 182–183; Mrs. Jos. Jenkins to Mrs. John H. Cornish, 1 June 1847, John Hamilton Cornish Papers, DU; and Wilma King, ed., *A Northern Woman in the Plantation South: Letters of Tryphena Blanche Holder Fox, 1856–1876* (Columbia: University of South Carolina Press, 1993), 53–63.

7. Joan E. Cashin, "The Structure of Antebellum Planter Families: 'The Ties that Bound Us Was Strong,'" *Journal of Southern History* 56 (Feb. 1990): 55. Historians who have focused on the medical events of birth have generally associated "social childbirth" with the colonial period, but for many women in the South, delivery—and the weeks afterwards—remained a social moment throughout the antebellum period.

8. Jane H. Pease and William H. Pease, *A Family of Women: The Carolina Petigrus in Peace and War* (Chapel Hill: University of North Carolina Press, 1999), 25–28; see also pp. 99 and 105.

9. Mahala P. H. Roach Diaries, Roach-Eggleston Family Papers, #2614, SHC. Entries for 6–9 July 1856 and 3–12 May 1859 record visitors after her own births; entries for 20 Mar. 1854, 9 June 1854, 30 June 1855, 3 July 1857, 2 Dec. 1857, 26 Feb. 1858, 1 Sept. 1858, 4 Sept. 1858, and 8 Jan. 1860 record reciprocal visits.

10. Roach Diary, 3–10 July 1856, SHC; Penelope Eliza Howard Alderman Diary, 20 Feb. 1855, Alderman Family Papers, #4479, SHC; and Journal of Sarah Ann Gayle, Sept. 1833, Degenre Papers, TU.

11. Deborah Gray White, *Ar'n't I a Woman?: Female Slaves in the Plantation South* (New York: W. W. Norton, 1999), chapter 4; and Marie Jenkins Schwartz, *Born in Bondage: Growing Up Enslaved in the Antebellum South* (Cambridge, MA: Harvard University Press, 2000), 19.

12. A few studies have given excellent insights into the lives of yeomen and poor whites in the South, including Victoria E. Bynum, *Unruly Women: The Politics of Social and Sexual Control in the Old South* (Chapel Hill: University

of North Carolina Press, 1992); and Laura F. Edwards, *Gendered Strife and Confusion: The Political Culture of Reconstruction* (Urbana: University of Illinois Press, 1997). But because these works often rely on legal records for evidence of this largely nonliterate population, they cannot penetrate into the normal, private experiences of such women in the birthing room. Margaret Hagood, *Mothers of the South: Portraiture of the White Tenant Farm Woman* (1939; reprint, New York: Greenwood Press, 1969), provides a more intimate insight into this group, but from a very different point in time, leaving historians of the antebellum period to conjecture what had changed over this interval.

13. Anita Dwyer Withers Diary, 4 July 1863, DAS.

14. Elisabeth Muhlenfeld, *Mary Boykin Chesnut: A Biography* (Baton Rouge: Louisiana State University Press, 1981), 48; and Ross, *First Lady of the South*, 66.

15. This move towards doctors and hospital births occurred only gradually, with much of the shift occurring in the early twentieth century. By the end of the nineteenth century only half of all births were attended by physicians, but by the 1930s, 85 percent of even poor white women in North Carolina had their births attended by doctors. This figure, however, was lower in more rural areas of the Deep South, and significantly lower among black women in the South. Judy Barrett Litoff, *American Midwives, 1860 to the Present* (Westport, CT: Greenwood Press, 1978), lx; Richard Wertz and Dorothy Wertz, *Lying-In: A History of Childbirth in America* (New Haven, CT: Yale University Press, 1989), 211; and Hagood, *Mothers of the South*, 113.

16. Rev. R. Q. Mallard to Rev. C. C. Jones, 27 Apr. 1860, and Mary Jones to Charles C. Jones Jr., 7 May 1861, in Myers, *Children of Pride*, 576, 675.

17. Withers Diary, 4 July 1863, DAS; and Virginia Ingraham Burr, ed., *The Secret Eye: The Journal of Ella Gertrude Clanton Thomas, 1848–1889* (Chapel Hill: University of North Carolina Press, 1990), 164.

18. King, *Northern Woman*, 127.

19. Erika L. Murr, ed., *A Rebel Wife in Texas: The Diary and Letters of Elizabeth Scott Neblett, 1852–1864* (Baton Rouge: Louisiana State University Press, 2001), 64.

20. Elizabeth W. Allston Pringle, *Chronicles of Chicora Wood* (Boston: Christopher Publishing House, 1940), 86. See also Pease and Pease, *Family of Women*, 26.

21. Sylvia Hoffert, "Childbearing on the Trans-Mississippi Frontier, 1830–1900," *Western Historical Quarterly* (Aug. 1991): 278.

22. Martha Carolyn Mitchell, "Health and the Medical Profession in the Lower South, 1845–1860," *Journal of Southern History* 10 (Nov. 1944): 440. The

plantation mistresses may have treated as many as 70 percent of the medical cases of enslaved people. Catherine Clinton, *The Plantation Mistress: Woman's World in the Old South* (New York: Pantheon Books, 1982), 118.

23. Philip N. Racine, ed., *Piedmont Farmer: The Journals of David Golightly Harris, 1855–1870* (Knoxville: University of Tennessee Press, 1990), 115, 143, 201, 207, 235, 301. Wertz and Wertz, *Lying-In*, 47, argue that "women ceased to be midwives also because of a change in the cultural attitudes about the proper place and activity for women in society. It came to be regarded as unthinkable to confront women with the facts of medicine or to mix men and women in training, even for such an event as birth." This does not seem to have been the case among these white midwives of the middling classes.

24. George Rawick, ed., *The American Slave: A Composite Autobiography* (Westport, CT: Greenwood Press, 1972), suppl. 2, vol. 10.9, 3911; vol. 7.1, 24; see also vol. 12.1, 103.

25. Rawick, suppl. 2, vol. 7.6, 2583.

26. Rawick, vol. 7.1, 252. The reliance on a midwife rather than a doctor to attend enslaved women is typical, although the race of this midwife is not; reliance on a black midwife, or *granny*, is described in Rawick, vol. 11.7, 232 and vol. 12.2, 63. See also Todd L. Savitt, "Black Health on the Plantation: Masters, Slaves, and Physicians," in *Science and Medicine in the Old South*, ed. Ronald L. Numbers and Todd L. Savitt (Baton Rouge: Louisiana State University Press, 1989), 355.

27. Frederick Law Olmsted, *A Journey in the Back Country* (New York: Mason Brothers, 1863), 78.

28. Rawick, vol. 17, 175; and suppl. 2, vol. 6, 2324.

29. Rawick, vol. 6.1, 256; vol. 16.3, 56; suppl. 1, vol. 7.2, 373; and vol. 12.1, 143.

30. African American midwives in the South continued to serve their communities, and hold an honored role, well into the twentieth century. As late as 1940 midwives attended over three-quarters of black women's births in Mississippi, South Carolina, Arkansas, Georgia, Florida, Alabama, and Louisiana. Linda Janet Holmes, "African American Midwives in the South," in *The American Way of Birth*, ed. Pamela Eakins (Philadelphia: Temple University Press, 1986); Sharon A. Robinson, "A Historical Development of Midwifery in the Black Community: 1600–1940," *Journal of Nurse-Midwifery* 29 (July/August 1984): 247; Jacquelyn S. Litt, *Medicalized Motherhood: Perspectives from the Lives of African-American and Jewish Women* (New Brunswick, NJ: Rutgers University Press, 2000), 73; Gertrude Jacinta Fraser, *African American Midwifery in the South: Dialogues of Birth, Race, and Memory* (Cam-

bridge, MA: Harvard University Press, 1998); and Molly C. Dougherty, "Southern Lay Midwives as Ritual Specialists," in *Women in Ritual and Symbolic Roles*, ed. Judith Hoch-Smith and Anita Spring (New York: Plenum Press, 1978), 151–164.

31. Rawick, vol. 17, 175 and vol. 11.7, 21; see also suppl. 1, vol. 4.2, 442; suppl. 1, vol. 7.2, 409; and suppl. 1, vol. 8.3, 1240.

32. Burr, *Secret Eye*, 164, 274.

33. Cited in Savitt, *Medicine and Slavery*, 183.

34. Rawick, vol. 11.7, 21.

35. Schwartz, *Born in Bondage*, 44.

36. Rawick, suppl. 2, vol. 7.6, 2875 and vol. 13.4, 177; and Kate E. R. Pickard, *The Kidnapped and the Ransomed; Being the Personal Recollections of Peter Still and His Wife 'Vina,' after Forty Years of Slavery* (1856; reprint, New York: Negro Universities Press, 1968), 356–357.

37. Frances Anne Kemble, *Journal of a Residence on a Georgia Plantation in 1838–1839* (Chicago: Afro-American Press, 1969), 28.

38. Jenny Carter and Thérèse Duriez, *With Child: Birth through the Ages* (Edinburgh: Mainstream, 1986), 54; and Judith Walzer Leavitt, *Brought to Bed: Childbearing in America, 1750–1950* (New York: Oxford University Press, 1986), 117.

39. *Ladies' Repository* 21 (Oct. 1861): 624.

40. Quoted in Leavitt, "Under the Shadow of Maternity," 143.

41. Elizabeth Scott Neblett of Texas gave birth to six children between 1853 and 1871. Murr, *Rebel Wife in Texas*, 75.

42. Charles C. Jones Jr. to Rev. and Mrs. C. C. Jones, 20 Jan. 1863, in Myers, *Children of Pride*, 1015; see also pp. 538, 675, 694, 790, 1139, and 1392.

43. Jan Lewis and Kenneth A. Lockridge, "'Sally Has Been Sick': Pregnancy and Family Limitation among Virginia Gentry Women, 1780–1830," *Journal of Social History* 22 (Fall 1988): 8; and Rawick, vol. 12.2, 123. See also Adrienne Rich, *Of Woman Born: Motherhood as Experience and Institution* (New York: Bantam Books, 1977), 152.

44. Martin S. Pernick, *A Calculus of Suffering: Pain, Professionalism, and Anesthesia in Nineteenth-Century America* (New York: Columbia University Press, 1985), 46; and Donald Caton, *What a Blessing She Had Chloroform: The Medical and Social Response to the Pain of Childbirth from 1800 to the Present* (New Haven, CT: Yale University Press, 1999), 21, 110. See also Elizabeth D. Clark, "'The Sacred Rights of the Weak': Pain, Sympathy, and the Culture of Individual Rights in Antebellum America," *Journal of American History* 82 (Sept. 1995): 472, 473.

45. Burr, *Secret Eye*, 215.

46. A British accoucheur held that "a consideration of their unimpaired constitutions and less exquisite feelings will likewise discover to us the reasons why the lower orders of women have more easy and favorable births, than those who live in affluence." He blamed this condition on the overindulgence of the upper classes. Quoted in Judith Schneid Lewis, *In the Family Way: Childbearing in the British Aristocracy, 1760–1860* (New Brunswick, NJ: Rutgers University Press, 1986), 155. Similar attitudes prevailed in the South toward blacks and natives, as well as poor women; see, for example, Mrs. Henry Rowe Schoolcraft, *Plantation Life: The Narratives of Mrs. Henry Rowe Schoolcraft* (1852–1860; reprint, New York: Negro Universities Press, 1969), 114. Martha Carolyn Mitchell points out the statistical inaccuracy of these assumptions in "Health and the Medical Profession," 434.

47. Lewis O. Saum, "Death in the Popular Mind of Pre–Civil War America," *American Quarterly* 26 (Dec. 1974): 477. Between 95 and 99 percent of births occurred without substantial danger to either mother or child. The 1850 census shows that death in childbed accounted for between 5.4 and 3.8 percent of white women's deaths. Statistics, however, are notoriously unreliable for this period and varied greatly by region. Marilyn Culpepper estimates that 1 out of every 154 live births claimed the life of the mother. Erika Murr puts that figure at 1 in 25 for southern women. In terms of the present volume, women's perceptions of the likelihood of death are more important than its statistical probability. Irvine Loudon, *Death in Childbirth: An International Study of Maternal Care and Maternal Mortality, 1800–1950* (Oxford: Clarendon Press, 1992), 340; Jacqueline S. Reiner, *From Virtue to Character: American Childhood, 1775–1850* (New York: Twayne, 1996), 225 n. 33; Marilyn Mayer Culpepper, *All Things Altered: Women in the Wake of Civil War and Reconstruction* (Jefferson, NC: McFarland, 2002), 219; and Murr, *Rebel Wife in Texas*, 9.

48. Burr, *Secret Eye*, 258.

49. Madaline Selima Edwards Journal, 1844, Folder 16, and Writing Book, 10 Nov. 1844, Folder 15, Charles William Bradbury Papers, #3011, SHC. See also Joan E. Cashin, *Our Common Affairs: Texts from Women in the Old South* (Baltimore: Johns Hopkins University Press, 1996), 148.

50. Maria Inskeep to Fanny Hampton, 22 January 1825, Fanny Leverich Eshleman Craig Collection, TU; and Mrs. R. Singleton to Marion and Angelica Singleton, 8 July 1830, 26 July 1830, and 19 Sept. 1830, Singleton Family Papers, LC.

51. S. Cassell to her sister, 9 Sept. 1861, Yonce Family Papers, DU; and Roach Diary, 31 Aug. 1856, SHC.

52. Theodore Rosengarten, ed., *Tombee: Portrait of a Cotton Planter; with The Journal of Thomas B. Chaplin* (New York: William Morrow, 1986), 569.

53. Andrew Cornish to John Cornish, 19 Sept. 1850, John Hamilton Cornish Papers, DU. John Cornish was an Episcopal minister in Aiken, SC; his brother Andrew was also a minister, in Pendleton, SC.

54. Charles C. Jones Jr. to Rev. C. C. Jones, 25 June to 4 July 1861, in Myers, *Children of Pride*, 701–715; and Edwin Adams Davis, ed., *Plantation Life in the Florida Parishes of Louisiana, 1836-1846; As Reflected in the Diary of Bennet H. Barrow* (New York: Columbia University Press, 1943), 362–367.

55. Roach Diaries, 29 Jan. 1854, 2 Aug. 1855, 2 Sept. 1857, 10 Aug. 1858, and 21 Aug. 1858, SHC.

56. King, *Northern Woman*, 97–99. See also Wilma King, "The Mistress and Her Maids: White and Black Women in a Louisiana Household, 1858–1868," in *Discovering the Women in Slavery: Emancipating Perspectives on the American Past*, ed. Patricia Morton (Athens: University of Georgia Press, 1996), 86, in which King suggests that pregnancy "created no special bonds between women." While that is certainly true in this case, birth did offer commonality for other women across status boundaries.

57. Burr, *Secret Eye*, 277.

58. Diary of Mary Jones and Mary Jones Mallard, 4 Jan. 1865, Charles Colcock Jones Papers, #154, TU.

59. Emma LeConte Diary, 1 Jan. 1865, DAS.

60. John Gunn, M.D., *Gunn's New Domestic Physician; or, Home Book of Health* (Cincinnati: Moore, Wilstach, Keys, 1859), 426.

61. Genteel northern and southern women followed a similar pattern, typically convalescing for about a month in the 1850s. Sylvia D. Hoffert, *Private Matters: Attitudes toward Childbearing and Infant Nurture in the Urban North* (Urbana: University of Illinois Press, 1989), 117.

62. Sarah Lois Wadley Diary, 6 Apr. to 11 May 1860, DAS; Beth G. Crabtree and James W. Patton, eds., *"Journal of a Secesh Lady": The Diary of Catherine Ann Devereux Edmondston, 1860-1866* (Raleigh: North Carolina Division of Archives and History, 1979), 105–107; F. M. B. to Susan Webb, 19 Sept. 1859, Webb Family Papers, #1900, SHC; and King, *Northern Woman*, 64. See also Brady, *George Washington's Beautiful Nelly*, 184.

63. Roach Diary, 14 May 1859, SHC.

64. Racine, *Piedmont Farmer*, 86–87.

65. Meta Morris Grimball Diary, 11 July 1861, DAS.

66. Susan Dabney Smedes, *A Southern Planter*, 4th ed. (New York: James Pott, 1890), 78.

67. Wadley Diary, 19 July 1864, DAS.

68. Racine, *Piedmont Farmer*, 50–57.

69. Rawick, vol. 2.2, 68.

70. Rawick, vol. 6.2, 166.

71. Rawick, vol. 11.8, 215 and suppl. 1, vol. 10, 2336.

72. See, for example, Rawick, vol. 5.4, 23; suppl. 2, vol. 3.2, 642–3; suppl. 2, vol. 6, 2298; and suppl. 2, vol. 9, 3541.

73. Rawick, vol. 14, 447.

74. Kemble, *Journal of a Residence*, 182–183; see also pp. 174, 245, 313. A report from North Carolina in the 1830s asserted: "They [enslaved women] are generally allowed four weeks after the birth of a child, before they are compelled to go into the field, they then take the child with them, attended sometimes by a little girl or boy, from the age of 4 to 6 . . . ." Quoted in Arthur W. Calhoun, *From Independence through the Civil War*, vol. 2 of *A Social History of the American Family, from Colonial Times to the Present* (New York: Barnes & Noble, 1945), 275.

75. Kemble, *Journal of a Residence*, 183.

76. See Sally McMillen, *Southern Women: Black and White in the Old South* (Arlington Heights, IL: Harlan Davidson, 1992), 63; Schwartz, *Born in Bondage*, 56, 60; and John Campbell, "Work, Pregnancy, and Infant Mortality among Southern Slaves," *Journal of Interdisciplinary History* 14, no. 4 (Spring 1984): 806.

77. Carey North Pettigrew (C. N. P.) to Minnie North, 10 Feb. 1855 and C. N. P. to "Lucia," 8 Feb. 1855, Folder 180, and C. N. P. to Louise North, 1 Mar. 1855, Folder 181, Pettigrew Family Papers, #592, SHC.

78. Carey North Pettigrew to Minnie North, 10 Feb. 1855, SHC; Murr, *Rebel Wife in Texas*, 424; Myers, *Children of Pride*, 675; Gabriela Huger to Marion Deveaux, 7 Oct. 1843, Singleton Family Papers, LC; Rawick, vol. 7.1, 24; and Brady, *George Washington's Beautiful Nelly*, 40. Susan Klepp discusses the changes in the language of birth around the time of the American Revolution. She argues that "the new vocabulary proclaimed a selfless, domestic womanhood while allowing expanded choices and a limitation of traditional obligation." Although I find the language choices of antebellum southerners less liberated than she suggests, I concur with her thesis that broader social concerns shape and are reflected in the language of birth. Klepp, "Revolutionary Bodies: Women and the Fertility Transition in the Mid-Atlantic Region, 1760–1820," *Journal of American History* 85 (Dec. 1998): 911.

79. "The Mutual Re-Action between Thought and Language," *Southern Planter* (Apr. 1861): 255. For discussions of the links between language, mean-

ing, and social structure, see Carroll Smith-Rosenberg, "Writing History: Language, Class, and Gender," in *Feminist Studies/Critical Studies*, ed. Teresa de Lauretis (Bloomington: Indiana University Press, 1986), 32; and Alexandra Dundas Todd and Sue Fisher, eds., *Gender and Discourse: The Power of Talk* (Norwood, NJ: Ablex, 1988), 6–9. For the uses of language in a southern context, see Drew Gilpin Faust, "The Rhetoric and Ritual of Agriculture in Antebellum South Carolina," *Journal of Southern History* 45 (Nov. 1979): 541; and Steven M. Stowe, "The Rhetoric of Authority: The Making of Social Values in Planter Family Correspondence," *Journal of American History* 73 (Mar. 1987): 918.

80. Burr, *Secret Eye*, 135.

81. Elizabeth F. Perry Diary, 28 Mar. 1838, #1642-z, SHC.

82. Alderman Diary, 16 Nov. 1851, SHC.

83. Murr, *Rebel Wife in Texas*, 420.

84. Nagueyalti Warren and Sally Wolff, eds., introduction to *Southern Mothers: Facts and Fictions in Southern Women's Writing* (Baton Rouge: Louisiana State University Press, 1999), 8; Wertz and Wertz, *Lying-In*, 79, suggest that the term "confinement" reflected the "shame and impropriety of exposure during pregnancy." I believe that for most women the sense of confinement had more to do with physical debilities and the restrictions of the social role than with modesty or shame.

85. Rawick, vol. 11.8, 170.

86. Ada Sterling, ed., *A Belle of the Fifties: Memoirs of Mrs. Clay of Alabama; Covering Social and Political Life in Washington and the South, 1853–1866* (New York: Da Capo Press, 1969), 96.

87. Roach Diary, 26 June 1855, SHC; Perry Diary, 14 Mar. 1838, SHC; and Wadley Diary, 13 Dec. 1861 and 15 Oct. 1862, DAS. Even in her sickbed, recovering from typhoid fever, Ellen Louis Power took time to record the birth of a son to a Mrs. Davis. Ellen Louis Power Diary, 1 Jan. 1862, #1459-z, SHC.

88. Cousin Anna to Mary Eliza Tillery, 1 Sept. 1847, Folder 2, Edward Conigland Papers, #859, SHC.

89. Mary E. Robarts to Rev. C. C. Jones, 26 Apr. 1858, in Myers, *Children of Pride*, 411 (my emphasis).

90. Harrison, *Best Companions*, 423; and Sally W. Taylor to Marion Singleton Deveaux, ca. 1837, Singleton Family Papers, LC. Such shared communication was, of course, not unique to the South. For example, Marilyn Ferris Motz, in *True Sisterhood: Michigan Women and Their Kin, 1820–1920* (Albany: State University of New York Press, 1983), 87–89, found a similar pattern in the lives of the women she studied.

91. Mary Bethell Diary, 3 Mar. to 17 May 1862, DAS.

92. Mary Jones to Mary S. Mallard, 15 May 1867 and 24 June 1867, in Myers, *Children of Pride*, 1381, 1385.

93. Webb, *Mistress of Evergreen Plantation*, 95, 102, 111, 194, 202, 224–225.

94. Webb, *Mistress of Evergreen Plantation*, 103–104.

95. Burr, *Secret Eye*, 138, 141.

96. Bertram Wyatt-Brown, *The Shaping of Southern Culture: Honor, Grace, and War, 1760s-1880s* (Chapel Hill: University of North Carolina Press, 2001), 33. Wyatt-Brown is referring to revolutionary rhetoric, but this observation is equally applicable to the language of birth. See also Murray Edelman, afterward to *Language, Symbolism, and Politics* (Boulder, CO: Westview Press, 1992), 307.

Chapter Four: Motherhood

1. Patricia Brady, ed., *George Washington's Beautiful Nelly: The Letters of Eleanor Parke Custis Lewis to Elizabeth Bordley Gibson, 1794–1851* (Columbia: University of South Carolina Press, 1991), 62; Journal of Sarah Ann Gayle, 27 Sept. 1833, Denegre Papers, #662, TU; and Beth G. Crabtree and James W. Patton, eds., *"Journal of a Secesh Lady": The Diary of Catherine Ann Devereux Edmondston, 1860–1866* (Raleigh: North Carolina Division of Archives and History, 1979), 199.

2. Sheila Kitzinger, *Ourselves as Mothers: The Universal Experience of Motherhood* (Reading, MA: Addison-Wesley, 1995), 233; and Joan E. Cashin, "The Structure of Antebellum Planter Families: 'The Ties that Bound Us Was Strong,'" *Journal of Southern History* 56 (Feb. 1990): 61, 68.

3. "Loose Thoughts on the Training of Children," *Southern Ladies' Book* 1 (Apr. 1840): 246–247. See also John C. Gunn, M.D., *Gunn's New Domestic Physician; or, Home Book of Health* (Cincinnati: Moore, Wilstach, Keys, 1859), 496.

4. Brady, *George Washington's Beautiful Nelly*, 191; and Elizabeth Allston Pringle, *Chronicle of Chicora Wood* (Boston: Christopher Publishing House, 1940), 82.

5. Mahala P. H. Roach Diary, 23 July 1856, Roach-Eggleston Family Papers, #2614, SHC. See also Wilma King, ed., *A Northern Woman in the Plantation South: Letters of Tryphena Blanche Holder Fox, 1856–1876* (Columbia: University of South Carolina Press, 1993), 129.

6. Marie Jenkins Schwartz, *Born in Bondage: Growing Up Enslaved in the Antebellum South* (Cambridge, MA: Harvard University Press, 2000), 98.

7. George Rawick, ed., *The American Slave: A Composite Autobiography* (Westport, CT: Greenwood Press, 1972), suppl. 2, vol. 8, 3332 and suppl. 1, vol. 8, 1215.

8. Mrs. Henry Rowe Schoolcraft, *Plantation Life: The Narratives of Mrs. Henry Rowe Schoolcraft* (1852–1860; reprint, New York: Negro Universities Press, 1969), 38; and Marie Jenkins Schwartz, "'At Noon, Oh How I Ran': Breastfeeding and Weaning on Plantation and Farm in Antebellum Virginia and Alabama," in *Discovering the Women in Slavery: Emancipating Perspectives on the American Past,* ed. Patricia Morton (Athens: University of Georgia Press, 1996), 242.

9. Duncan Clinch Heyward, *Seed of Madagascar* (Chapel Hill: University of North Carolina Press, 1937), 102, 177. See also John Q. Anderson, ed., *Brokenburn: The Journal of Kate Stone, 1861–1868* (Baton Rouge: Louisiana State University Press, 1972), 6.

10. Edmund Kirke, *Among the Pines; or, South in Secession Times*, 7th ed. (New York: J. R. Gilmore, 1862), 209.

11. Emily P. Burke, *Reminiscences of Georgia* (Oberlin, OH: James M. Fitch, 1850), 234.

12. Fredrika Bremer, *The Homes of the New World; Impressions of America,* trans. Mary Howitt (New York: Harper & Bros., 1854), vol. 2, 449.

13. Rawick, vol. 2.1, 119; for other descriptions of similar care patterns see vol. 5.3, 35 and 56; suppl. 1, vol. 1, 449; suppl. 1, vol. 7, 349; and suppl. 1, vol. 8, 1058.

14. Rawick, vol. 6.1, 429. See also vol. 4.1, 76; vol. 19, 17; and suppl. 2, vol. 5, 1733. In her memoirs of her time on her husband's Georgia plantation, Fannie Kemble also notes that the caregivers for enslaved infants were themselves four to ten years of age. Frances Anne Kemble, *Journal of a Residence on a Georgia Plantation in 1838–1839* (Chicago: Afro-American Press, 1969), 31.

15. Rawick, vol. 4.1, 205; vol. 6.1, 426; vol. 7.2, 13; and vol. 12.2, 93.

16. Rawick, vol. 6.1, 87; see also suppl. 1, vol. 6.1, 248; and suppl. 1, vol. 8.3, 6899.

17. Kate E. R. Pickard, *The Kidnapped and the Ransomed; Being the Personal Recollections of Peter Still and His Wife 'Vina,' after Forty Years of Slavery* (1856; reprint, New York: Negro Universities Press, 1968), 163–165. See also Rawick, suppl. 1, vol. 5.1, 65.

18. Rawick, vol. 14, 88; see also suppl. 1, vol. 8.3, 855.

19. C. Richard King, ed., *A Victorian Lady on the Texas Frontier: The Journal of Ann Raney Coleman* (Norman: University of Oklahoma Press, 1971), 103.

20. Rawick, vol. 12.1, 174.

21. Allie Bayne Windham Webb, ed., *Mistress of Evergreen Plantation: Rachel O'Connor's Legacy of Letters, 1823–1845* (Albany: State University of New York Press, 1983), 242, 149; see also p. 49.

22. Virginia Ingraham Burr, ed., *The Secret Eye: The Journal of Ella Gertrude Clanton Thomas, 1848–1889* (Chapel Hill: University of North Carolina Press, 1990), 193.

23. Rawick, vol. 4.1, 205.

24. Quoted in Arthur W. Calhoun, *From Independence through the Civil War*, vol. 2 of *A Social History of the American Family, from Colonial Times to the Present* (New York: Barnes & Noble, 1945), 22. See also Laura F. Edwards, *Scarlett Doesn't Live Here Anymore: Southern Women in the Civil War Era* (Urbana: University of Illinois Press, 2000), 40. The poor white women Margaret Hagood interviewed sixty years after emancipation still considered this a reward. Many felt they could stop laboring in the fields when they had "enough children of full working age who, the mother feels, 'take her place.'" Hagood, *Mothers of the South: Portraiture of the White Tenant Farm Woman* (1939; reprint, New York: Greenwood Press, 1969), 87.

25. Kirke, *Among the Pines*, 210.

26. Kirke, *Among the Pines*, 169.

27. Bremer, *Homes of the New World*, vol. 2, 491 (my emphasis).

28. Evelyn Nakano Glenn, "Social Constructions of Mothering: A Thematic Overview," in *Mothering: Ideology, Experience, and Agency*, ed. Evelyn Nakano Glenn, Grace Cheng, and Linda Rennie Forcey (New York: Routledge, 1994), 7.

29. Anita Dwyer Withers Diary, 6 May 1860 and 19–23 Aug. 1860, DAS.

30. Roach Diary, 11 Dec. 1857, SHC.

31. Ada Sterling, ed., *A Belle of the Fifties: Memoirs of Mrs. Clay of Alabama; Covering Social and Political Life in Washington and the South, 1853–1866* (New York: Da Capo Press, 1969), 56.

32. Roach Diaries, 31 Jan. 1857, 23 July 1857, and 7 Nov. 1857, SHC.

33. Eliza Cope Harrison, ed., *Best Companions: Letters of Eliza Middleton Fisher and Her Mother, Mary Hering Middleton, from Charleston, Philadelphia, and Newport, 1839–1846* (Columbia: University of South Carolina Press, 2001), 416.

34. Miriam Badger Hilliard Diary (transcript), 4 Feb. 1850, M1031, TU. Mrs. Polk was the former Frances Ann Deveraux, wife of Bishop Leonidas Polk.

35. Harrison, *Best Companions*, 248; and Roach Diaries, 27 Dec. 1856, 7 Feb. 1857, and 9 Nov. 1857, SHC.

36. Caroline Lee Hentz, *The Planter's Northern Bride* (1854; reprint, Chapel Hill: University of North Carolina Press, 1970), 533, 402; see also pp. 205 and 440.

37. Rev. C. C. Jones to Mary Jones Mallard, 9 Aug. 1861, in Robert Manson Myers, ed., *The Children of Pride: A True Story of Georgia and the Civil War*

(New Haven, CT: Yale University Press, 1972), 735. A similar situation is described in the letters of the Singleton family of South Carolina. See especially Mrs. Rebecca Singleton to Marion and Angelica Singleton, 7 Dec. 1830, Singleton Family Papers, LC.

38. Stephanie Cole, "A White Woman, of Middle Age, Would be Preferred: Children's Nurses in the Old South," in *Neither Lady nor Slave: Working Women of the Old South*, ed. Susanna Delfino and Michele Gillespie (Chapel Hill: University of North Carolina Press, 2002), 76.

39. Jane H. Pease and William H. Pease, *A Family of Women: The Carolina Petigrus in Peace and War* (Chapel Hill: University of North Carolina Press, 1999), 103, 122; and Pringle, *Chronicle of Chicora Wood*, 24. See also Charles M. McGee and Ernest M. Lander, eds., *A Rebel Came Home: The Diary and Letters of Floride Clemson, 1863–1866* (Columbia: University of South Carolina Press, 1989), 5.

40. Frederick Law Olmsted, *Journeys and Explorations in the Cotton Kingdom: A Traveller's Observation on Cotton and Slavery in the American Slave States* (London: Sampson Low, Son, 1861), vol. 2, 166.

41. Mary Jones to Rev. C. C. Jones, 25 Nov. 1859, in Myers, *Children of Pride*, 542. See also Brady, *George Washington's Beautiful Nelly*, 237.

42. Anya Jabour, "Between Mistress and Slave: Elizabeth Wirt's White Housekeepers, 1808–1825," in *Beyond Image and Convention: Explorations in Southern Women's History*, ed. Janet L. Coryell, Martha H. Swain, Sandra Gioia Treadway, and Elizabeth Hayes Turner (Columbia: University of Missouri Press, 1998), 28–52. Although Jabour focuses on housekeepers, the chapter suggests some of the contentions which could arise between slaveholding women and the white women hired to care for their children.

43. G. W. Henry, *Tell Tale Rag, and Popular Sins of the Day* (Oneida, NY: published and bound by the author, 1861), vol. 1, 16.

44. Susan Dabney Smedes, *A Southern Planter* (New York: James Pott, 1890), 108. See also Pringle, *Chronicle of Chicora Wood*, 90.

45. Deborah Gray White, *Ar'n't I a Woman?: Female Slaves in the Plantation South* (New York: W. W. Norton, 1999).

46. Rawick, vol. 6.1, 72.

47. Elizabeth F. Perry Diary, 6 June 1848, #1642-z, SHC.

48. Rawick, vol. 6.2, 13.

49. Rawick, vol. 7.1, 138; see also vol. 4.1, 249; vol. 9.3, 345; and suppl. 1, vol. 12, 169.

50. Quoted in Orville Vernon Burton, *In My Father's House Are Many Mansions: Family and Community in Edgefield, South Carolina* (Chapel Hill: University of North Carolina Press, 1985), 164. See also Drew Gilpin Faust,

"Culture, Conflict, and Community: The Meaning of Power on an Ante-Bellum Plantation," *Journal of Social History* 14 (Fall 1980): 83–97.

51. Thomas R. R. Cobb, *An Inquiry into the Law of Negro Slavery in the United States of America* (1858; reprint, New York: Negro Universities Press, 1968), ccxx.

52. John Hammond Moore, ed., *The Plantation Mistress on the Eve of the Civil War: The Diary of Keziah Goodwyn Hopkins Brevard, 1860–1861* (Columbia: University of South Carolina Press, 1993), 38, 50.

53. Eliza Frances Andrews, *The War-Time Journal of a Georgia Girl, 1864–1865* (New York: D. Appleton, 1908), 179.

54. Webb, *Mistress of Evergreen Plantation*, 185, 204, 247.

55. Rawick, suppl. 1, vol. 9.4, 1732.

56. Rawick, vol. 5.4, 144; suppl. 2, vol. 7, 2755; and vol. 3.3, 2.

57. Rawick, suppl. 1, vol. 1, 144; suppl. 2, vol. 8, 3265; see also vol. 5.4, 30; suppl. 1, vol. 5.2, 461; and suppl. 1, vol. 10, 2364.

58. Quoted in Thelma Jennings, "'Us Colored Women Had to Go Through Plenty': Sexual Exploitation of African-American Slave Women," *Journal of Women's History* 1 (Winter 1990): 59.

59. Evidence of the various "involvements" or "interferences" may be found in the narratives of ex-slaves. See Rawick, vol. 6.2, 76; vol. 17, 213; vol. 18, 117; suppl. 1, vol. 3, 42; and suppl. 1, vol. 7, 341.

60. Rawick, suppl. 1, vol. 1, 267. A similar Sunday ritual is described in Virginia V. Clayton, *White and Black under the Old Regime* (1899; reprint, Freeport, NY: Books for Libraries Press, 1970), 58.

61. Kemble, *Journal of a Residence*, 64.

62. Gunn, *Gunn's New Domestic Physician*, 481; James Ewell, *The Planter's and Mariner's Medical Companion* (Philadelphia: printed by John Bioren, 1807), 265–266; William P. Dewees, *A Compendious System of Midwifery, Chiefly Designed to Facilitate the Inquiries of Those Who May Be Pursuing This Branch of Study*, 4th ed. (Philadelphia: Carey & Lea, 1830), 203; Sally McMillen, "Mothers' Sacred Duty: Breast-Feeding Patterns among Middle- and Upper-Class Women in the Antebellum South," *Journal of Southern History* 51 (Aug. 1985): 337, 342; and Schwartz, *Born in Bondage*, 67. See also Marylynn Salmon, "The Cultural Significance of Breastfeeding and Infant Care in Early Modern England and America," *Journal of Social History* 28 (1994): 254.

63. Harrison, *Best Companions*, 238, 263, 240. Geography and class-position may have affected Mary Middleton's attitude. She raised her own children in South Carolina and in Europe, where the use of a wet-nurse and/or night-

nurse was more common. See also Paula A. Treckel, "Breastfeeding and Maternal Sexuality in Colonial America," *Journal of Interdisciplinary History* 20 (Summer 1989): 48.

64. Maria Inskeep to Fanny Hampton, 20 Mar. 1848, Fanny Leverich Eshleman Craig Collection, #225, TU; and Caroline North Pettigrew to Jane North, 1 Mar. 1855, Pettigrew Family Papers, #592, SHC.

65. Anita Dwyer Withers Diary, 25 Feb. 1864, DAS; Harrison, *Best Companions*, 202; and Penelope Eliza Howard Alderman Diary, 23 Aug. 1854 and 18 Aug. 1856, Alderman Family Papers, #4479, SHC. See also Sarah Wadley on her mother weaning her baby brother, Sarah Lois Wadley Diary, 2 Nov. 1861, DAS.

66. Anne Webb to Anne Moore, 9 Apr. 1840, Webb Family Papers, #1900, SHC. See also McMillen, "Mother's Sacred Duty," 349–350.

67. Jane Amelia Petigru, quoted in Pease and Pease, *A Family of Women*, 28; Burr, *Secret Eye*, 218. A discussion of southern views on using a wet-nurse may be found in Janet Golden, *A Social History of Wet Nursing in America: From Breast to Bottle* (Cambridge: Cambridge University Press, 1996), 25–27, 72–74.

68. Mrs. R. Singleton to Marion and Angelica Singleton, 19 Sept. 1830 and 7 Dec. 1830, Singleton Family Papers, LC.

69. Mary Jones to Dr. Joseph Jones, 13 May 1858, in Myers, *Children of Pride*, 415. For a discussion of a white woman's motivation for nursing black infants, see McMillen, "Mother's Sacred Duty," 345; and William Hampton Adams, "Health and Medical Care on Antebellum Southern Plantations," *Plantation Society* 2 (May 1989): 272.

70. Smedes, *Southern Planter*, 70.

71. Rawick, vol. 8.1, 241.

72. Rawick, vol. 8.1, 113 and vol. 9.4, 244.

73. McMillen, "Mother's Sacred Duty," 336.

74. Kemble, *Journal of a Residence*, 23.

75. McMillen, "Mother's Sacred Duty," 353.

76. Henry, *Tell Tale Rag*, 15–16. See also Carol Mossman, *Politics and Narratives of Birth: Gynocolonization from Rousseau to Zola* (Cambridge: Cambridge University Press, 1993), 159.

77. Caroline Gilman, *Recollections of a Southern Matron* (New York: Harper & Brothers, 1838), 16; and Smedes, *Southern Planter*, 20, 86.

78. Heyward, *Seed of Madagascar*, 188.

79. Withers Diary, 3 Sept. 1863, 29 Sept. 1863, 1 Oct. 1863, 1 Nov. 1863, and 15 Mar. 1864, DAS.

80. Erika L. Murr, ed., *A Rebel Wife in Texas: The Diary and Letters of Elizabeth Scott Neblett, 1852–1864* (Baton Rouge: Louisiana State University Press, 2001), 192, 18 [for background and age].

81. King, *Victorian Lady*, 77.

82. Burr, *Secret Eye*, 271; Edwin Adams Davis, ed., *Plantation Life in the Florida Parishes of Louisiana, 1836–1846; As Reflected in the Diary of Bennet H. Barrow* (New York: Columbia University Press, 1943), 113; Journal of Sarah Ann Gayle, 7 Apr. 1835, Denegre Papers, #662, TU; and Rev. C. C. Jones to Charles C. Jones Jr., 24 Mar. 1862, in Myers, *Children of Pride*, 865. See also Cole, "A White Woman," 80–82.

83. Caroline Merrick, *Old Times in Dixie Land: A Southern Matron's Memories* (New York: Grafton Press, 1901), 20–22.

84. Glenn, "Social Constructions of Mothering," 7.

85. The actual number of women designated as mammies, or child nurses, was relatively small. On large plantations one woman might find herself entirely devoted to the care of white children, while on smaller plantations or in urban households mammies would almost certainly be expected to cook or clean while tending small children. On farms with only a few slaves, any provision of child-care would be ad hoc, secondary to laboring in the field. In such situations, it was perhaps more likely that the white mistress would tend to children, both black and white, so enslaved women could do more physically demanding work. Both White, *Ar'n't I a Woman?*, 49–55, and the Roach Diary, 31 Jan. 1857 and 7 Nov. 1857, SHC, suggest how a small household of women shifted the jobs of cleaning, caregiving, and cooking to meet the demands of the household. For references to white women being the principal caregivers, see Rawick, vol. 8.1, 1; vol. 14, 88; suppl. 1, vol. 5.2, 361; and suppl. 1, vol. 8.3, 924.

86. Rawick, vol. 5.4, 166; see also vol. 11.7, 201; vol. 12.1, 64; and vol. 16.6, 67.

87. Elizabeth Keckley, *Behind the Scenes: Thirty Years a Slave and Four Years in the White House* (New York: Arno Press and New York Times, 1968), 19–20.

88. Rawick, vol. 8.1, 301.

89. Rawick, vol. 6.2, 193.

90. Pickard, *Kidnapped and the Ransomed*, 122.

91. Rawick, suppl. 1, vol. 5.1, 194.

92. Mary H. Eastman, *Aunt Phillis's Cabin; or, Southern Life As It Is* (Philadelphia: Lippincott, Grambo, 1852), 43–44.

93. Burr, *Secret Eye*, 274.

94. Andrews, *War-Time Journal*, 252.

95. Crabtree and Patton, "*Journal of a Secesh Lady*," 463.

Chapter Five: Fatherhood and the Southern Patriarchy

1. Jane H. Pease and William H. Pease, *A Family of Women: The Carolina Petigrus in Peace and War* (Chapel Hill: University of North Carolina Press, 1999), 103–104.

2. Judith Schneid Lewis, *In the Family Way: Childbearing in the British Aristocracy, 1760–1860* (New Brunswick, NJ: Rutgers University Press, 1986), 61; and Adrienne Rich, *Of Woman Born: Motherhood as Experience and Institution* (New York: Bantam Books, 1977), 193. Overt preferences for male infants still exist in strongly patriarchal societies such as those in India and Korea. See, for example, Sheila Kitzinger, *Rediscovering Birth* (New York: Pocket Books, 2000), 31–33; and Eun-Shils Kim, "Female Gender Subjectivity Constructed by 'Son-Birth': Need for Feminisms?" *Asian Journal of Women's Studies* 1 (1995): 33–57.

3. Orville Vernon Burton, *In My Father's House Are Many Mansions: Family and Community in Edgefield, South Carolina* (Chapel Hill: University of North Carolina Press, 1985), 101; Laura F. Edwards, *Scarlett Doesn't Live Here Anymore: Southern Women in the Civil War Era* (Urbana: University of Illinois Press, 2000), 25; Michael P. Johnson, "Planters and Patriarchy: Charleston, 1800–1860," *Journal of Southern History* 46 (1980): 64; and Stephanie McCurry, "Producing Dependence: Women, Work, and Yeomen Households in Low-Country South Carolina," in *Neither Lady nor Slave: Working Women of the Old South*, ed. Susanna Delfino and Michele Gillespie (Chapel Hill: University of North Carolina Press, 2002), 62.

4. Caroline North Pettigrew to Charles Pettigrew, 16 June 1854, Folder 172, Pettigrew Family Papers, #592, SHC.

5. James A. Smith to Levi Lewis, 16 May 1834, Levi Lewis Papers, DU.

6. Elizabeth F. Perry Diary, 11 Feb. 1838, #1642-z, SHC; Burton, *In My Father's House*, 102; Erika L. Murr, ed., *A Rebel Wife in Texas: The Diary and Letters of Elizabeth Scott Neblett, 1852–1864* (Baton Rouge: Louisiana State University Press, 2001), 87; and Joan E. Cashin, *Our Common Affairs: Texts from Women in the Old South* (Baltimore: Johns Hopkins University Press, 1996), 64.

7. Eliza Cope Harrison, ed., *Best Companions: Letters of Eliza Middleton Fisher and Her Mother, Mary Hering Middleton, from Charleston, Philadelphia, and Newport, 1839–1846* (Columbia: University of South Carolina Press, 2001), 174, 197, 228, 372.

8. Thomas Kennedy to Nancy Kennedy, 12 Mar. 1833 and 14 Apr. 1833, Kennedy, Moore, and Southgate Papers, SHC.

9. Fredrika Bremer, *The Homes of the New World; Impressions of America*, trans. Mary Howitt (New York: Harper & Bros., 1854), vol. 1, 337. See also John

Q. Anderson, ed., *Brokenburn: The Journal of Kate Stone, 1861–1868* (Baton Rouge: Louisiana State University Press, 1972), 157.

10. Margaret Law Callcott, ed., *Mistress of Riversdale: The Plantation Letters of Rosalie Stier Calvert, 1795–1821* (Baltimore: Johns Hopkins University Press, 1991), 254.

11. Murr, *Rebel Wife in Texas*, 116, 150, 70.

12. See, for example, Kate E. R. Pickard, *The Kidnapped and the Ransomed: Being the Personal Recollections of Peter Still and His Wife 'Vina,' after Forty Years of Slavery* (1856; reprint, New York: Negro Universities Press, 1968), 121; Richard Hildreth, *The Slave; or, Memoirs of Archy Moore* (1836; reprint, Upper Saddle River, NJ: Gregg Press, 1968), vol. 2, 48; and Harriet A. Jacobs, *Incidents in the Life of a Slave Girl*, ed. and with an intro. by Jean Fagan Yellin, (Cambridge, MA: Harvard University Press, 1987), 77.

13. George Rawick, ed., *The American Slave: A Composite Autobiography* (Westport, CT: Greenwood Press, 1972), vol. 6.1, 87; vol. 6.1, 216; suppl. 2, vol. 10, 3959; and vol. 8.2, 42. Free black communities may prove the exception to the rule on sex preferences. Many such men adopted normative gender roles and signs of patriarchal authority as a claim to respectability. James Oliver Horton, "Freedom's Yoke: Gender Conventions among Antebellum Free Blacks," *Feminist Studies* 12 (1986): 55, 70.

14. "The Negro Race," *Southern Literary Messenger* 31 (July 1860): 3; and Hon. A. H. Stephens, "African Slavery, the Corner-Stone of the Southern Confederacy," delivered at the Atheneum, Savannah, 22 Mar. 1861, reprinted in *Echoes from the South, Comprising the Most Important Speeches, Proclamations, and Public Acts Emanating from the South During the Late War* (1866; reprint, Westport, CT: Negro Universities Press, 1970), 88–89.

15. Hildreth, *The Slave*, vol. 1, 19. Walter Johnson, in "The Slave Trader, the White Slave, and the Politics of Racial Determination in the 1850s," *Journal of American History* (June 2000): 13–38, suggests some of the complexities of using the rhetoric of blood to determine racial identity and status.

16. Elizabeth Keckley, *Behind the Scenes: Thirty Years a Slave and Four Years in the White House* (New York: Arno Press and New York Times, 1968), 47.

17. "Slavery in the Southern States," *Southern Quarterly Review* (Oct. 1845): 352.

18. Interrelationships between white women and black men, while much rarer, did exist. Such relationships were even more problematic to southern society, both because they challenged the ideal of white womanhood and because any offspring would be legally free. Indeed, it was so troubling that most southern social commentators were silent on the subject. See Martha Hodes, *White*

Women, Black Men: Illicit Sex in the Nineteenth-Century South (New Haven, CT: Yale University Press, 1997).

19. Judge Chancellor Harper, "Memoir on Slavery," *Southern Literary Journal and Magazine of Arts* (Feb. 1838): 96, 97.

20. Thomas R. R. Cobb, *An Inquiry into the Law of Negro Slavery in the United States of America* (1858; reprint, New York: Negro Universities Press, 1968), ccxix.

21. Quoted in Burton, *In My Father's House*, 187.

22. Jacobs, *Incidents in the Life*, 28. For fictionalized accounts of forced immodesty and slaveholders' lasciviousness directed toward black women, see Martha Griffith, *Autobiography of a Female Slave* (1857; reprint, New York: Negro Universities Press, 1969), 48; and Pickard, *Kidnapped and the Ransomed*, 167.

23. Pickard, *Kidnapped and the Ransomed*, 167.

24. Frances Anne Kemble, *Journal of a Residence on a Georgia Plantation in 1838–1839* (Chicago: Afro-American Press, 1969), 227.

25. Cited in Arthur W. Calhoun, *From Independence through the Civil War*, vol. 2 of *A Social History of the American Family, from Colonial Times to the Present* (New York: Barnes & Noble, 1945), 309.

26. C. Vann Woodward, ed., *Mary Chesnut's Civil War* (New Haven, CT: Yale University Press, 1981), 343. See also Nell Irvin Painter, "Of *Lily*, Linda Brent, and Freud: A Non-Exceptionalist Approach to Race, Class, and Gender in the Slave South," *Georgia Historical Quarterly* 76 (Summer 1992): 242; Catherine Clinton, *The Plantation Mistress: Woman's World in the Old South* (New York: Pantheon Books, 1982), 73, 111; and Burton, *In My Father's House*, 140.

27. Virginia Ingraham Burr, ed., *The Secret Eye: The Journal of Ella Gertrude Clanton Thomas, 1848–1889* (Chapel Hill: University of North Carolina Press, 1990), 152.

28. Elizabeth Fox-Genovese, *Within the Plantation Household: Black and White Women of the Old South* (Chapel Hill: University of North Carolina Press, 1988), 9.

29. John Hammond Moore, ed., *The Plantation Mistress on the Eve of the Civil War: The Diary of Keziah Goodwyn Hopkins Brevard, 1860–1861* (Columbia: University of South Carolina Press, 1993), 95.

30. Rawick, vol. 5.3, 243 and suppl. 2, vol. 8, 3292.

31. Murr, *Rebel Wife in Texas*, 148. See also Allie Bayne Windham Webb, ed., *Mistress of Evergreen Plantation: Rachel O'Connor's Legacy of Letters, 1823–1845* (Albany: State University of New York Press, 1983), 71.

32. Woodward, *Mary Chesnut's Civil War*, 29; Nell Irvin Painter, introduction to Burr, *Secret Eye*, 30, 39; and Callcott, *Mistress of Riversdale*, 150. See also Kemble, *Journal of a Residence*, 15.

33. Woodward, *Mary Chesnut's Civil War*, 54.

34. Rawick, suppl. 1, vol. 4.2, 343; and Kent Anderson Leslie, "Amanda America Dickson: An Elite Mulatto Lady in Nineteenth-Century Georgia," in *Southern Women: Histories and Identities*, ed. Virginia Bernhard, Betty Brandon, Elizabeth Fox-Genovese, and Theda Perdue (Columbia: University of Missouri Press, 1992), 71–86. See also Rawick, vol. 8.2, 118 and suppl. 2, vol. 1, 315.

35. Rawick, vol. 5.4, 80.

36. Rawick, suppl. 1, vol. 2, 102. See also Rawick, vol. 2.1, 150; and William Wells Brown, *The Narrative of William Wells Brown, a Fugitive Slave; and A Lecture Delivered before the Female Anti-Slavery Society of Salem* (1848; reprint, Reading, MA: Addison-Wesley, 1969), 18.

37. Rawick, vol. 12.2, 50.

38. Rawick, vol. 18, 3.

39. Hildreth, *The Slave*, vol. 1, 15.

40. Griffith, *Autobiography of a Female Slave*, 9.

41. William Wells Brown, *Clotel; or, The President's Daughter: A Narrative of Slave Life in the United States* (London: Partridge & Oakey, 1853), 102. Despite Brown's claim, Jefferson's children with Sally Hemming did ultimately achieve freedom. See Annette Gordon-Reed, *The Hemingses of Monticello: An American Family* (New York: W. W. Norton, 2008), 643.

42. "Domestic Slavery," *Southern Literary Messenger* 5 (Oct. 1839): 678.

43. Quoted in Anne Firor Scott, *The Southern Lady: From Pedestal to Politics, 1830–1930* (Chicago: University of Chicago Press, 1970), 101. See also Bertram Wyatt-Brown, *Southern Honor: Ethics and Behavior in the Old South* (New York: Oxford University Press, 1982).

44. Woodward, *Mary Chesnut's Civil War*, 32.

45. Quoted in Burton, *In My Father's House*, 99. See also Johnson, "Planters and Patriarchy," 46; Stephanie McCurry, "The Two Faces of Republicanism: Gender and Proslavery Politics in Antebellum South Carolina," *Journal of American History* 78 (Mar. 1992): 1254; and Jacqueline Jones, *Labor of Love, Labor of Sorrow: Black Women, Work, and the Family from Slavery to the Present* (New York: Basic Books, 1985), 25.

46. Angela Boswell, *Her Act and Deed: Women's Lives in a Rural Southern County, 1837–1873* (College Station: Texas A&M University Press, 2001), 4.

47. Woodward, *Mary Chesnut's Civil War*, xxxiv, 261; and Mrs. Henry Rowe Schoolcraft, *Plantation Life: The Narratives of Mrs. Henry Rowe Schoolcraft* (1852–1860; reprint, New York: Negro Universities Press, 1969), 543.

48. Christine Jacobson Carter, ed., *The Diary of Dolly Lunt Burge, 1848–1879* (Athens: University of Georgia Press, 1997), 65; and Johnson, "Planters and Patriarchy," 48. See also Mary Ann Mason, *From Father's Property to Children's Rights: The History of Child Custody in the United States* (New York: Columbia University Press, 1994), 6. Despite the potential it offers to illuminate larger power structures, the historiography of fatherhood remains relatively scant, with most of the work on American fatherhood focused on the late nineteenth- to mid-twentieth-century period. See, for example, Robert L. Griswold, *Fatherhood in America: A History* (New York: Basic Books, 1993).

49. Beth G. Crabtree and James W. Patton, eds., *"Journal of a Secesh Lady": The Diary of Catherine Ann Devereux Edmondston, 1860–1866* (Raleigh: North Carolina Division of Archives and History, 1979), 107.

50. Jan Lewis and Kenneth Lockridge, "'Sally Has Been Sick': Pregnancy and Family Limitation among Virginia Gentry Women, 1780–1830," *Journal of Social History* 22 (Fall 1988): 10; and Janet Farrell Brodie, *Contraception and Abortion in Nineteenth-Century America* (Ithaca, NY: Cornell University Press, 1994), 34–37, 291–293.

51. Murr, *Rebel Wife in Texas*, 153.

52. Philip N. Racine, ed., *Piedmont Farmer: The Journals of David Golightly Harris, 1855–1870* (Knoxville: University of Tennessee Press, 1990), 201.

53. Obstetrical Record Book of Dr. C. A. Hentz, 8 Oct. 1853, Folder 27, Hentz Family Papers, #332, SHC. See also J. Jill Suitor, "Husbands' Participation in Childbirth: A Nineteenth-Century Phenomenon," *Journal of Family History* (Fall 1981), 278–293.

54. Nancy Kennedy to Thomas Kennedy, 8 Jan. 1838, Folder 5, Kennedy, Moore, and Southgate Papers, #4416, SHC.

55. James T. McIntosh and Lynda Lasswell Crist, eds., *The Papers of Jefferson Davis* (Baton Rouge: Louisiana State University Press, 1983), vol. 4, 291.

56. Sally McMillen, "Antebellum Southern Fathers and the Health Care of Children," *Journal of Southern History* 60 (Aug. 1994): 517–518.

57. "Causes of Diseases of Children," *Southern Planter* 10 (May 1850): 154.

58. Theodore Rosengarten, ed., *Tombee: Portrait of a Cotton Planter; with The Journal of Thomas B. Chaplin* (New York: William Morrow, 1986), 546. See also Edwin Adams Davis, ed., *Plantation Life in the Florida Parishes of Louisiana, 1836–1846; As Reflected in the Diary of Bennet H. Barrow* (New York: Columbia University Press, 1943), 368.

59. Burton, *In My Father's House*, 105. See also McMillen, "Antebellum Southern Fatherhood," 516. Fredrika Bremer observed that "better, more

affectionate family-fathers than the men of America I have seen nowhere in the world." Bremer, *Homes of the New World*, vol. 1, 337. See also Jacqueline S. Reiner, *From Virtue to Character: American Childhood, 1775–1850* (New York: Twayne, 1996), 24.

60. Thomas Kennedy to Nancy Kennedy, 12 Mar. 1833, Folder 5, Kennedy, Moore, and Southgate Papers, SHC.

61. Patricia Brady, ed., *George Washington's Beautiful Nelly: The Letters of Eleanor Parke Custis Lewis to Elizabeth Bordley Gibson, 1794–1851* (Columbia: University of South Carolina Press, 1991), 184. See also Carter, *Diary of Dolly Lunt Burge*, 18; Webb, *Mistress of Evergreen Plantation*, 52; and Sarah Lois Wadley Diary, 22 Feb. 1864, DAS.

62. George M. Southgate to Elizabeth Southgate, 10 Sept. 1828, Folder 2, Kennedy, Moore, and Southgate Papers, SHC. See also McMillen, "Antebellum Southern Fathers," 524, 530.

63. Racine, *Piedmont Farmer*, 225.

64. McIntosh, *Papers of Jefferson Davis*, vol. 6, 130.

65. Brady, *George Washington's Beautiful Nelly*, 134.

66. Rev. Benjamin Morgan Palmer, "The South: Her Peril and Her Duty," in *Southern Pamphlets on Secession, November 1860–April 1861*, ed. Jon L. Wakelyn (Chapel Hill: University of North Carolina Press, 1996), 69. Also see the discussion of the Manigault family's use of this metaphor in Jeffery R. Young, "Ideology and Death on a Savannah River Rice Plantation, 1833–1867: Paternalism amidst 'a Good Supply of Disease and Pain,'" *Journal of Southern History* 59 (Nov. 1993): 677.

67. Caroline Lee Hentz, *The Planter's Northern Bride* (1854; reprint, Chapel Hill: University of North Carolina Press, 1970), 332.

68. William H. Holcombe, "Characteristics and Capabilities of the Negro Race," *Southern Literary Messenger* 33 (Dec. 1861): 405.

69. Frederick Law Olmsted, *Journeys and Explorations in the Cotton Kingdom: A Traveller's Observation on Cotton and Slavery in the American Slave States* (London: Sampson Low, Son, 1861), vol. 1, 54.

70. Cobb, *Inquiry into the Law*, 245; and Gustave de Beaumont, Appendix A in *Marie; or, Slavery in the United States; A Novel of Jacksonian America*, trans. Barbara Chapman (Stanford, CA: Stanford University Press, 1958), 190. Abolitionists also adopted the limits on marriage and the subsequent lack of paternal authority as a theme; see, for example, William Goodell, *The American Slave Code in Theory and Practice: Its Statutes, Judicial Decisions, and Illustrative Facts* (1853; reprint, New York: Johnson Reprint, 1968), 248–249.

71. Brown, *Narrative of William Wells Brown*, 1. See also Frederick Douglass, *My Bondage and My Freedom* (1855; reprint, New York: Arno Press and New York Times, 1968), 51.

72. Plantation Records, folder 1, pp. 1, 8; folder 2, p. 28; and folder 5, p. 15, Manigault Family Papers, #484, SHC. See also Judith Kelleher Schafer, "New Orleans Slavery in 1850 as Seen in Advertisements," *Journal of Southern History* 47 (Feb. 1981): 37; and Elizabeth Regosin, *Freedom's Promise: Ex-Slave Families and Citizenship in the Age of Emancipation* (Charlottesville: University Press of Virginia, 2002), 141.

73. Regosin, *Freedom's Promise*, 115.

74. Marie Jenkins Schwartz, *Born in Bondage: Growing Up Enslaved in the Antebellum South* (Cambridge, MA: Harvard University Press, 2000), 199; and Pickard, *Kidnapped and the Ransomed*, 113, 117.

75. Hildreth, *The Slave*, vol. 2, 48–49. See also Mary B. Harlan, *Ellen; or, The Chained Mother and Pictures of Kentucky Slavery, Drawn from Real Life* (Cincinnati: published for the author, Applegate, 1855), 80.

76. Burton, *In My Father's House*, 163–164.

77. Louis Hughes, *Thirty Years a Slave: From Bondage to Freedom; The Institution of Slavery as Seen on the Plantation and in the Home of the Planter* (Milwaukee: South Side Printing, 1897), 191. See also Horton, "Freedom's Yoke," 55.

78. Rawick, vol. 7.1, 316; see also vol. 15.2, 119 and suppl. 2, vol. 6.5, 2167.

79. Kemble, *Journal of A Residence*, 60.

80. Rawick, suppl. 1, vol. 9.4, 1801; see also vol. 5.4, 188 and suppl. 1, vol. 8, 1212.

81. Rawick, suppl. 2, vol. 9, 3473; see also vol. 4.1, 299.

82. Rawick, suppl. 1, vol. 8, 841.

83. Rawick, suppl. 1, vol. 1, 295.

84. Rawick, vol. 4.1, 236.

85. Rawick, vol. 4.2, 45.

86. Rawick, vol. 5.3, 24.

Chapter Six: Birth and Professional Identity in the Antebellum South

1. Quoted in William Hampton Adams, "Health and Medical Care on Antebellum Southern Plantations," *Plantation Society* 2 (May 1989): 273; N. B. P., "Treatment of Slaves in the Southern States," *Southern Quarterly Review* (Jan. 1852), 216; and Thomas R. R. Cobb, *An Inquiry into the Law of Negro Slavery in the United States of America* (1858; reprint, New York: Negro Universities Press, 1968), 69.

2. Barbara Katz Rothman, *In Labor: Women and Power in the Birthplace* (New York: W. W. Norton, 1982), 33. For further discussions of the medicalization of birth narratives, see Karen L. Michaelson, "Childbirth in America: A Brief History and Contemporary Issues," in *Childbirth in America: Anthropological Perspectives*, ed. Karen Michaelson and contributors (South Hedley, MA: Bergan & Garvey, 1988), 10; Jo Murphy-Lawless, "The Obstetric View of Feminine Identity: A Nineteenth-Century Case History of the Use of Forceps on Unmarried Women in Ireland," in *Gender and Discourse: The Power of Talk*, ed. Alexandra Dundas Todd and Sue Fisher (Norwood, NJ: Ablex, 1988), 178, 195; Sheila Kitzinger, *Ourselves as Mothers: The Universal Experience of Motherhood* (Reading, MA: Addison-Wesley, 1995), 141–143; and Ann Oakley, *The Captured Womb: A History of the Medical Care of Pregnant Women* (Oxford: Basil Blackwell, 1984), 1–3.

3. Frederick Law Olmsted, *Journeys and Explorations in the Cotton Kingdom: A Traveller's Observation on Cotton and Slavery in the American Slave States* (London: Sampson Low, Son, 1861), vol. 2, 89; and Charles D. Meigs, *An Introductory Lecture, Delivered to the Class of Midwifery and Diseases of Women and Children, in Jefferson Medical College, Oct. 18th, 1848, Published by the Class* (Philadelphia: C. Sherman, 1848), 12. A large percentage of this class were from the South.

4. Steven M. Stowe, *Doctoring the South: Southern Physicians and Everyday Medicine in the Mid-Nineteenth Century* (Chapel Hill: University of North Carolina Press, 2004), 4.

5. Marie Jenkins Schwartz, *Birthing a Slave: Motherhood and Medicine in the Antebellum South* (Cambridge, MA: Harvard University Press, 2006).

6. William P. Dewees, M.D., *A Treatise on the Physical and Medical Treatment of Children* (Philadelphia: Carey, Lea, & Carey, 1829), 39. Although in cities such as Philadelphia doctors had become the primary birth attendants by the mid-nineteenth century, these statistics are not representative of the experience in the rural South. As late as 1910 midwives still attended half of all births in the United States. The figure was even higher for black and/or southern women; in the 1940s midwives still attended 75 percent of black women's births in the states of the Deep South. Female friends also continued to attend childbirths until birth moved to the hospital. Judy Barrett Litoff, *American Midwives, 1860 to the Present* (Westport, CT: Greenwood Press, 1978), lx; and Sharon A. Robinson, "A Historical Development of Midwifery in the Black Community: 1600–1940," *Journal of Nurse-Midwifery* 29 (July/Aug. 1984): 247. For Philadelphia doctor/midwife ratios, see Irvine Loudon, *Death in Childbirth: An International Study of Maternal Care and Maternal Mortality, 1800–1950* (Oxford: Clarendon Press, 1992), 281.

7. Obstetrical Records of Dr. C. A. Hentz, 3 Mar. 1858, Folder 27, Hentz Family Papers, #332, SHC; and Madaline Selima Edwards Diary, 25 Apr. 1844, 13 Jan. 1845, and 9 Apr. 1845, Folders 16 and 17, Charles William Bradbury Papers, #3011, SHC.

8. William P. Dewees, M.D., *A Compendious System of Midwifery, Chiefly Designed to Facilitate the Inquiries of Those Who May be Pursuing This Branch of Study*, 4th ed. (Philadelphia: Carey & Lea, 1830), 69. See John C. Gunn, M.D., *Gunn's New Domestic Physician; or, Home Book of Health* (Cincinnati: Moore, Wilstach, Keys, 1859), 431, for a list of the observable signs of pregnancy. Histories of birth control and infertility indicate that nineteenth-century physicians had a limited understanding of conception. Janet Farrell Brodie, *Contraception and Abortion in Nineteenth-Century America* (Ithaca, NY: Cornell University Press, 1994), 85–86; and Margaret Marsh, "Motherhood Denied: Women and Infertility in Historical Perspective," in *Mothers and Motherhood: Readings in American History*, ed. Rima Apple and Janet Golden (Columbus: Ohio State University Press, 1997), 220.

9. Theodore Rosengarten, ed., *Tombee: Portrait of a Cotton Planter; with The Journal of Thomas B. Chaplin* (New York: William Morrow, 1986), 659; Stowe, *Doctoring the South*, 47–48, 53; and Deborah Kuhn McGregor, *From Midwives to Medicine: The Birth of American Gynecology* (New Brunswick, NJ: Rutgers University Press, 1998), 14, 19.

10. Thomas Ewell, *Letters to Ladies, Detailing Important Information, Concerning Themselves and Infants* (Philadelphia: printed by the author, 1817), 26; and Meigs, *Introductory Lecture*, 3.

11. Gunn, *Gunn's New Domestic Physician*, 418; Dewees, *Compendious System of Midwifery*, xii; and Henry Miller, quoted in Steven M. Stowe, "Obstetrics and the Work of Doctoring in the Mid-Nineteenth-Century American South," *Bulletin of the History of Medicine* 64 (Winter 1990): 551.

12. For an overview of the anesthesia debate, see Martin S. Pernick, *A Calculus of Suffering: Pain, Professionalism, and Anesthesia in Nineteenth-Century America* (New York: Columbia University Press, 1985), 36–47; and Donald Caton, *What a Blessing She Had Chloroform: The Medical and Social Response to the Pain of Childbirth from 1800 to the Present* (New Haven, CT: Yale University Press, 1999), 91.

13. In a career that spanned forty-three years he recorded 493 births. In contrast, the Maine midwife Martha Ballard attended 816 births in her twenty-seven-year career, an average of thirty births per year. Hentz Obstetrical Records, SHC; and Laurel Thatcher Ulrich, *A Midwife's Tale: The Life of Martha Ballard, Based on Her Diary, 1785–1812* (New York: Vintage Books, 1991). See also Stowe, "Obstetrics and the Work of Doctoring," 548.

14. Steven M. Stowe, "Seeing Themselves at Work: Physicians and the Case Narrative in the Mid-Nineteenth-Century American South," *American Historical Review* 101 (Feb. 1996): 41–79.

15. Meigs, *Introductory Lecture*, 3.

16. Gunn, *Gunn's New Domestic Physician*, 412; *Harper's*, quoted in John B. Blake, "Women and Medicine in Ante-Bellum America," *Bulletin of the History of Medicine* 39 (Mar./Apr. 1965): 111; James Ewell, *The Planter's and Mariner's Medical Companion* (Philadelphia: printed by John Bioren, 1807), 118–119; and Carroll Smith-Rosenberg and Charles Rosenberg, "The Female Animal: Medical and Biological Views of Women and Their Role in Nineteenth-Century America," *Journal of American History* 60 (1973/74): 335.

17. Ewell, *Planter's and Mariner's Medical Companion*, 12–13, 256; and Gunn, *Gunn's New Domestic Physician*, 426, 480. Of course, despite their dictates about cleanliness, nineteenth-century physicians had no knowledge of germ theory.

18. Stowe, "Obstetrics and the Work of Doctoring," 544.

19. Hentz Obstetrical Records, 8 Apr. 1860 and 5 Feb. 1865, SHC.

20. Stowe, "Obstetrics and the Work of Doctoring," 542, 563.

21. John S. Haller, "The Negro and the Southern Physician: A Study of Medical and Racial Attitudes 1800–1860," *Medical History* 16 (July 1972): 238.

22. Ewell, *Planter's and Mariner's Medical Companion*, 13–14.

23. Martha Carolyn Mitchell, "Health and the Medical Profession in the Lower South, 1845–1860," *Journal of Southern History* 10 (Nov. 1944): 434. Dr. Charles Hentz's obstetrical records indicated that he attended a significantly higher percentage of difficult labors for black women than white women. Although he was perhaps more likely to be called in to assist white women in normal deliveries, and only asked to attend problematic situations in the case of enslaved women, his observation of these difficulties should still have raised questions about the ease with which black women gave birth. Hentz attended the births of 178 women in the antebellum period, 26 percent of whom were black. While he indicated that 58 percent of the white women he attended had "natural" births, he characterized only 28 percent of black women's births in this way. He intervened with positive results in 39 percent of the births of enslaved women (compared to 22 percent of white women's births), and another 33 percent of black women's births ended with the death of either the infant or the mother (versus 20 percent of white women's births). Hentz Obstetrical Records, SHC.

24. Frances Anne Kemble, *Journal of a Residence on a Georgia Plantation in 1838–1839* (Chicago: Afro-American Press, 1969), 135–136.

25. Quoted in Stowe, "Obstetrics and the Work of Doctoring," 545. See also Olmsted, *Journeys and Explorations*, vol. 1, 118.

26. Ariela J. Gross, *Double Character: Slavery and Mastery in the Antebellum Southern Courtroom* (Princeton, NJ: Princeton University Press, 2000), 123, 132.

27. McGregor, *From Midwives to Medicine*, 48–50, 61; Diana Axelsen, "Women as Victims of Medical Experimentation: J. Marion Sims' Surgery on Slave Women, 1845–1850," *SAGE* 2 (Fall 1985): 10–12; and Terri Kapsalis, "Mastering the Female Pelvis: Race and the Tools of Reproduction," in *Skin Deep, Spirit Strong: The Black Female Body in the American Culture*, ed. Kimberly Wallace-Sanders (Ann Arbor: University of Michigan Press, 2002), 263–277. See Todd L. Savitt, "The Uses of Blacks for Medical Experimentation and Demonstration in the Old South," *Journal of Southern History* 48 (Aug. 1982): 331–348, for a more general discussion of the uses of enslaved bodies, dead and alive, for experimentation.

28. Mitchell, "Health and the Medical Profession," 440.

29. Adams, "Health and Medical Care," 275; W. W. Watts Physician's Ledger, p. 47 (Nov. 1861), p. 85 (5 May 1862), and p. 103 (22 Oct. 1861), DU; and Levi Smithwick Yates Ledger, p. 132 (22 Oct. 1861), DU. I am grateful to the staff of Duke's Special Collections who pointed out this overlap.

30. Plantation records often included recipes for medicines. The Manigault Plantation Record Books, for example, contained a treatment recipe for "venerial" disease. Caroline Gilman's novel, based on her experiences living on a southern plantation, suggested that a man did not feel prepared to inherit a large estate until "he attended medical and surgical lectures, that he might supply with advice the accidental wants of his people[.]" Many real-life planters did the same. Gunn, "Recommendatory" in *Gunn's New Domestic Physician*, unnumbered page; Plantation Record Books, Folder 2, p. 55, Manigault Family Papers, #484, SHC; and Caroline Gilman, *Recollections of a Southern Matron* (New York: Harper & Brothers, 1838), 202. See also Elizabeth Barnaby Keeney, "Unless Powerful Sick: Domestic Medicine in the Old South," in *Science and Medicine in the Old South*, ed. Ronald L. Numbers and Todd L. Savitt (Baton Rouge: Louisiana State University Press, 1989), 278; and John Duffy, "Medical Practice in the Ante-Bellum South," *Journal of Southern History* 25 (Feb. 1959): 65.

31. Margaret Law Callcott, ed., *Mistress of Riversdale: The Plantation Letters of Rosalie Stier Calvert, 1795–1821* (Baltimore: Johns Hopkins University Press, 1991), 162.

32. Richard Wertz and Dorothy Wertz, *Lying-In: A History of Childbirth in America* (New Haven, CT: Yale University Press, 1989); Jan Lewis and Kenneth

A. Lockridge, "'Sally Has Been Sick': Pregnancy and Family Limitation among Virginia Gentry Women, 1780–1830," *Journal of Social History* 22 (Fall 1988): 5–19; Catherine Scholten, *Childbearing in American Society: 1650–1850* (New York: New York University Press, 1985); and Judith Walzer Leavitt, *Brought to Bed: Childbearing in America, 1750–1950* (New York: Oxford University Press, 1986). Both Wertz and Wertz and Lewis and Lockridge argue that women chose medical assistance as their best option. Catherine Scholten believes that doctors took over the women-centered birth event, while Judith Leavitt suggests that women continued to orchestrate their experiences until births moved to the hospital.

33. Hentz Obstetrical Records, 3 Aug. 1858, 24 Nov. 1857, 18 Mar. 1858, and 22 Sept. 1861, SHC. Irvine Loudon writes that American doctors' opposition to midwives "was expressed in a series of unrelenting attacks so vitriolic they take your breath away." I find, however, that such animosity largely occurred in the early twentieth century when, in their newfound professionalism, doctors sought to eliminate any competition. Loudon, *Death in Childbirth*, 322.

34. Such was the case in the deliveries of both Anita Withers and Gertrude Clanton. See Anita Dwyer Withers Diary, 4 July 1863, DAS; and Virginia Ingraham Burr, ed., *The Secret Eye: The Journal of Ella Gertrude Clanton Thomas, 1848–1889* (Chapel Hill: University of North Carolina Press, 1990), 163–164.

35. Philip N. Racine, ed., *Piedmont Farmer: The Journals of David Golightly Harris, 1855–1870* (Knoxville: University of Tennessee Press, 1990), 50.

36. Gunn, *Gunn's New Domestic Physician*, 419.

37. George Rawick, ed., *The American Slave: A Composite Autobiography* (Westport, CT: Greenwood Press, 1972), vol. 11.7, 21.

38. John Duffy, "A Note on Ante-Bellum Southern Nationalism and Medical Practice," *Journal of Southern History* 34 (May 1968): 268–269; and Reginald Horsman, *Josiah Nott of Mobile: Southerner, Physician, and Racial Theorist* (Baton Rouge: Louisiana State University Press, 1987).

39. Stowe, "Obstetrics and the Work of Doctoring," 545; and J. S. Wilson, "The Negro—His Peculiarities as to Disease," *American Cotton Planter & Soil of the South* 3 (July 1859): 228. This development is discussed in Duffy, "Note on Ante-Bellum Southern Nationalism," 267–268; and John Harley Warner, "The Idea of Southern Medical Distinctiveness: Medical Knowledge and Practice in the Old South," in *Science and Medicine in the Old South*, ed. Ronald L. Numbers and Todd L. Savitt (Baton Rouge: Louisiana State University Press, 1989), 180. See also John Duffy, "Sectional Conflict and Medical Education in Louisiana," *Journal of Southern History* 23 (Aug. 1957): 291. Darrett B. Rutman and Anita H. Rutman, "Of Agues and Fevers: Malaria in the Early Chesapeake,"

William and Mary Quarterly (Jan. 1976): 31–60, examine some climate-related health issues in the South.

40. Quoted in Duffy, "Sectional Conflict," 302.

41. From the New Orleans *Daily Delta*, June 9, 1860, quoted in Duffy, "Sectional Conflict," 299.

42. Susan Klepp, "Revolutionary Bodies: Women and the Fertility Transition in the Mid-Atlantic Region, 1760–1820," *Journal of American History* 85 (Dec. 1998): 917. See also Mary Fissell, "Gender and Generation: Representing Reproduction in Early Modern England," *Gender & History* 7 (Nov. 1995): 435.

43. Stephanie McCurry, "Producing Dependence: Women, Work, and Yeoman Households in Low-Country South Carolina," in *Neither Lady nor Slave: Working Women of the Old South*, ed. Susanna Delfino and Michele Gillespie (Chapel Hill: University of North Carolina Press, 2002), 62.

44. "The Rights of Women," *Southern Planter* (June 1860): 384.

45. Beverly Guy-Sheftall, "The Body Politic: Black Female Sexuality and the Nineteenth-Century Euro-American Imagination," in *Skin Deep, Spirit Strong*, ed. Wallace-Sanders, 18; and Kathy Peiss and Christina Simmons, "Passion and Power: An Introduction," in *Passion and Power: Sexuality in History*, ed. Kathy Peiss and Christina Simmons (Philadelphia: Temple University Press, 1989), 6.

46. Theodore Weld, in his anti-slavery tract, collected advertisements for runaways which made clear references to pregnancy as well as to the condition of some enslaved women's breasts. Theodore Dwight Weld, *American Slavery As It Is: Testimony of a Thousand Witnesses* (1839; reprint, New York: Arno Press, 1968), 154; J. H. Easterby, ed., *The South Carolina Rice Plantation, as Revealed in the Papers of Robert F. W. Allston* (Chicago: University of Chicago Press, 1945), 68–73; "Farm Management—Diseases of Slaves—Treatment," *Southern Planter* (Aug. 1847): 226; and Olmsted, *Journeys and Explorations*, vol. 2, 43. See also Freddie L. Parker, ed., *Stealing a Little Freedom: Advertisements for Slave Runaways in North Carolina, 1791–1840* (New York: Garland, 1994), 119, 229, 380, 460, 800.

47. William H. Holcombe, "Characteristics and Capabilities of the Negro Race," *Southern Literary Messenger* (Nov. 1861): 406; another doctor, John Wilson, made similar references to the "inferior animal natures" of African Americans in "The Peculiarities & Diseases of Negroes," quoted in James O. Breeden, ed., *Advice among Masters: The Ideal in Slave Management in the Old South* (Westport, CT: Greenwood Press, 1980), 243; John Pendleton Kennedy, *Swallow Barn; or, A Sojourn in the Old Dominion*, 2nd ed. (1853; reprint, New York: Hafner 1962), 437–439, 452; and Rawick, suppl. 2, vol. 10, 4327.

48. John R. McKivigan, ed., *The Roving Editor; or, Talks with Slaves in the Southern States, by James Redpath* (1859; reprint, University Park: Pennsylvania State University Press, 1996), 223.

49. Klepp, "Revolutionary Bodies," 917, 927; Olmsted, *Journeys and Explorations*, vol. 1, 57, 59; and Breeden, *Advice among Masters*. In this collection of advice for masters, for example, one may find references to "pregnancy," "lying-in," "accouchment," and even "amalgamation and intercourse," but generally not to "breeding."

50. Richard Sutch uses demographic data to suggest that breeding for sale to the South's western territories existed. He argues that 250,000 slaves were exported from the top eight "selling states" to the six "buying states" in the last decade of slavery, and that the ratio of children under fourteen years of age to grown women was higher in the selling states (323 per 1,000 women) than in the buying states (268.8 per 1,000 women). Based on her own analysis of the statistics, Catherine Clinton similarly argues that "we cannot assume, as some scholars have suggested, that slaveowners merely let nature take its course. The reproduction of the slave labor force was too vital for planters to leave such matters to the slave themselves." In contrast, Richard Lowe and Randolph Campbell conclude from their demographic data "that there was little regional specialization in the buying and selling of slaves." They note that the age-sex ratio was similar in both buying and selling states, hovering around 50 percent of the women, with between 22 and 24 percent of the women being of "breeding" age in both areas. They also argue that there is no clear pattern regarding fertility rates. While Virginia, a selling state, had a rate of 178 infants per 1,000 childbearing women, the rate in the buying state of Texas was only minimally lower, at 170 infants per 1,000 childbearing women. Richard Sutch, "The Breeding of Slaves for Sale and the Westward Expansion of Slavery, 1850–1860," in *Race and Slavery in the Western Hemisphere: Quantitative Studies*, ed. Stanley L. Engerman and Eugene Genovese (Princeton, NJ: Princeton University Press and Center for Advanced Study in the Behavioral Sciences at Stanford, 1975), 173–210; Richard G. Lowe and Randolph B. Campbell, "The Slave-Breeding Hypothesis: A Demographic Comment on the 'Buying' and 'Selling' States," *Journal of Southern History* 42 (Aug. 1976): 401–412; Robert W. Fogel and Stanley L. Engerman, "The Slave Breeding Thesis," in *Without Consent or Contract: The Rise and Fall of American Slavery*, ed. Robert W. Fogel and Stanley L. Engerman (New York: W. W. Norton, 1992), vol. 2, 455–472; and Catherine Clinton, "'Southern Dishonor': Flesh, Blood, Race, and Bondage," in *In Joy and In Sorrow: Women, Family, and Marriage in the Victorian South, 1830–1900*, ed. Carol Bleser (New York: Oxford University Press, 1991), 54.

51. Jacqueline Jones makes a similar point about the "breeding" debate in *Labor of Love, Labor of Sorrow: Black Women, Work, and the Family from Slavery to the Present* (New York: Basic Books, 1985), 34.

52. Rawick, vol. 8.2, 44; vol. 15.2, 77–78; vol. 16.1, 12; and vol. 15.2, 77–78. For other links between breeding and animal metaphors, see vol. 2.1, 173; vol. 4.2, 42, 163; vol. 6.1, 107, 258; vol. 8.1, 211; and vol. 18, 1.

53. Rawick, vol. 8.2, 92; see also vol. 8.1, 25 and vol. 10.5, 243. It is interesting that most of the comments that follow this pattern come from interviews conducted in Arkansas by black interviewers, perhaps representing the interests or biases of an interviewer or one of the state's departments. Such comments, however, could also stem from the desire of enslaved parents to protect their children from this sort of knowledge. These informants would have been small children when slavery ended.

54. Rawick, vol. 5.4, 189; vol. 10.6, 222; vol. 11.8, 214; vol. 12.1, 228; vol. 16.2, 34; and suppl. 2, vol. 3, 709.

55. Rawick, vol. 17, 127.

56. Rawick, vol. 9.3, 374.

57. Rawick, vol. 5.4, 188. Many former slaves remarked on the profitability and the market interests of their masters in encouraging the breeding of enslaved women without making explicit animal metaphors. See, for example, vol. 6.1, 191; vol. 6.2, 116; vol. 8.2, 15; vol. 11.7, 30; vol. 13.3, 116; vol. 16.2, 74; vol. 17, 167; suppl. 1, vol. 5.2, 327; suppl. 1, vol. 7.2, 423; and suppl. 2, vol. 9, 3641.

58. Rawick, vol. 2.2, 11.

59. Rawick, vol. 11.7, 16.

60. Rawick, vol. 12.1, 24–25. This account also includes the whipping of a pregnant woman. In this case Sylvia, Avery's grandmother, escaped to the woods for two weeks with the assistance of her husband, and while there she gave birth to twins.

61. Dr. Collins' chapter "On the Breeding of Negroes" provides a notable exception, but his book was published early in the nineteenth century and was intended for the Sugar Colonies rather than American planters. Some Caribbean islands actually developed an official policy of encouraging slave reproduction in response to low birthrates among slaves; this was never the case in the southern states. Dr. Collins, *Practical Rules for the Management and Medical Treatment of Negro Slaves, in the Sugar Colonies, by a Professional Planter* (1811; reprint, Freeport, NY: Books for Libraries Press, 1971), 130–150; Barbara Bush, "Hard Labor: Women, Childbirth, and Resistance in British Caribbean Slave Societies," in *More than Chattel: Black Women and Slavery in the Americas*, ed. David Barry Gaspar and Darlene Clark Hine (Bloomington: Indiana

University Press, 1996), 199; and Richard S. Dunn, "A Tale of Two Plantations: Slave Life at Mesopotamia in Jamaica and Mount Airy in Virginia, 1799 to 1828," *William and Mary Quarterly* 34 (Jan. 1977): 32–65.

62. Thomas Jefferson to Joel Yancey, 17 Jan. 1819, in Edwin Morris Betts, ed., *Thomas Jefferson's Farm Book* (Princeton, NJ: Princeton University Press, 1953), 43; William Trotter, quoted in Gross, *Double Character*, 117; and John R. Turner, "Plantation Hygiene," *Southern Cultivator* (May and June 1857), quoted in Breeden, *Advice among Masters*, 195.

63. Nathan Bass, "Essay on the Treatment and Management of Slaves," *Southern Central Agricultural Society of Georgia*, 1851, quoted in Breeden, *Advice among Masters*, 15.

64. Rawick, vol. 4.1, 180.

65. Rawick, suppl. 2, vol. 5.4, 1556 and suppl. 2, vol. 8, 3369; see also vol. 7.2, 4 and vol. 14.1, 360.

66. Quoted in Breeden, *Advice among Masters*, 13.

67. Quoted in Arthur W. Calhoun, *From Independence through the Civil War*, vol. 2 of *A Social History of the American Family, from Colonial Times to the Present* (New York: Barnes & Noble, 1945), 275. The work of John Campbell suggests that this easing of labor demands in the last trimester was actually at the least useful time in terms of the health of mother and infant. This misallocation of respite, however, probably stemmed more from a lack of medical knowledge than a particular maliciousness on the part of the slaveowner. John Campbell, "Work, Pregnancy, and Infant Mortality among Southern Slaves," *Journal of Interdisciplinary History* 14 (Spring 1984): 809.

68. Quoted in John Spencer Bassett, *The Southern Plantation Overseer: As Revealed in His Letters* (Northampton, MA: Smith College, 1925), 29.

69. Araby Plantation Journal, p. 194, Haller Nutt Papers, DU.

70. Quoted in Todd L. Savitt, *Medicine and Slavery: The Diseases and Health Care of Blacks in Antebellum Virginia* (Urbana: University of Illinois Press, 1978), 117.

71. This comparison is made in Christopher Morris, "The Articulation of Two Worlds: The Master-Slave Relationship Reconsidered," *Journal of American History* 85 (Dec. 1998): 982.

72. See Michael Tadman, "The Demographic Cost of Sugar: Debates on Slave Societies and Natural Increase in the Americas," *American Historical Review* 105 (Dec. 2000): 1534–1575; and Sutch, "Breeding of Slaves for Sale."

73. Olmsted, *Journeys and Explorations*, vol. 2, 188 [*Agriculturalist* quote], 187 [Phillips quote]; and Betts, *Thomas Jefferson's Farm Book*, 43.

74. Bassett, *Southern Plantation Overseer*, 116, 152.

75. Drew Gilpin Faust, "The Rhetoric and Ritual of Agriculture in Antebellum South Carolina," *Journal of Southern History* 45 (Nov. 1979): 544. See also Anne Norton, *Alternative Americas: A Reading of Antebellum Political Culture* (Chicago: University of Chicago Press, 1986), 105, 116. Notably, farm journals were one of the few locally produced forms of literature in the South before the 1850s. Jay B. Hubbell, *The South in American Literature, 1607–1900* (Durham, NC: Duke University Press, 1954), 690.

76. Peter W. Bardaglio, *Reconstructing the Household: Families, Sex, and the Law in the Nineteenth-Century South* (Chapel Hill: University of North Carolina Press, 1995), xvii. See also Mark V. Tushnet, *The American Law of Slavery, 1810–1860: Considerations of Humanity and Interest* (Princeton, NJ: Princeton University Press, 1981), 19; and Alan Watson, *Slave Law in the Americas* (Athens: University of Georgia Press, 1989), 6. Several abolitionists made the same connection between laws and values in the antebellum period. William Goodell, for example, examined the laws of slavery "to test the moral character of American slaveholding." Goodell, *The American Slave Code in Theory and Practice: Its Statutes, Judicial Decisions, and Illustrative Facts* (1853; reprint, New York: Johnson Reprint, 1968), 17. See also George M. Stroud, *A Sketch of the Laws Relating to Slavery in the Several States of the United States of American*, 2d ed. (1856; reprint, New York: Negro Universities Press, 1968).

77. "Study of the Law," *Southern Literary Messenger* 3 (Jan. 1837): 31; Laura F. Edwards, "Law, Domestic Violence, and the Limits of Patriarchal Authority in the Antebellum South," in *Gender and the Southern Body Politic*, ed. Nancy Bercaw (Jackson: University Press of Mississippi, 2000), 60, 75; and Thomas D. Morris, *Southern Slavery and the Law, 1619–1860* (Chapel Hill: University of North Carolina Press, 1996), 2–3.

78. See, for example, *Fanny v. Bryant* (KY, 1830) and *Preston v. M'Gaughey* (TN, 1812), both cited in Jacob D. Wheeler, *A Practical Treatise on the Law of Slavery* (1837; reprint, New York: Negro Universities Press, 1968), 34, 24; Marie Jenkins Schwartz, *Born in Bondage: Growing Up Enslaved in the Antebellum South* (Cambridge, MA: Harvard University Press, 2000), 49; and Wilbert E. Moore, "Slave Law and Social Structure," *Journal of Negro History* 26 (Apr. 1941): 191–202.

79. The Virginia legislature reaffirmed this principle in 1748. Morris, *Southern Slavery and the Law*, 43; June Purcell Guild, *Black Laws of Virginia: A Summary of the Legislative Acts of Virginia Concerning Negroes from Earliest Times to the Present* (1936; reprint, New York: Negro Universities Press, 1969), 22, 56; Cobb, *An Inquiry into the Law*, 68–69; Wheeler, *A Practical Treatise*, 24; and Helen Tunnicliff Catterall, ed., *Judicial Cases Concerning American*

Slavery and the Negro (Washington, DC: Carnegie Institution, 1929), vol. 3, 10. A number of southern states never explicitly legislated *partus sequitur ventrem*, although all generally accepted its principles. The two notable exceptions include Maryland between 1664 and 1681 and two cases heard by the Alabama Supreme Court in the antebellum period. Morris, *Southern Slavery and the Law*, 47–48; and Catterall, *Judicial Cases*, vol. 3, 127.

80. Moore, "Slave Law and Social Structure," 187–190; Tushnet, *American Law of Slavery*, 147; and James F. Davis, *Who is Black? One Nation's Definition* (University Park: Pennsylvania State University Press, 1991), 34.

81. Cobb, *Inquiry into the Law*, 73.

82. Bardaglio, *Reconstructing the Household*, 81; and Mary Ann Mason, *From Father's Property to Children's Rights: The History of Child Custody in the United States* (New York: Columbia University Press, 1994), xvi.

83. Joan Rezner Gundersen, "The Double Bonds of Race and Sex: Black and White Women in a Colonial Virginia Parish," *Journal of Southern History* (Aug. 1986): 360.

84. Bardaglio, *Reconstructing the Household*, xiii.

85. Cited in Martha Albertson Fineman, "The Neutered Mother," in *Language, Symbolism, and Politics*, ed. Richard M. Merelman (Boulder, CO: Westview Press, 1992), 171.

86. Michael Grossberg uses a particularly contentious public hearing from Philadelphia in the late 1830s to explore the changing patterns of legal custody in this era. Michael Grossberg, *A Judgment for Solomon: The d'Hauteville Case and Legal Experience in Antebellum America* (Cambridge: Cambridge University Press, 1996), especially pp. 50–56, 68.

87. Jamil S. Zainaldin, "The Emergence of a Modern American Family Law: Child Custody, Adoption, and the Courts, 1796–1851," *Northwestern University Law Review* 73 (Feb. 1979): 1062.

88. *Bryan v. Bryan* (AL, 1859), cited in Jane Turner Censer, "'Smiling Through Her Tears': Ante-Bellum Southern Women and Divorce," *American Journal of Legal History* 25 (1981): 45.

89. "Review: Women Physiologically Considered by Alexander Walker," *Southern Quarterly Review* (Oct. 1842): 310–311.

90. Mason, *From Father's Property*, 50. As early as 1830, women's rights advocates in both Britain and the United States made the mother's right to the custody of her children part of their platform. This change, however, occurred slowly; a bill establishing the equal rights and responsibilities of parents in Britain was not passed until 1925. Elizabeth K. Helsinger, Robin Lauterbach Sheets, and William Weeder, *Social Issues*, vol. 2 of *The Woman Question: Society and*

Literature in Britain and America, 1837–1883 (Chicago: University of Chicago Press, 1983), 8–13.

91. Zainaldin, "Emergence of a Modern American Family Law," 1052, 1067, 1069.

92. Case cited in Censer, "'Smiling Through Her Tears,'" 44.

93. Quoted in Censer, "'Smiling Through Her Tears,'" 44–45.

94. Mason, *From Father's Property*, 10; and Sophonisba Breckinridge, ed., *The Family and the State: Selected Documents* (1934; reprint, New York: Arno Press, 1972), 417.

95. Cited in Censer, "'Smiling Through her Tears,'" 42.

96. Susan Newcomer, in "Out of Wedlock Childbearing in an Ante-Bellum Southern County," *Journal of Family History* 15, no. 3 (1990): 357–368, examines the use of these bonds in Wake County, NC.

97. Elizabeth Regosin, *Freedom's Promise: Ex-Slave Families and Citizenship in the Age of Emancipation* (Charlottesville: University Press of Virginia, 2002), 114–115; and Cobb, *Inquiry into the Law*, 260.

98. Cobb, *Inquiry into the Law*, 99, 86.

99. Eva Saks, "Representing Miscegenation Law," *Raritan* 8 (Fall 1988): 58; Tushnet, *American Law of Slavery*, 147; and Catterall, *Judicial Cases*, vol. 2, 385. For a specific case that struggled with these principals, see Walter Johnson, "The Slave Trader, the White Slave, and the Politics of Racial Determination in the 1850s," *Journal of American History* (June 2000): 13–38.

100. Martha Hodes, *White Women, Black Men: Illicit Sex in the Nineteenth-Century South* (New Haven, CT: Yale University Press, 1997), 1–15. Hodes has found a degree of toleration for these unions in the antebellum period. This is in part attributable to the assumption that most white women who engaged in these unions were of the lowest classes and thus already morally suspect, according to the southern ideal. See also Diane Miller Sommerville, "The Rape Myth in the Old South Reconsidered," *Journal of Southern History* 61 (Aug. 1995): 481–518.

101. Edwards, "Law, Domestic Violence, and Limits," 69.

102. Tushnet, *American Law of Slavery*, 19.

103. Drew Gilpin Faust, "Culture, Conflict, and Community: The Meaning of Power on an Ante-Bellum Plantation," *Journal of Social History* 14 (Fall 1980): 89.

Chapter Seven: Birth, Motherhood, and the Sectional Crisis

1. *Correspondence between Lydia Maria Child, and Gov. Wise and Mrs. Mason, of Virginia* (New York: American Anti-Slavery Society, 1860), 16–26. This

correspondence began when Mrs. Child wrote Governor Wise in October 1859, asking for permission to nurse the captive John Brown.

2. Ebenezer Davies, *American Scenes, and Christian Slavery: A Recent Tour of Four Thousand Miles in the United States* (1849; reprint, New York: AMS Press, 1973), 56; and William Wells Brown, *Clotel; or, The President's Daughter; A Narrative of Slave Life in the United States* (London: Partridge & Oakey, 1853), 62. For a discussion of this abolitionist tactic, see Elizabeth D. Clark, "'The Sacred Rights of the Weak': Pain, Sympathy, and the Culture of Individual Rights in Antebellum America," *Journal of American History* 82 (Sept. 1995): 482; and Gillian Brown, *Domestic Individualism: Imagining Self in Nineteenth-Century America* (Berkeley: University of California Press, 1990), 20.

3. Quoted in Elizabeth Ammons, "Heroines in *Uncle Tom's Cabin*," in *Critical Essays on Harriet Beecher Stowe*, ed. Elizabeth Ammons (Boston: G. K. Hall, 1980), 152.

4. Harriet Beecher Stowe, *Uncle Tom's Cabin* (1851–1852; reprint, New York: Bantam Books, 1981), 441. A number of scholars have explored Stowe's use of maternal symbolism. See, for example, Elizabeth Ammons, "Stowe's Dream of the Mother and Savior: *Uncle Tom's Cabin* and American Women Writers before the 1920s," in *New Essays on* Uncle Tom's Cabin, ed. Eric J. Sundquist (Cambridge: Cambridge University Press, 1986); and Minrose C. Gwin, *Black and White Women of the Old South: The Peculiar Sisterhood in American Literature* (Knoxville: University of Tennessee Press, 1985), 32–34.

5. Fredrika Bremer, *The Homes of the New World; Impressions of America*, trans. Mary Howitt (New York: Harper & Bros., 1854), vol. 2, 108 (my emphasis).

6. William Wells Brown, *The Narrative of William Wells Brown, A Fugitive Slave; and A Lecture Delivered before the Female Anti-Slavery Society of Salem* (1848; reprint, Reading, MA: Addison-Wesley, 1969), 97.

7. Kate E. R. Pickard, *The Kidnapped and the Ransomed; Being the Personal Recollections of Peter Still and His Wife 'Vina,' after Forty Years of Slavery* (1856; reprint, New York: Negro Universities Press, 1968), 346.

8. Stowe, *Uncle Tom's Cabin*, chapters 7 and 8; and G. W. Henry, *Tell Tale Rag, and Popular Sins of the Day* (Oneida, NY: published and bound by the author, 1861), vol. 1, 18. See also Brown, *Narrative of William Wells Brown*, 10.

9. Martha Griffith, *Autobiography of a Female Slave* (1857; reprint, New York: Negro Universities Press, 1969), 14, 75. See also Mary B. Harlan, *Ellen; or, The Chained Mother and Pictures of Kentucky Slavery, Drawn from Real Life* (Cincinnati: published for the author, by Applegate, 1855), 210–211.

10. John R. McKivigan, ed., *The Roving Editor; or, Talks with Slaves in the Southern States, by James Redpath* (1859; reprint, University Park: Pennsylvania State University Press, 1996), 51.

11. Henry, *Tell Tale Rag*, vol. 1, 22–23.

12. Brown, *Clotel*, 5; and Theodore Dwight Weld, *American Slavery As It Is: Testimony of a Thousand Witnesses* (1839; reprint, New York: Arno Press, 1968), 175.

13. Rev. William Goodell, *The American Slave Code in Theory and Practice: Its Statutes, Judicial Decisions, and Illustrative Facts* (1853; reprint, New York: Johnson Reprint, 1968), 82–83, 106. See also Weld, *American Slavery As It Is*, 110, 182; and Harlan, *Ellen*, 67. Interestingly, another condemnation of slavery presented in *American Slavery As It Is* was that slavery's abuses could cause limited fecundity and even infertility. This argumentation, however, was less common in anti-slavery writing than accusations of forced reproduction. See Weld, *American Slavery As It Is*, 37, 38, 133.

14. Harriet A. Jacobs, *Incidents in the Life of a Slave Girl*, ed. and with an intro. by Jean Fagan Yellin (Cambridge, MA: Harvard University Press, 1987), 28. For fictionalized accounts of forced immodesty and slaveholders' lasciviousness directed toward black women, see Griffith, *Autobiography of a Female Slave*, 48; and Pickard, *Kidnapped and the Ransomed*, 167.

15. Weld, *American Slavery As It Is*, 153. See also McKivigan, *Roving Editor*, 217; and Ronald G. Walters, "The Erotic South: Civilization and Sexuality in American Abolitionism," *American Quarterly* 25 (May 1973): 180, 182–184.

16. Dana D. Nelson, *The Word in Black and White; Reading 'Race' in American Literature, 1638–1867* (New York: Oxford University Press, 1992), 66. Lydia Maria Child garnered this sort of criticism from white Bostonians after the publication of her *An Appeal in Favor of That Class of Americans Called Africans*. Historian Frances Foster suggests that the discussion of sexual abuse, which appeared in almost every anti-slavery narrative, might have done more harm than good, perpetuating the image that black women had limited sexual purity. James McPherson, preface to L. M. Child, *An Appeal in Favor of That Class of Americans Called Africans* (1836; reprint, New York: Arno Press and New York Times, 1968); and Frances S. Foster, "Ultimate Victims: Black Women in Slave Narratives," *Journal of American Culture* 1 (Winter 1978): 847–848.

17. Weld, *American Slavery As It Is*, 20; see also pp. 46, 90.

18. Pickard, *Kidnapped and the Ransomed*, 359.

19. George Rawick, ed., *The American Slave: A Composite Autobiography* (Westport, CT: Greenwood Press, 1972), suppl. 1, vol. 2, 115 and suppl. 2, vol. 5, 1885. See also the memoir of former slave Louis Hughes, *Thirty Years a Slave:*

From Bondage to Freedom; The Institution of Slavery as Seen on the Plantation and in the Home of the Planter (Milwaukee: South Side Printing, 1897), 79.

20. Bremer, *Homes of the New World*, vol. 1, 276.

21. Harlan, *Ellen*, 8.

22. Angelina Emily Grimké, *Appeal to the Christian Women of the South* (1836; reprint, New York: Arno Press, 1969), 26. See also George Bourne, *Slavery Illustrated in Its Effects upon Woman and Domestic Society* (1837; reprint, Freeport, NY: Books for Libraries Press, 1972), 95–106. Grimké may have based her rhetoric on her troubled relationship with her own mother, a South Carolina slave mistress. See Charles Wilbanks, ed., *Walking by Faith: The Diary of Angelina Grimké, 1828–1853* (Columbia: University of South Carolina Press, 2003), 47, 56, 88.

23. McKivigan, *Roving Editor*, 223.

24. Goodell, *American Slave Code*, 111.

25. Pickard, *Kidnapped and the Ransomed*, 159.

26. Griffith, *Autobiography of a Female Slave*, 75. Mattie Griffith Browne was a white woman from Kentucky who had owned a number of slaves before her conversion to the abolitionist cause. She avowed that everything she wrote in her novel stemmed from her experiences and observations as a slaveowner.

27. Stowe, *Uncle Tom's Cabin*, 153.

28. Brown, *Narrative of William Wells Brown*, 91.

29. "Slavery in the Southern States," *Southern Quarterly Review* (Oct. 1845): 319.

30. Quoted in Arthur W. Calhoun, *From Independence through the Civil War*, vol. 2 of *A Social History of the American Family, from Colonial Times to the Present* (New York: Barnes & Noble, 1945), 316.

31. Caroline Lee Hentz, *The Planter's Northern Bride* (1854; reprint, Chapel Hill: University of North Carolina Press, 1970), 108. See also "The Caucasian Master and the African Slave," *Southern Literary Messenger* 10 (June 1844): 333–334.

32. Caroline Rush's novel presents the comfort of southern slaves compared to a poverty-stricken northern mother forced to sell her child to a southern couple because she cannot afford to keep her: "Talk of the separation of parents and children at the South: can you find one more touching, more sad than this. Say what you will, the affections of the negro are never so strong as those of the white man. The tenderness that is but natural in the breast of a white mother, is very much lessened in the blacks, and I have here convinced you that the bondage of poverty, forces a lady to give up her child to the care of strangers, with scarcely a hope of ever seeing her again." Caroline E. Rush, *The North and*

South; or, Slavery and Its Contrasts; A Tale of Real Life (1852; reprint, New York: Negro Universities Press, 1968), 238.

33. Mary H. Eastman, *Aunt Phillis's Cabin; or, Southern Life As It Is* (Philadelphia: Lippincott, Grambo, 1852), 44.

34. Eastman, *Aunt Phillis's Cabin*, 43–44.

35. Mrs. Henry Rowe Schoolcraft, *Plantation Life: The Narratives of Mrs. Henry Rowe Schoolcraft* (1852–1860; reprint, New York: Negro Universities Press, 1969), 45.

36. John Pendleton Kennedy, *Swallow Barn; or, A Sojourn in the Old Dominion*, 2nd ed. (1853; reprint, New York: Hafner, 1962), 456. The Louisiana legislature set the age at which a child no longer needed its mother at ten years old, forbidding separation by sale until that age. There is evidence, however, that this law was easily disregarded. Judith Kelleher Schafer, "New Orleans in 1850 as Seen in Advertisements," *Journal of Southern History* 47 (Feb. 1981): 36.

37. Caroline Gilman, *Recollections of a Southern Matron* (New York: Harper & Bros., 1838), 81.

38. "Diversity of the Races," *Southern Quarterly Review* (Apr. 1851): 403. See other examples of this rhetoric in Stephanie McCurry, "The Two Faces of Republicanism: Gender and Proslavery Politics in Antebellum South Carolina," *Journal of American History* 78 (Mar. 1992): 1250.

39. Rev. J. H. Thornwell, *The Rights and the Duties of Masters: A Sermon Preached at the Dedication of a Church, Erected in Charleston, S.C., for the Benefit and Instruction of the Coloured Population* (Charleston, SC: Walker & James, 1850), 14.

40. Python, "The Relative Moral and Social Status of the North and the South," *DeBow's Review* 22 (Mar. 1857): 244.

41. George F. Holmes, "Review of *Uncle Tom's Cabin*," *Southern Literary Messenger* 18 (Oct. 1852): 631. See also "*Uncle Tom's Cabin*," *Southern Literary Messenger* 18 (Dec. 1852): 722, 731.

42. "Northern Mind and Character," *Southern Literary Messenger* 31 (Nov. 1860): 343–344. See also John Pendleton Kennedy, "The Border States: Their Power and Duty in the Present Disordered Condition of the Country" (Philadelphia: J. B. Lippincott, 1861), reprinted in *Southern Pamphlets on Secession, November 1860–April 1861*, ed. Jon L. Wakelyn (Chapel Hill: University of North Carolina Press, 1996), 241.

43. "Northern Mind and Character," 349.

44. "Domestic Slavery," *Southern Literary Messenger* 5 (Oct. 1839): 679; and Margaret Law Callcott, ed., *Mistress of Riversdale: The Plantation Letters of Rosalie Stier Calvert, 1795–1821* (Baltimore: Johns Hopkins University Press, 1991), 348.

45. Edmund Kirke, *Among the Pines; or, South in Secession Times*, 7th ed. (New York: J. R. Gilmore, 1862), 62.

46. Hentz, *Planter's Northern Bride*, 218, 549.

47. Sarah Lois Wadley Diary, 18 Dec. 1862, DAS.

48. "Northern Mind and Character," 346.

49. Eliza Frances Andrews, *The War-Time Journal of a Georgia Girl, 1864–1865* (New York: D. Appleton, 1908), 148.

50. Brown, *Clotel*, 130.

51. McKivigan, *Roving Editor*, 85.

52. "Northern Mind and Character," 346.

53. William Shepperson, *War Songs of the South* (Richmond: West & Johnston, 1862), Documenting the American South Collection, University of North Carolina at Chapel Hill, 40, 103.

54. Suzanne L. Bunkers, ed., *The Diary of Caroline Seabury, 1854–1863* (Madison: University of Wisconsin Press, 1991), 74. Seabury, a New York native, traveled to Mississippi in 1854 to teach at the Columbus Female Institute.

55. Drew Gilpin Faust, *The Creation of Confederate Nationalism: Ideology and Identity in the Civil War South* (Baton Rouge: Louisiana State University Press, 1988), 21, 84.

56. Quoted in Orville Vernon Burton, *In My Father's House Are Many Mansions: Family and Community in Edgefield, South Carolina* (Chapel Hill: University of North Carolina Press, 1985), 100, 366 n. 157.

57. William Gilmore Simms, "Oh, The Sweet South!"; "The Spirit of '60"; James Randall, "My Maryland"; John Collins M'Cabe, "Maryland Our Mother!"; and "Prosopopeia," all reprinted in Shepperson, *War Songs of the South*, 15–16, 58–59, 138–139, 142–143, 96–97.

58. Marshall L. DeRosa, ed., *The Politics of Dissolution: The Quest for National Identity and the American Civil War* (New Brunswick, NJ: Transaction, 1998), 225.

59. "Speech of President Davis, at Richmond, June 1st, 1861," in *Echoes from the South, Comprising the Most Important Speeches, Proclamations, and Public Acts Emanating from the South During the Late War* (1866; reprint, Westport, CT: Negro Universities Press, 1970), 148. See also Stephanie McCurry, "Citizens, Soldiers' Wives, and 'Hiley Hope Up' Slaves: The Problem of Political Obligation in the Civil War South," in *Gender and the Southern Body Politic*, ed. Nancy Bercaw (Jackson: University Press of Mississippi, 2000), 106.

60. Anne Norton, *Alternative Americas: A Reading of Antebellum Political Culture* (Chicago: University of Chicago Press, 1986), 171; and McCurry, "Citizens, Soldiers' Wives," 98.

61. "Speech of Ex-Governor Henry A. Wise, June 1st, 1860," in *Echoes from the South*, 151.

62. Virginia Ingraham Burr, ed., *The Secret Eye: The Journal of Ella Gertrude Clanton Thomas, 1848–1889* (Chapel Hill: University of North Carolina Press, 1990), 207.

63. Rev. James Henley Thornwell, "The State of the Country" (New Orleans: *True Witness & Sentinel* Office, 1861), in *Southern Pamphlets on Secession*, ed. Wakelyn, 177.

64. McCurry, "Citizens, Soldiers' Wives," 112.

65. Quoted in Angela Boswell, *Her Act and Deed: Women's Lives in a Rural Southern County, 1837–1873* (College Station: Texas A&M University Press, 2001), 93.

66. Ada Sterling, ed., *A Belle of the Fifties: Memoirs of Mrs. Clay of Alabama; Covering Social and Political Life in Washington and the South, 1853–1866* (New York: Da Capo Press, 1969), 202, 144.

67. Ellen A. Moriarty, "My Only Boy," in Shepperson, *War Songs of the South*, 169–170.

68. Caroline Merrick, *Old Times in Dixie Land: A Southern Matron's Memories* (New York: Grafton Press, 1901), 33.

69. See William H. Pease and Jane H. Pease, *James Louis Petigru: Southern Conservative, Southern Dissenter* (Columbia: University of South Carolina Press, 2002), 1.

70. Frederick Douglass, letter to Thomas Auld, Sept. 3, 1848, in *Frederick Douglass: Selected Speeches and Writings*, ed. Philip Foner (Chicago: Lawrence Hill Books, 1999), 111.

71. Marilyn Mayer Culpepper, *All Things Altered: Women in the Wake of Civil War and Reconstruction* (Jefferson, NC: McFarland, 2002), 284.

Conclusion

1. Rev. Benjamin Morgan Palmer, "The South: Her Peril and Her Duty" (New Orleans: *True Witness & Sentinel* Office, 1860), reprinted in *Southern Pamphlets on Secession, November 1860–April 1861*, ed. Jon L. Wakelyn (Chapel Hill: University of North Carolina Press, 1996), 77; and Victoria V. Clayton, *White and Black under the Old Regime* (1899; reprint, Freeport, NY: Books for Libraries Press, 1970), 21.

2. Margaret Hagood, *Mothers of the South: Portraiture of the White Tenant Farm Woman* (1939; reprint, New York: Greenwood Press, 1969), 118.

3. Judy Barrett Litoff, *American Midwives, 1860 to the Present* (Westport, CT: Greenwood Press, 1978), 27; and Molly C. Dougherty, "Southern Lay

Midwives as Ritual Specialists," in *Women in Ritual and Symbolic Roles*, ed. Judith Hoch-Smith and Anita Spring (New York: Plenum Press, 1978), 151–164.

4. Letter from Spotswood Rice to his children, St. Louis, MO, 3 Sept. 1864, and letter from Spotswood Rice to Kitty Diggs, 3 Sept. 1864, quoted in Ira Berlin and Leslie S. Rowland, eds., *Families and Freedom: A Documentary History of African-American Kinship in the Civil War Era* (New York: New Press, 1997), 195–197. See also Herbert G. Gutman, *The Black Family in Slavery and Freedom, 1750–1925* (New York: Vintage Books, 1976), 414–418.

5. Berlin and Rowland, *Families and Freedom*, 171.

6. Berlin and Rowland, *Families and Freedom*, 172.

7. Elizabeth Regosin, *Freedom's Promise: Ex-Slave Families and Citizenship in the Age of Emancipation* (Charlottesville: University Press of Virginia, 2002), 119, 154–155.

8. Laura F. Edwards, *Gendered Strife and Confusion: The Political Culture of Reconstruction* (Urbana: University of Illinois Press, 1997), 147. See also Grace Elizabeth Hale, *Making Whiteness: The Culture of Segregation in the South, 1890–1940* (New York: Pantheon Books, 1998), 32; and Evelyn Brooks Higginbotham, *Righteous Discontent: The Women's Movement in the Black Baptist Church, 1880–1920* (Cambridge, MA: Harvard University Press, 1993), 96, 192.

9. Eliza Frances Andrews, *The War-Time Journal of a Georgia Girl, 1864–1865* (New York: D. Appleton, 1908), 347, 293.

10. Andrews, *War-Time Journal*, 277.

11. Quoted in George C. Rable, *Civil Wars: Women and the Crisis of Southern Nationalism* (Urbana: University of Illinois Press, 1989), 260.

12. Wilma King, ed., *A Northern Woman in the Plantation South: Letters of Tryphena Blanche Holder Fox, 1856–1876* (Columbia: University of South Carolina Press, 1993), 139.

13. Virginia Ingraham Burr, ed., *The Secret Eye: The Journal of Ella Gertrude Clanton Thomas, 1848–1889* (Chapel Hill: University of North Carolina Press, 1990), 268. See also Leslie A. Schwalm, *A Hard Fight for We: Women's Transition from Slavery to Freedom in South Carolina* (Urbana: University of Illinois Press, 1997), 51.

14. Karin L. Zipf, *Labor of Innocents: Forced Apprenticeship in North Carolina, 1715–1919* (Baton Rouge: Louisiana State University Press, 2005), 40.

15. King, *Northern Woman*, 208.

16. Marilyn Mayer Culpepper, *All Things Altered: Women in the Wake of Civil War and Reconstruction* (Jefferson, NC: McFarland, 2002), 88, 97; Edwards, *Gendered Strife*, 39; Regosin, *Freedom's Promise*, 133; Rable, *Civil Wars*, 259; and Michael Grossberg, *Governing the Hearth: Law and the Family in Nineteenth-Century America* (Chapel Hill: University of North Carolina Press,

1985), 263–268. Grossberg points out that these apprenticeship laws had traditionally been applied to poor whites. In the Reconstruction period, however, their application became aimed at black children.

17. Burr, *Secret Eye*, 343.

18. Burr, *Secret Eye*, 269.

19. King, *Northern Woman*, 148.

20. Quoted in Culpepper, *All Things Altered*, 134.

21. Caroline E. Janney, *Burying the Dead but Not the Past: Ladies' Memorial Associations and the Lost Cause* (Chapel Hill: University of North Carolina Press, 2008), 50.

22. Karen L. Cox, *Dixie's Daughters: The United Daughters of the Confederacy and the Preservation of Confederate Culture* (Gainesville: University Press of Florida, 2003), 123. This work provides a full study of both the intentions and the methods of the UDC. See also W. Fitzhugh Brundage, "'Woman's Hand and Heart and Deathless Love': White Women and the Commemorative Impulse in the New South," in *Monuments to the Lost Cause: Women, Art, and the Landscapes of Southern Memory*, ed. Cynthia Mills and Pamela H. Simpson (Knoxville: University of Tennessee Press, 2003), 64–82; and LeeAnn Whites, *The Civil War as a Crisis in Gender: Augusta, Georgia 1860–1890* (Athens: University of Georgia Press, 1995), 160–198.

The narratives that southern women created about their own birth experiences are at the core of this book. Fortunately, archival repositories throughout the South have preserved many of the diaries and letters in which southern women recorded and shared this information. My research is based on archival collections held in the Southern Historical Collection at the University of North Carolina at Chapel Hill (SHC); the Manuscript Department of the William R. Perkins Library at Duke University (DU); the South Carolina Historical Society (SCHS); Special Collections at the Howard-Tilton Memorial Library, Tulane University (TU); and the Library of Congress (LC). The digitization of many primary sources by the Documenting the American South Project at the University of North Carolina at Chapel Hill (DAS) provides an invaluable remote access to additional resources. Published diaries and collections of letters furnished another source of narratives on the birth experience. Useful examples include Patricia Brady, ed., *George Washington's Beautiful Nelly: The Letters of Eleanor Parke Custis Lewis to Elizabeth Bordley Gibson, 1794–1851* (Columbia: University of South Carolina Press, 1991); Virginia Ingraham Burr, ed., *The Secret Eye: The Journal of Ella Gertrude Clanton Thomas, 1848–1889* (Chapel Hill: University of North Carolina Press, 1990); and Erika L. Murr, ed., *A Rebel Wife in Texas: The Diary and Letters of Elizabeth Scott Neblett, 1852–1864* (Baton Rouge: Louisiana State University Press, 2001).

Unfortunately, a limited amount of archival sources exist that offer the perspective of African American southerners. The interviews with former slaves conducted by the Works Progress Administration and collected in George Rawick, ed., *The American Slave: A Composite Autobiography* (Westport, CT: Greenwood Press, 1972), provide valuable access to the experience of the enslaved in their own words. However, these interviews must be used with great caution because of numerous problems with the methods in which they were collected and recorded. Memoirs written by former or escaped slaves such as Frederick Douglass, *My Bondage and My Freedom* (1855; reprint, New York: Arno Press, 1968); William Wells Brown, *The Narrative of William Wells*

Brown, a Fugitive Slave; and A Lecture Delivered before the Female Anti-Slavery Society of Salem (1848; reprint, Reading, MA: Addison-Wesley, 1969); and Louis Hughes, *Thirty Years a Slave: From Bondage to Freedom; The Institution of Slavery as Seen on the Plantation and in the Home of the Planter* (Milwaukee: South Side Printing, 1897), present another source of firsthand accounts into the experience of the enslaved. Although these are often mediated through white editors and publishers, when used with caution they provide insight into an important facet of the southern experience.

Literary sources often supplied their readers with instruction on appropriate behaviors and social ideals. Journals such as the *Southern Ladies' Book: A Magazine of Literature, Science, and Arts* (1840–1842); the *Southern Literary Journal* (1836–1838); the *Southern Literary Messenger* (1834–1860); and the *Southern Quarterly Review* (1842–1857) contained prescriptive articles, stories, and poetry to edify their readership. Similarly, the growing field of domestic fiction, including novels such as Caroline Lee Hentz, *The Planter's Northern Bride* (1854; reprint, Chapel Hill: University of North Carolina Press, 1970), also provided models of proper behavior for men and women in the South. Literary scholars Nina Baym, *Woman's Fiction: A Guide to Novels by and about Women in America, 1820–1870*, 2nd ed. (Urbana: University of Illinois Press, 1993); Kathryn Lee Seidel, *The Southern Belle in the American Novel* (Tampa: University of South Florida Press, 1985); Minrose C. Gwin, *Black and White Women of the Old South: The Peculiar Sisterhood in American Literature* (Knoxville: University of Tennessee Press, 1985); and Dana D. Nelson, *The Word in Black and White: Reading 'Race' in American Literature, 1638–1867* (New York: Oxford University Press, 1992), provide models for understanding how these fictional works shaped understandings of gender and race relations within southern society.

The first histories of American birth were generally written from a medical perspective. Catherine Scholten, *Childbearing in American Society: 1650–1850* (New York: New York University Press, 1985); Judith Walzer Leavitt, *Brought to Bed: Childbearing in America, 1750–1950* (New York: Oxford University Press, 1986); and Richard Wertz and Dorothy Wertz, *Lying-In: A History of Childbirth in America* (New Haven, CT: Yale University Press, 1989), all focus on the negotiations between women and the medical community over the control of birth. Sociological and anthropological studies—such as Barbara Katz Rothman, *In Labor: Women and Power in the Birthplace* (New York: W. W. Norton, 1982); and Robbie E. Davis-Floyd and Carolyn F. Sargent, eds., *Childbirth and Authoritative Knowledge: Cross-Cultural Perspectives* (Berkeley: University of California Press, 1997)—have suggested the need to understand birth in its particular cultural context. Similarly, the study of motherhood has been a focus of feminist scholars, including Adrienne Rich, *Of Woman Born: Motherhood as Experience and Institution* (New York: Bantam Books, 1977); and Sheila Kitzinger, *Ourselves as Mothers: The Universal Experience of Motherhood* (Reading, MA: Addison-Wesley, 1995). Birth and motherhood have also been examined from a political perspective by W. Penn Handwerker, ed., *Birth and Power: Social Change and the Politics of Reproduction* (Boulder, CO: Westview Press, 1990); and Carol A. Mossman, *Politics and Narratives of Birth: Gynocolonization from Rousseau to Zola* (Cambridge: Cambridge University Press, 1993).

More recent historical studies of birth and motherhood have focused on specific contexts, recognizing the variations of experience in different regions and in different periods. Rima Apple and Janet Golden, eds., *Mothers and Motherhood: Readings in American History* (Columbus: Ohio State University Press, 1997), provide an overview of the multiplicity of meanings and experiences of motherhood in American history. Birth in the nineteenth-century North is explored in Sylvia D. Hoffert, *Private Matters: Attitudes toward Childbearing and Infant Nurture in the Urban North* (Urbana: University of Illinois Press, 1989). The birth experiences of elite white southern women is the focus of Sally McMillen, *Motherhood in the Old South: Pregnancy, Childbirth, and Infant Rearing* (Baton Rouge: Louisiana State University Press, 1990). Marie Jenkins Schwartz, *Birthing a Slave: Motherhood and Medicine in the Antebellum South* (Cambridge, MA: Harvard University Press, 2006); and Jennifer L. Morgan, *Laboring Women: Reproduction and Gender in New World Slavery* (Philadelphia: University of Pennsylvania Press, 2004), examine some of the meanings of birth and motherhood within the enslaved community. Other reproductive issues, from infertility to illegitimacy to contraception, have also garnered historical attention, including Margaret Marsh and Wanda Rommer, *The Empty Cradle: Infertility in America from Colonial Times to the Present* (Baltimore: Johns Hopkins University Press, 1997); Susan Newcomer, "Out of Wedlock Childbearing in an Ante-Bellum Southern County," *Journal of Family History* 15, no. 3 (1990): 357–368; and Janet Farrell Brodie, *Contraception and Abortion in Nineteenth-Century America* (Ithaca, NY: Cornell University Press, 1994).

The history of reproduction is grounded in the larger field of gender and sexuality. Two seminal articles outline the prescriptive modes of behavior: Barbara Welter, "The Cult of True Womanhood: 1820–1860," *American Quarterly* 18 (1966): 151–174; and Nancy F. Cott, "Passionless: An Interpretation of Victorian Sexual Ideology, 1790–1850," *Signs* (Winter 1978): 219–236. Subsequent studies, including Charles E. Rosenberg, "Sexuality, Class, and Role in 19th-Century America," *American Quarterly* 25 (May 1973): 131–153; Carl N. Degler, "What

Ought To Be and What Was: Women's Sexuality in the Nineteenth Century," *American Historical Review* 79 (Dec. 1974): 1467–1490; and Estelle B. Freedman, "Sexuality in Nineteenth-Century America: Behavior, Ideology, and Politics," *Reviews in American History* (Dec. 1982): 196–215, sought to reconcile ideals with actual behaviors. The unique experiences of African American women are suggested in studies such as Thelma Jennings, "'Us Colored Women Had to Go Though a Plenty': Sexual Exploitation of African-American Slave Women," *Journal of Women's History* 1 (Winter 1990): 45–74; and Diane Miller Sommerville, *Rape and Race in the Nineteenth-Century South* (Chapel Hill: University of North Carolina Press, 2004). A good introduction to and overview of the entire field is provided by John D'Emilio and Estelle B. Freedman, *Intimate Matters: A History of Sexuality in America* (New York: Harper & Row, 1988).

Although much of the study of sex and gender has taken a national perspective, regional variations in values and behaviors are often significant. The field of southern women's history has grown geometrically since the publication of Anne Firor Scott's *The Southern Lady: From Pedestal to Politics, 1830–1930* (Chicago: University of Chicago Press, 1970). Catherine Clinton, *The Plantation Mistress: Woman's World in the Old South* (New York: Pantheon Books, 1982); and Elizabeth Fox-Genovese, *Within the Plantation Household: Black and White Women of the Old South* (Chapel Hill: University of North Carolina Press, 1988), remain touchstones in the field. More recent works building on this subject include Margaret Ripley Wolfe, *Daughters of Canaan: A Saga of Southern Women* (Lexington: University Press of Kentucky, 1995); and Marli Weiner, *Mistresses and Slaves: Plantation Women in South Carolina, 1830–80* (Urbana: University of Illinois Press, 1998).

The work of scholars such as Suzanne Lebsock, *The Free Women of Petersburg: Status and Culture in a Southern Town, 1784–1860* (New York: W. W. Norton, 1984); Victoria E. Bynum, *Unruly Women: The Politics of Social and Sexual Control in the Old South* (Chapel Hill: University of North Carolina Press, 1992); and Laura F. Edwards, *Scarlett Doesn't Live Here Anymore: Southern Women in the Civil War Era* (Urbana: University of Illinois Press, 2000), have added immensely to our understanding of the complex interaction of gender and class in the southern experience. For the particular situation of southern women during the Civil War and Reconstruction, see Drew Gilpin Faust, *Mothers of Invention: Women of the Slaveholding South in the American Civil War* (Chapel Hill: University of North Carolina Press, 1996); Marilyn Mayer Culpepper, *All Things Altered: Women in the Wake of Civil War and Reconstruction* (Jefferson, NC: McFarland, 2002); George C. Rable, *Civil Wars: Women and the Crises of Southern Nationalism* (Urbana: University of Illinois Press, 1989); and LeeAnn Whites, *The Civil War as a Crisis in*

Gender: Augusta, Georgia 1860–1890 (Athens: University of Georgia Press, 1995).

The study of the unique circumstances of African American and enslaved women has also been a burgeoning field in the last few decades, led by Deborah Gray White, *Ar'n't I a Woman?: Female Slaves in the Plantation South* (New York: W. W. Norton, 1999). Other important works for understanding the experiences of enslaved women include David Barry Gaspar and Darlene Clark Hine, *More than Chattel: Black Women and Slavery in the Americas* (Bloomington: Indiana University Press, 1996); Jacqueline Jones, *Labor of Love, Labor of Sorrow: Black Women, Work, and the Family from Slavery to the Present* (New York: Basic Books, 1985); and Leslie A. Schwalm, *A Hard Fight for We: Women's Transition from Slavery to Freedom in South Carolina* (Urbana: University of Illinois Press, 1997).

Women's birth experiences occurred within, and created, the bonds of family in the antebellum South. Studies of family structures of white antebellum southerners include Joan E. Cashin, "The Structure of Antebellum Planter Families: 'The Ties that Bound Us Was Strong,'" *Journal of Southern History* 56 (Feb. 1990): 55–70; Jane Turner Censer, *North Carolina Planters and Their Children, 1800–1860* (Baton Rouge: Louisiana State University Press, 1984); and Jan Lewis, *The Pursuit of Happiness: Family and Values in Jefferson's Virginia* (Cambridge: Cambridge University Press, 1983). Herbert G. Gutman, *The Black Family in Slavery and Freedom, 1750–1925* (New York: Vintage Books, 1976), remains one of the most important works on the history of the enslaved family. The "southern family, black and white" has formed an important basis for insightful studies of southern household structures, including Peter W. Bardaglio, *Reconstructing the Household: Families, Sex, and the Law in the Nineteenth-Century South* (Chapel Hill: University of North Carolina Press, 1995); Orville Vernon Burton, *In My Father's House Are Many Mansions: Family and Community in Edgefield, South Carolina* (Chapel Hill: University of North Carolina Press, 1985); Steven M. Stowe, *Intimacy and Power in the Old South: Ritual in the Lives of the Planters* (Baltimore: Johns Hopkins University Press, 1987); and Stephanie McCurry, *Masters of Small Worlds: Yeoman Households, Gender Relations, and the Political Culture of the Antebellum South Carolina Low Country* (New York: Oxford University Press, 1995).

Close examination of southern household structures reminds us that men as well as women had a stake in this domestic institution. Control of the household was key to men's claims of patriarchal authority and honor. The foundation laid by Bertram Wyatt-Brown, *Southern Honor: Ethics and Behavior in the Old South* (New York: Oxford University Press, 1982), in understanding southern masculinity has been enhanced by more recent works, such as Lorri Glover,

Southern Sons: Becoming Men in the New Nation (Baltimore: Johns Hopkins University Press, 2007). Michael P. Johnson, "Planters and Patriarchy: Charleston, 1800–1860," *Journal of Southern History* 46 (1980): 45–72, also provides a valuable model for understanding these relationships. Although fatherhood formed an important facet of the patriarchal identity, relatively little has been written about this role. A notable exception is Robert L. Griswold, *Fatherhood in America: A History* (New York: Basic Books, 1993).

Men's roles in the newly developing professions in the nineteenth century have received more attention. The evolution of professional medicine in the South is most closely linked to an understanding of the patterns of birth narratives. Steven Stowe, *Doctoring the South: Southern Physicians and Everyday Medicine in the Mid-Nineteenth Century* (Chapel Hill: University of North Carolina Press, 2006), provides an invaluable examination of the emerging professional identity of southern doctors. Marie Jenkins Schwartz, *Birthing a Slave: Motherhood and Medicine in the Antebellum South* (Cambridge, MA: Harvard University Press, 2006), offers an excellent examination of the intersection of race, birth, and medicine. The study of southern medical development has a long history, going back to Martha Carolyn Mitchell, "Health and the Medical Profession in the Lower South, 1845–1860," *Journal of Southern History* 10 (Nov. 1944): 424–446; and John Duffy, "Sectional Conflict and Medical Education in Louisiana," *Journal of Southern History* 23 (Aug. 1957): 289–306. A collection of more recent studies is presented in Ronald L. Numbers and Todd L. Savitt, eds., *Science and Medicine in the Old South* (Baton Rouge: Louisiana State University Press, 1989). Slavery has been a particular focus of historians interested in uniquely southern medical practices, including Todd L. Savitt, *Medicine and Slavery: The Diseases and Health Care of Blacks in Antebellum Virginia* (Urbana: University of Illinois Press, 1978); and Katherine Bankole, *Slavery and Medicine: Enslavement and Medical Practices in Antebellum Louisiana* (New York: Garland, 1998). Reginald Horsman, *Josiah Nott of Mobile: Southerner, Physician, and Racial Theorist* (Baton Rouge: Louisiana State University Press, 1987), provides a good case study of how racist assumptions shaped the practice of medicine in the antebellum South.

The emergence of the fields of gynecology and obstetrics has been another focus of historians of medicine. These developments are outlined in Deborah Kuhn McGregor, *From Midwives to Medicine: The Birth of American Gynecology* (New Brunswick, NJ: Rutgers University Press, 1998). Donald Caton, *What a Blessing She Had Chloroform: The Medical and Social Response to the Pain of Childbirth from 1800 to the Present* (New Haven, CT: Yale University Press, 1999), explores a particular subspeciality of this practice from a medical perspective. Other works, such as Judy Barrett Litoff, *American Midwives, 1860* to the Present (Westport, CT: Greenwood Press, 1978); and Amanda Carson Banks, *Birth Chairs, Midwives, and Medicine* (Jackson: University Press of Mississippi, 1999), have focused on the continuity of midwifery alongside the growth of obstetrics in the late nineteenth century. This continuity was particularly important in the African American community, as evidenced by Gertrude Jacinta Fraser, *African American Midwifery in the South: Dialogues of Birth, Race, and Memory* (Cambridge, MA: Harvard University Press, 1998); and Linda Janet Holmes, "African American Midwives in the South," in *The American Way of Birth*, ed. Pamela S. Eakins (Philadelphia: Temple University Press, 1986), 273–291.

Legal history also provides a structure for understanding the unique context of southern social relations. A number of published sources allow access to primary resources, such as legal codes and court documents, including Thomas R. R. Cobb, *An Inquiry into the Law of Negro Slavery in the United States of America* (1858; reprint, New York: Negro Universities Press, 1968); Helen Tunnicliff Catterall, ed., *Judicial Cases Concerning American Slavery and the Negro* (Washington, DC: Carnegie Institution, 1929); and June Purcell Guild, *Black Laws of Virginia: A Summary of the Legislative Acts of Virginia Concerning Negroes from Earliest Times to the Present* (1936; reprint, New York: Negro Universities Press, 1969). Some historians have directly linked the law to family and household structures, including Michael Grossberg, *Governing the Hearth: Law and the Family in Nineteenth-Century America* (Chapel Hill: University of North Carolina Press, 1985); and Mary Ann Mason, *From Father's Property to Children's Rights: The History of Child Custody in the United States* (New York: Columbia University Press, 1994). The legal repercussions of slavery have also proved to be rich ground for historians and legal scholars in works such as Ariela J. Gross, *Double Character: Slavery and Mastery in the Antebellum Southern Courtroom* (Princeton, NJ: Princeton University Press, 2000); Mark V. Tushnet, *The American Law of Slavery, 1810–1860: Considerations of Humanity and Interest* (Princeton, NJ: Princeton University Press, 1981); Alan Watson, *Slave Law in the Americas* (Athens: University of Georgia Press, 1989); and Thomas D. Morris, *Southern Slavery and the Law, 1619–1860* (Chapel Hill: University of North Carolina Press, 1996).

The majority of southerners worked on the land during the nineteenth century. The particular agricultural perspective of the antebellum South is suggested in Drew Gilpin Faust, "The Rhetoric and Ritual of Agriculture in Antebellum South Carolina," *Journal of Southern History* 45 (Nov. 1979): 541–568. Several contemporary journals, such as the *Southern Planter* (1841–1861); *American Cotton Planter & Soil of the South* (1857–1859); and *DeBow's Review* (1846–1869), provide insight into agricultural interests. James O. Breeden, ed.,

Advice among Masters: The Ideal in Slave Management in the Old South (West-port, CT: Greenwood Press, 1980), contains a collection of documents created by those running southern plantations. Similar viewpoints are represented in a number of published primary collections, such as John Spencer Bassett, *The Southern Plantation Overseer: As Revealed in His Letters* (Northampton, MA: Smith College, 1925); and J. H. Easterby, ed., *The South Carolina Rice Planta-tion, as Revealed in the Papers of Robert F. W. Allston* (Chicago: University of Chicago Press, 1945).

In the late antebellum period, a growing war of words emerged between anti-slavery advocates and those intent on defending the slave system. Fortu-nately, many of the documents written on both sides of the debate have been reprinted and made available for historians. Some of the anti-slavery docu-ments offering a particular insight on the use of birth and motherhood in this debate include Harriet A. Jacobs, *Incidents in the Life of a Slave Girl*, edited and with an introduction by Jean Fagan Yellin (Cambridge, MA: Harvard Univer-sity Press, 1987); Theodore Dwight Weld, *American Slavery As It Is: Testimony of a Thousand Witnesses* (1839; reprint, New York: Arno Press, 1968); Angelina Emily Grimké, *Appeal to the Christian Women of the South* (1836; reprint, New York: Arno Press, 1969); and George Bourne, *Slavery Illustrated in its Effects upon Woman and Domestic Society* (1837; reprint, Freeport, NY: Books for Li-braries Press, 1972). On the other side of the debate, works such as George Fit-zhugh, *Sociology of the South; or, The Failure of Free Society* (1854; reprint, New York: Burt Franklin, 1965); D. R. Hundley, *Social Relations in Our Southern States* (1860; reprint, New York: Arno Press, 1975); and Mrs. Henry Rowe Schoolcraft, *Plantation Life: The Narratives of Mrs. Henry Rowe Schoolcraft* (1852–1860; reprint, New York: Negro Universities Press, 1969), offered a vigor-ous defense of antebellum southern society.

The emergence of a southern identity and the development of Confederate nationalism are perhaps the two most contested issues in southern historiogra-phy. Older works, such as Avery O. Craven, *The Growth of Southern National-ism, 1848–1861* (Baton Rouge: Louisiana State University Press, 1953); and David Potter, *The South and the Sectional Conflict* (Baton Rouge: Louisiana State University Press, 1968), suggest a largely political genesis to these issues. However, more recent works have looked to a complex of social, cultural, and political factors in constructing these identities. Notable work on the Confeder-ate identity has been undertaken in Drew Gilpin Faust, *The Creation of Confed-erate Nationalism: Ideology and Identity in the Civil War South* (Baton Rouge: Louisiana State University Press, 1988); and Anne Sarah Rubin, *A Shattered Nation: The Rise and Fall of the Confederacy, 1861–1868* (Chapel Hill: University of North Carolina Press, 2005). A broader perspective on the meaning of southern identity is offered by W. Fitzhugh Brundage, *The Southern Past: A Clash of Race and Memory* (Cambridge, MA: Harvard University Press, 2005); and James C. Cobb, *Away Down South: A History of Southern Identity* (New York: Oxford University Press, 2005).

southern fiction, 11–12. *See also* writers, pro-southern

southern household, 7; nuclearization of, 193

southern identity, 3–4, 6, 158; in postbellum era, 189. *See also* regional identity

Southern Ladies' Book, 11, 85

Southern Literary Journal, 10

Southern Literary Messenger, 4, 24, 179; on domesticity, 10; on illegitimacy, 21; on maternal ideal, 33; on miscegenation, 126; on regional identity, 180, 182; on slave system, 27, 118

Southern Planter, 79, 129, 149

southern politicians: and conservatism, 179; maternal symbolism used by, 176, 178, 187. *See also* rhetoric, pro-slavery

Southern Quarterly Review: on birthrates, 14; on child custody, 162–63; on enslaved reproduction, 137; on miscegenation, 119; on slave system, 176, 178

Southgate, George, 130

State v. Paine, 161

Stephens, Alexander H., 118

Stowe, Harriet Beecher, *Uncle Tom's Cabin*, 12, 169, 170, 175; southern reaction to, 179

support networks, during recovery period, 60–61

Susan (slave in Jones household), 106

Susan (slave in Thomas household), 67, 110

Sutton, Katie, 108

Swallow Barn (Kennedy), 12, 26, 31, 149–50

Taylor, Letha, 50

Taylor, Sally, 81

Terrill, J. W., 124

Thomas, Gertrude, 23, 55, 80, 83, 90, 110, 123; on anesthesia, 70; and birth control, 39; and black caregivers, 106; on breastfeeding, 102; childbirths of, 62, 66; on former slaves, 192; miscarriages of, 73; on miscege-

nation, 122; political loyalties of, 185, 194; on postbellum hardships, 194; pregnancies of, 45, 48

Thornwell, J. H., 179, 185

Tillery, Mary Eliza, 81

Towns, Phil, 18

Trotter, William, *History and Defense of African Slavery*, 153–54

Tucker, George, *Valley of the Shenandoah*, 20, 36

Uncle Tom's Cabin (Stowe), 12, 169, 170, 175, 179

United Daughters of the Confederacy (UDC), 195

Valley of the Shenandoah (Tucker), 20, 36

Vanhook, Winger, 64

Wadley, Sarah, 75, 77, 181

Walker, Clara, 66, 67, 147

Walson, Henry, 153

Washington, George, 131

Watts, W. W., 145

weaning. *See* breastfeeding

Webb, Anne, 102

Webb, Susan, 75

Weeks, William, 98

Weld, Theodore, *American Slavery As It Is*, 172

Wells, Easter, 134

Weston, P. C., 18, 156

wet-nurses, 101–4. *See also* breastfeeding

white infants: breastfed by black women, 103–4; devotion of, to black nurses, 105

Wigfall, Louis, 115

Williams, Lou, 51, 108

Williams, Willie, 152

Wilson, Lulu, 40

Winfield, Cornelia, 67

Wise, Henry, 184

Withers, Anita, 92–93; and black caregivers, 105; childbirths of, 62; pregnancies of, 44, 46, 53; and support networks, 61; weaning by, 101

Witherspoon, Silvia, 88

writers, anti-slavery, 13, 150, 175; on sexual abuse of enslaved women, 171–72. *See also* abolition movement; Brown, William Wells; Griffith, Martha; Henry, G. W.; Hildreth, Richard; Pickard, Kate; Redpath, James; Stowe, Harriet Beecher; Weld, Theodore

writers, pro-southern, 176, 177. *See also* Eastman, Mary; Hentz, Caroline; Kennedy, John Pendleton; Tucker, George

Yancey, Joel, 153, 157
Yates, Levi Smithwick, 145
Young, Dink Walton, 18